John H. Skinner, EdD, is Associate Professor and Graduate Program Director of the University of South Florida, Department of Gerontology. He received his doctoral degree from Columbia University, and has contributed to the development of gerontology serving in leadership roles in policy, program development, and research. He is a Fellow of the Gerontological Society of America and was Vice-president of the Gerontological Society of America, Associate Commissioner of the Administration of Aging, and founding Director of the USF Aging Studies Program. His research interests include minority aging, service access and utilization, program evaluation, and program outcomes.

Jeanne A. Teresi, EdD, PhD is a senior research scientist at Columbia University Stroud Center and the New York State Psychiatric Institute of the Office of Mental Health. She is also a senior associate of the Research Division of the Hebrew Home for the Aged at Riverdale. Her doctorates are in gerontology and measurement and statistics. She is on the editorial board of several journals reflecting these disciplines. Her publications are in the areas of measurement statistics, assessment and aging, epidemiology of disorders in the elderly, family caregiving, dementia care, health services research and minority issues. She has numerous publications related to measurement as it relates to ethnically diverse groups. She is Director or Co-Director of several multi-site NIH projects, including the National Institute on Aging Coordinating Center for the Collaborative Studies of Dementia Special Care; and the Center for Medicare and Medicaid Services Coordinating Center for the Diabetes Telemedicine Project. Finally, she is the Director of the Methods and Data Core of the Columbia University Resource Center for Minority Aging Research.

Douglas Holmes, PhD, has been PI, Co-PI, or Senior Scientist on more than 50 Federally-funded studies and has had more than 35 years' experience in project administration, conceptual design, and data management and analysis. Among the studies he has conducted have been a number which have resulted in the initiation of national services to at risk constituencies, most notably the elderly, and minority group members. He was the first person to evaluate Operation Head Start (in the Summer of 1965), was the evaluator of the National Parent-child Center Program, and the National Children's Advocacy Program. He undertook the evaluation of the New York City child abuse and neglect programs, working under the auspices of the Mayor's Task Force on Child Abuse and Neglect. He is the author of over 100 papers which have appeared in peer-reviewed journals, and has given presentations before many professional societies and groups.

Sidney M. Stahl, PhD, is Chief of Behavioral Medicine at the National Institute on Aging, National Institutes of Health (NIH). He is responsible for research on health promotion and social and psychological factors in health and illness for older Americans as well as for research on elder abuse, end-of-life issues, long-term care, and caregiving. Dr. Stahl came to NIH in 1996 after having served as a research and professor of medical sociology and social gerontology at Purdue University. He has published four books and over 50 articles and chapters on the health of older Americans, social science factors in chronic disease, and on statistical methods for the measurement of health in aging populations. He served as consultant to the World Health Organization in Geneva and Beijing as well as to several health care delivery organizations on the role of the social sciences in the delivery of services to older populations. He is active professionally in the Gerontological Society of America, the Academy for Health Services Research and Health Policy, the American Public Health Association, and the American Sociological Association, and the Society for Behavioral Medicine.

Anita L. Stewart, PhD, has over 25 years of experience in the conceptualization and measurement of health, functioning, well-being, and other health-related concepts. She coordinated the development of the Medical Outcomes Study (MOS) measures of functioning and well-being (developed to be appropriate for patients with chronic physical and mental conditions). Dr. Stewart has discussed issues in measuring health-related quality of life (HRQL) in older populations and facilitated the development of self-report measures for special subgroups of older adults. She has contributed to the development of measures of health outcomes and self-efficacy for health promotion programs. She has studied the HRQL outcomes of smoking cessation and the impact of physical activity on functioning and well-being. Dr. Stewart completed psychometric analyses of self-report measures of interpersonal processes of care; she is further testing these measures in a larger, more representative sample of over 1,600 patients from four diverse groups. She developed a review paper outlining the issues in assessing HRQL in diverse populations. She also recently published a new measure of physical activity appropriate for community-based interventions to promote physical activity in older adults. Dr. Stewart has been PI of the measurement core of the Centers for Aging in Diverse Communities, one of the RCMAR programs.

Multicultural Measurement in Older Populations

John H. Skinner, EdD

Jeanne A. Teresi, EdD, PhD

Douglas Holmes, PhD

Sidney M. Stahl, PhD

Anita L. Stewart, PhD

Editors

Springer Publishing Company

Springer Publishing Company, Inc.
536 Broadway
New York, NY 10012-3955

Acquisitions Editor: Helvi Gold
Production Editor: Sara Yoo
Cover design by Joanne Honigman

01 02 03 04 05 / 5 4 3 2 1

Library of Congress Cataloging-in-Publication-Data

Multicultural measurement in older populations / John H. Skinner, Jeanne A. Teresi,
   Douglas Holmes, editors.
    p. cm.
   Published also as v. 7, no. 1, spring 2001, of the Journal of mental health and aging.
   Includes bibliographical references and index.
   ISBN 0-8261-2246-9
    1. Minority aged—Research—Methodology.   2. Health and race—Research—
   Methodology.   3. Gerontology—Statistical methods.   I. Skinner, John H., Ed. D.
   II. Holmes, Douglas.   III. Stahl, Sidney M.   IV. Journal of mental health and aging.

   HQ1061.M816 2003
   305.26'07'2—dc21

                                                2002075791

Printed in the United States of America by Maple-Vail Book Manufacturing Group.

Contents

Part III: Cognitive Function Measures and Cross-Cultural Variation

Part IV: Measurement of Health, Mental Health and Quality of Life

Part V: Religiosity and Ethnicity

Contributors

Ronald J. Angel, PhD
University of Texas at Austin
Austin, Texas

Denise Burnette, PhD
Columbia University School of Social
    Work
New York, New York

Ameera Butler, BS
Resource Center for African American
    Aging Research
Detroit, Michigan

Linda M. Chatters, PhD
University of Michigan
Ann Arbor, Michigan

Li Mei Chen, MSW
Columbia University School of Social
    Work
New York, New York

Marvella E. Ford, PhD
Resource Center for African American
    Aging Research
Detroit, Michigan

Michelle L. Frisco, PhD
University of Texas at Austin
Austin, Texas

Barry J. Gurland, MD
Columbia University Stroud Center
New York, New York

Suzanne Havstad, MA
Resource Center for African American
    Aging Research
Detroit, Michigan

Deanna Hill, MPH
Resource Center for African American
    Aging Research
Detroit, Michigan

Rafael Lantigua, MD
Columbia University Stroud Center
Department of General Medicine
New York, New York

Jersey Liang, PhD
School of Public Health and Institute
    of Gerontology
University of Michigan
Ann Arbor, Michigan

Karen D. Lincoln, MSW, MA
University of Michigan
Ann Arbor, Michigan

Kyriakos S. Markides, PhD
Department of Preventive Medicine &
    Community Health
University of Texas Medical Branch
Galveston, Texas

Ada C. Mui, PhD
Columbia University School of Social
    Work
New York, New York

Elizabeth J. Mutran, PhD
Center on Minority Aging
University of North Carolina at
    Chapel Hill
Chapel Hill, North Carolina

Anna M. Nápoles-Springer, PhD
University of California
Center for Aging in Diverse
    Communities
San Francisco, California

Mildred Ramírez, PhD
Hebrew Home for the Aged
Riverdale, New York

Peter S. Reed, MPH
Center on Minority Aging
University of North Carolina at
    Chapel Hill
Chapel Hill, North Carolina

Laura Rudkin, PhD
Department of Preventive Medicine &
    Community Health
University of Texas Medical Branch
Galveston, Texas

Stephanie Silver, MPH
Hebrew Home for the Aged
Riverdale, New York

S. Sudha, PhD
Center on Minority Aging
University of North Carolina at
    Chapel Hill
Chapel Hill, North Carolina

Robert Joseph Taylor, PhD, MSW
University of Michigan
Ann Arbor, Michigan

Preface

Measurement in Older Ethnically Diverse Populations

Without culture-fair measures, advancements in health and social services research will be limited. Data that are not reliable and valid can result in biased multivariate results and biased estimates of the prevalence and of the magnitude of risk factors in epidemiological research. In multivariate studies that attempt to identify determinants of health, biases in self-reported measures of the determinants and health outcomes can lead to erroneous conclusions. For example, observed differences between two cultural groups in self-reported health may reflect true differences, or may instead reflect cultural bias in measures used to measure health. Similarly, screening measures used to estimate prevalence of disorder across groups may indicate differing risk factors and etiology; however, one cannot assume without question that such differences reflect true differences in the prevalence of the underlying attribute measured by the screen. If different prevalence ratios are artifacts of the assessment methods, or if different determinants of health outcomes are the result of cultural bias in measures, erroneous conclusions drawn from the results can hinder identification of the disease process, understanding of the effects of environmental stressors on illness, and/or the refinement of interventions to improve outcomes.

The Resource Centers for Minority Aging Research (RCMARS) constitute an effort by the National Institute on Aging (NIA) to redress disparities in health outcomes and delivery. Within the RCMARs, measurement is considered so important that one of the four RCMAR Cores at each site is devoted to this topic. Many of the authors or associate editors of the book are RCMAR investigators or associates. Stahl (see afterword) reviews the history, goals and early achievements of the RCMARs, pointing out that "valid measurement is a prerequisite to accurate assessment of medical needs and outcomes."

We are fortunate with this book to have as authors or as associate editors, many experts in measurement among ethnically diverse populations. Thus, we are grateful to Bob DeVellis for acting as associate editor of the methods section, to Ron Abeles, Bill Haley and Jennifer Manly for oversight of the section on measurement of acculturation, ethnic identity, socioeconomic status, and social support; and to Ana Abraido-Lanza, Steve Albert, Neal Krause, Jennifer Manly, Harold Neighbors and Al Siu for serving as associate editors for the sections on health, mental health, cognition and religion.

Methodological Issues in Cross-Cultural Assessment

Over the past decade advances have been made in the methodologies used to evaluate measures; moreover, methods long used for detection of item bias in educational testing have become more widely applied to measures of health, mental health and cognition. At the same time, some of the well-known caveats regarding use of standard or traditional measurement statistics have been forgotten. Three chapters in the methods section provide a background for the evaluation of the performance of measures. Teresi and Holmes provide some guidelines and caveats regarding the comparison of summary statistics such as corrected item-total correlations, alphas, sensitivities and specificities. The chapter by Liang discusses cross-cultural invariance in the context of structural equation modeling. He discusses the hierarchy of invariance from conceptual to metric to structural. The lowest level of evidence for factorial invariance is whether the factor structure (number of factors and item loadings on the factors) is equivalent. A second level refers to whether the loadings and measurement error variances and factor means are equivalent. An important issue is whether exact metric invariance is scientifically reasonable or whether configural invariance is the most that can be expected. Configural invariance implies that the pattern of zero and non-zero loadings are the same across groups but are not necessarily equal. Liang argues that metric equivalence remains the standard for valid comparisons.

The chapter by Teresi reviews the different methods for examining differential item functioning (DIF), focusing on studies of the elderly and health and mental health constructs. Both item response theory (IRT) and other methods are reviewed; while IRT-methods are generally preferred theoretically, some other methods can be useful first steps in identifying items that may show DIF.

Acculturation, Ethnic Identity, Socioeconomic Status and Social Support

Several chapters address the issues of acculturation, ethnic identification, socioeconomic status, and social support. The chapter by Skinner reviews acculturation measures developed over the past two decades; of these only 11 provided evidence for both reliability and validity. He underlines the point that scoring high on a measure of adherence to the native culture does not necessarily mean rejection of the dominant culture. Rather, he suggests that a bicultural approach measuring the degree of adoption of elements of both cultures should be the goal. He also calls for a multidimensional approach to the measurement of acculturation and suggests that more attention be given to developing a measure of the dominant American culture. Skinner cautions against inclusion of items that relate to childhood practices that do not therefore change over time, as such items compromise the ability to examine the process of acculturation over time.

Socioeconomic status (SES) has been linked to health outcomes in numerous studies. Rudkin and Markides describe the ways in which SES has been measured (a) over the years (b) in different epidemiological studies and (c) among different minority groups. They recommend as minimum requirements for adequate measurement of SES among ethnically diverse groups the inclusion of years of schooling, occupational status, income and financial status. However, also recommended for some groups is measurement of literacy, sources of current income and assets. Because of the sensitive nature of questions about income, the authors recommend reducing non-response by using the "bracketing" technique, where those who refuse are asked to indicate either a category of income or whether their income is above or below a certain amount. They recommend oversampling of higher SES minority elderly and of lower SES majority members because of the large SES disparities between ethnic groups that render statistical control inadequate. Rudkin and Markides conclude by emphasizing that ethnicity and minority status are primary determinants of SES differences across groups, and therefore of health outcomes associated with SES differences.

Social support has been linked to positive health and mental health outcomes. However, Mutran, Reed and Sudha point out that differences in definition of social support constructs pose an obstacle to measurement research in this area. They found few studies that examined the properties of social support measures among elderly minority group members, and call for studies examining scales that already exist in terms of performance across different ethnic and racial groups.

Cognitive Function

Two chapters review the findings with respect to possible item and test bias in cognitive functioning measures. Teresi and colleagues examine the few studies using modern psychometric methods to examine the properties of cognitive screening scales and neuropsychological tests. While most scales contain items that show some differential item functioning (DIF), there are scales that contain items that exhibit relatively greater magnitudes of DIF. Because of the growing body of consistent and compelling evidence of DIF with respect to some items, experts are beginning to agree that they are probably culturally biased. Several new scales show promise for use in cross-cultural comparisons.

While item bias is important, the criterion validity of cognitive scales is also important. Several important caveats in evaluating criterion validity are reviewed, including the fact that the diagnostic criterion can also be biased. Ramírez and colleagues review 18 studies, nearly all published in the 1990's, examining the sensitivity, specificity and predictive values of screening tests against a diagnostic "gold standard." Although summary statistics are variously affected by factors such as base rate, study design and sampling, some guidelines are provided for selecting scales that may perform better in a multicultural environment.

Health, Mental Health and Quality of Life

While self-report and performance measures of functional capacity generally agree, the level of their association is only moderate. However, both are related to poor outcomes, for example, morbidity. The attenuated mutual association may reflect the fact that they are measuring different constructs and contributing different unique information, or that self-report measures are influenced by extraneous factors such as depression, older age, culture or language. As reviewed by Angel and Frisco, some studies show that self-report measures overestimate functional capacity, for example, one large study of Mexican-Americans found that some individuals who reported that they could walk across a small room were unable to actually perform the task. Angel and Frisco conclude that there is little work that examines either cultural invariance in health and ADL measures or how "culture, language, and social class interact with factors that influence responses to survey probes and performance on tests of functional capacity."

Mui, Burnette and Chen point out that sociocultural factors such as "differences in perception, interpretation, valuation, expression, and tolerance of symptoms" may contribute to bias in measures of depression. Somatic symptoms in particular have been found to be problematic, either inflating estimates among older people in general or exhibiting differential item response among different ethnic/racial groups. The authors review two widely-used depression measures that have been applied cross-culturally among the elderly. While one of the measures developed among younger groups for use in epidemiological studies has been subjected to extensive confirmatory factor analyses among ethnically diverse populations, little evidence of cross-cultural criterion validity is available. The other measure, developed for clinical screening for geriatric depression, has been subjected to numerous analyses of the sensitivity, specificity and predictive value across different racial/ethnic groups, but few factor analyses. Cross-cultural criterion validity coefficients were only modest for this latter scale. While depression is an area that has been (relatively) better studied in terms of cross-cultural invariance, more work is still needed.

Health-related quality-of-life constructs are frequently measured as outcomes in studies of chronic disease. However, Nápoles-Springer and Stewart found only 16 studies that examined health-related quality of life measures among elderly ethnically diverse groups, and report that many suffered from one or more deficiencies in measurement adequacy. The authors discuss the fact that there are no clear guidelines regarding explicit methods for dealing with differences in measurement characteristics across groups when they are observed.

Coping and Religiosity

Coping and health locus of control are two constructs that may be linked with health-promoting behavior and outcomes. Ford, Hill, Butler and Havstad review measures of these two constructs, noting that despite the fact that the John Henry Active Coping Theory grew out of studies of hypertension among African Americans, the scale has not been evaluated systematically among large samples of African Americans. The authors call for more research examining the conceptual equivalence and factorial invariance of the measure.

Increasing attention has been focused on the role of religion as a coping mechanism that can influence health outcomes. Measurement of religious constructs was a focus of a workgroup of experts in measurement of religion sponsored by the Fetzer Institute and the National Institute on Aging. The result was a multidimensional measure of religiousness and spirituality; however, few large epidemiological studies include more than one or two items measuring religion. Chatters, Taylor and Lincoln discuss the lack of research in the mental health literature that deals with religious coping, a potentially important mediating variable related to health outcomes. They conclude that, despite the long-investigated role of religion in the lives of African Americans, few studies include sufficient numbers of African Americans to investigate adequately the measures of religion among this group.

Conclusions

In conclusion, we feel that this book constitutes an important compilation of chapters addressing the state-of-the art in multicultural measurement. The authors (and the associate editors) are well-established researchers who collectively represent the best thinking in this field. What is apparent from their chapters is that in many substantive areas, there is a dearth of cross-cultural measurement research. The most studied areas are cognition and depression. If disparities in health, mental health and service delivery are to be reduced, an important first step is their accurate assessment. Hopefully, this book sets the conceptual stage for more work toward this goal.

John H. Skinner, EdD
Jeanne A. Teresi, EdD, PhD
Douglas Holmes, PhD
Sidney M. Stahl, PhD
Anita L. Stewart, PhD

Part I

Methodological Issues in Cross-Cultural Assessment

1

Some Methodological Guidelines for Cross-Cultural Comparisons

Jeanne A. Teresi, Douglas Holmes

The purpose of this chapter is to review and revisit some methodological issues of relevance to cross-cultural research. Companion chapters by Liang and Teresi in this book discuss statistical invariance issues and the role of Confirmatory Factor Analyses and Item Response Theory in such research. Below are several guidelines related to interpretation of reliability and validity coefficients that are well addressed in the measurement and biostatistics literature, but that are frequently ignored in common practice. Some of these guidelines are based on conclusions presented in the psychometric literature over 70 years ago, but have since been forgotten (or were never learned).

1. Avoid omission and translation bias.

Measurement error will result from inadequate representation of a construct. Bias can result from differential definition and operationalization of relevant constructs; poor item structure; idiosyncratic patterns of item selection across administrations and raters; and/or inadequate criteria. The use of different items or wordings and problems in the interpretation of wording when used in translations will lead to error. An example of this is provided by the cognitive test item, "repeating no if's, and's, or but's": the item has been found to be easier for Latinos interviewed in Spanish than for those interviewed in English. This may be because there is no literal Spanish translation for the item and the alternatives do not measure adequately the intended construct, language (see Teresi, Holmes, Ramirez, Gurland & Lantigua in this book.)

2. Avoid phrases like "the test is reliable"; "the measure has proven reliability for _____(subgroup)."

A measure should be described in terms of the type of reliability estimated, and the context in which the measurement occurred. Reliability must be reexamined for every subsample and, if possible, for different score (disability) groups. Omnibus statistics (one coefficient for the entire group of individuals) do not present a complete picture of the performance of a test because an assumption (usually unrealistic) is that equal errors of measurement are made across all individuals, regardless of their standing on the latent attribute (see Hambleton, Swaminathan, & Rogers, 1991). (Modern psychometric theory, in contrast to classical test theory, allows estimates of precision across the disability continuum.)

Reliability theory was developed under the assumption of normally distributed variables. Moreover, it is assumed that a measure is developed using a random sample of individuals representing the target population. In educational testing, these assumptions are often met. Under such circumstances, and assuming that new samples are similar, one might compare the reliability coefficient obtained in a sample to the normative sample using a well-known test $[1-\alpha_1 / 1-\alpha_2]$, distributed as an F statistic with $N1-_1$ and $N2-_1$ degrees of freedom (see Feldt, 1969; Feldt and Ankenmann, 1998). However, the case is very different for most measures used in health science research. First, normally distributed variables are not the rule, and the development samples may or may not have been large random samples. Therefore, it is not meaningful to talk in terms of the "reliability" of a measure; a more meaningful description would be "the reliability estimate for this sample using Cronbach's alpha (Cronbach, 1951) was .70. This sample differs from other samples in that the average item prevalence was .15." There is an unfortunate practice among some to report the reliability of a measure as that which is reported in the literature, rather than that which is the case for the current sample. The arguments related to how reliability coefficients should be discussed recently have been revisited (e.g., Sawilowsky, 2000; Thompson & Vacha-Haase, 2000).

3. Avoid comparing Cronbach's alpha across different racial/ethnic groups; never use comparison of means and corrected item-total correlations as evidence for (or against) differential item performance across subgroups. The same caution applies to other measures of reliability as well.

Reliant as they are on average interitem correlations and thus on degree of heterogeneity in a particular sample, reliability coefficients such as Cronbach's alpha, a measure of internal consistency, will vary across populations varying in item prevalences, rendering problematic comparisons across samples drawn from these populations. Inspection of the definition of classical test theory reliability ($1-(\sigma^2_e /\sigma^2_x)$, where σ^2_e is the error variance, and $\sigma^2 x$ is the variance of the measure or item sum, shows that the more homogeneous the sample, the lower the reliability estimate (see Lord and Novick, 1968). Health-related scales are often comprised of dichotomous items or symptoms with low occurrence. Examination of the formula for the KR-20 (equivalent to Cronbach's alpha) applied to binary items shows explicitly the influence of base-rate or item prevalence on the reliability estimate. KR-20 = $n / n\text{-}1\ (1 - \Sigma p_i q_i / \sigma^2_x)$, where p_i is the proportion with the health symptom and q_i equals $(1\text{-}p_i)$ and σ^2_x is as defined above. If item difficulties are equivalent, the numerator reduces to npq, where n is the number of items, p and q are the average p and q values for the item set, and $p_i q_i$ is the item variance. The denominator is comprised of the sum of the item variances added to the sum of the item covariances. As is obvious from these formulas, the smaller the item p values, the smaller the variances and covariances and the smaller the correlation (analogous to Cronbach's alpha). Values for coefficients will vary from sample to sample and from subgroup to subgroup without necessarily reflecting true differences in reliability. The issue of comparing reliabilities becomes especially problematic in the health sciences where items with low prevalences, indicative of greater severity, for example, thoughts of suicide, blurred vision, high systolic blood pressure can be the norm. For example, in a clinic population, prevelances for a suicide item will be greater than in the general population. Similarly, the item prevalences for hypertension-related items will be higher in samples of African Americans than of Latinos, resulting in lower item variances, covariances, corrected item-total correlations and alpha coefficients for the group with lower item prevalences. Comparing these coefficients as evidence of differential item functioning will be meaningless. This is not to say that they should not be computed for each sample. The byproducts of these analyses can help to ensure that there are no coding errors. For example, if negative corrected-item total correlations are observed, this may be the result of coding errors, and as such provide a good diagnostic test to make sure that items are scored correctly. Or varying alphas can indicate that the item prevalences are different between groups.

An example of such differences is provided by Teresi and Holmes (1994) using two samples of older community-resident elderly of different age cohorts. The observed alphas for several scales in the first community sample were .87, .84, .95, while in the other sample, the comparable alphas were .74, .51, .84. Coefficient alpha is a function of the number of items and of the average interitem correlation; given a constant number of items, differences in item base rates can result in different alphas. In the first study the estimated prevalence ratios for depression, cognitive impairment and activity limitation were .10, .05, .20, respectively. In the other study the prevalences for these scales were .03, .02, .07. The observed estimates of the average interitem correlations for the first samples were .19, .35, .35. Given the lower item prevalences, the average interitem correlation in the second study is about one half of the original estimate, resulting in lower possible (maximum) observed alphas. Carmine and Zeller (1979) provide a table showing that, given an average interitem correlation of .2, a four item scale will have an alpha of .50, a 10-item scale a value of .71. Similarly, if the average interitem correlation is .4, the 4-item scale will have an alpha of .73, the 10-item scale .87.

While in educational testing items with floor or ceiling effects in a normative sample will be considered poor items, offering little information about a construct, this is not the case for the health assessment. Items with low prevalences may be important indicators of the underlying latent attribute measured, and cannot be summarily rejected, or the convergent validity with a diagnostic criterion may be compromised. On the other hand, it is true that measures with a lower maximum alpha will as a result have lower associations with outcome measures, because low reliability attenuates correlation-based construct validity coefficients. (See also DeVellis [1991] for a discussion of the effects of scale reliability on statistical power and sample size.)

As concluded over 50 years ago by McNemar (1949), "The researcher who is cognizant of the assumptions requisite for a given interpretation of a correlation coefficient and who is also fully aware of the many factors which may affect its magnitude will not regard the correlational technique as an easy road to scientific discovery." (McNemar, 1949, p. 187).

The same situation obtains for interrater reliability coefficients such as kappa (Cohen, 1960). Kraemer and Bloch (1988) and Feinstein and Cicchetti (1990) show how marginal totals can affect both the maximum value of P_o (observed total agreement $a + d/N$) and P_e (the correction factor for chance agreement calculated using marginal probabilities). They show that two reliability studies with the same percent agreement and symmetrically balanced marginal totals, but with different base rates (prevalence estimates), yield different kappas. All measures of reliability which are based on classical test theory suffer from the base rate problem. In homogeneous samples (with low baserates), the true score variance (estimated in the numerator of many reliability equations) will be small; thus the same error rates will yield smaller reliability estimates. In analysis of variance terminology, this means that the between-subject (subject to subject) variation is low, resulting in a smaller numerator in calculation of statistics such as the intraclass correlation coefficient (ICC; see Bartko, 1994).

Several authors (Shrout, Spitzer, & Fleiss [1987] and Bartko [1994]) argue that settings yielding homogeneous samples offer little test of the reliability of a measure across the full range of possibilities (scale scores or classification situations), and therefore do not provide a good basis for assessing the reliability of a measure. This reasoning is problematic because the true prevalence of a condition may be low, and artificially increasing the numbers of cases and controls or variance of a measure will not present a true picture of how the measure is operating in the real world, where the base rate is low. Muller and Buttner (1994) present a real world example—that of systolic blood pressure measurements which yield higher ICCs than do diastolic blood pressure measurements because the former have a wider range, and thus more variation. There is no evidence that diastolic blood pressure is harder to measure or that it is less "truly reliable" than is systolic blood pressure; thus the lower ICCs are more likely an artifact of the classical test theory methods of estimating reliability.

The reliance of reliability estimates on the base rate of the state or trait in the sample has long been known; however, it is sometimes forgotten or ignored in evaluating the psychometric properties of measures. The lack of invariance is less of a problem when prevalences and correlations are higher (prevalences above .2 and correlations of .4 and higher), as is typically the case with more normally distributed variables, for example, some personality variables. However, the problem is particularly relevant to clinical constructs, such as depression, affect, cognitive impairment, and many chronic illnesses. Education and ethnicity can be important factors affecting item performance because of their different prevalence ratios across these subgroups.

4. Don't automatically assume that because a test is correlated with education or other sociodemographic characteristics that it is biased.

As discussed above, a measure can be unbiased for a subgroup of interest, for example, education and still be correlated with education in a specific sample because the measure is distributed differently in the education subgroups (see Kraemer, Moritz, & Yesavage, 1998).

5. Avoid phrases like "the test is sensitive and specific"; "the sensitivity for the measure is .90 for African Americans."

It is well-known that sensitivity and specificity vary with cut-scores, with the proportion rated positive in the sample, and with the nature of the symptomatology extant in the population studied (e.g., depression symptoms are more or less severe indicators, depending upon whether a clinic or community or older or younger sample is studied). This latter source of error is sometimes referred to as spectrum bias (see also Guggenmoos-Holzmann and van Houwelingen, (2000). Moreover, sensitivities will be inflated in two-stage screening studies if the majority of cases referred for diagnosis score positive on the screening test. Kraemer and colleagues (1998) review several criteria for evaluation of a measure; one criterion used in the literature is that a measure should have equivalent sensitivities and specificities across subgroups. However, examining subgroup differences between sensitivities and specificities at specific cut-points of a scale distribution is not the optimal method for evaluating scale performance; rather, the entire receiver operating curve (ROC) should be compared for one test versus another (a plot of the sensitivity on the vertical axis and the specificity on the horizontal axis for different cut-point on the scale). This is because the absolute location (sensitivity and specificity) on the ROC curve may vary across groups due to characteristics unrelated to the test performance (Kraemer et al., 1998). While preferable to examining sensitivity and specificity at selected cut-points, even the area under the ROC curves cannot be used to rank the performance of a diagnostic test in a prevalence-free manner; all practical methods of examining the relative merits of diagnostic tests are affected by the prevalence of the disease in the sample (Hilden, 2000).

6. Do not assume that it is always a good idea to adjust scores statistically or to mechanically adjust cut-scores based on membership in an educational or racial/ ethnic subgroup.

A frequently recommended practice in dealing with inequalities in measure performance across subgroups is to construct measures which are adjusted for age and education using regression techniques. Kraemer, Moritz and Yesavage (1998) show that statistically adjusted scores actually can perform worse than unadjusted scores. Examination of adjustments for premorbid intelligence (empirically found in one study to be a proxy for age and education) indicates that such adjustments are more important in clinical practice than in research involving case ascertainment (Lindeboom et al., 1996). There is a need for more research, particularly using longitudinal data, regarding the utility of adjustments.

7. Be cautious in applying cut scores to measures.

Cut-scores are typically derived by examining the sensitivity, specificity, positive and negative predictive value of a scale against a criterion; these statistics are variously affected by the base (case) rate or marginal distribution, and by the reliability of the measure in the normative population, and will not necessarily cross-validate with a sample differing in base rate. Even in the instance of the most rigorous form of validity testing against an accepted criterion variable, it can be shown that, holding reliability constant, the positive predictive value is attenuated by low prevalence (Shrout and Fleiss, 1981). Shrout & Fleiss (1981) show that even at reliabilities as high as .80, the maximum positive predictive value for prevalences ratios below .05 is less than .70.

Because cut-scores are not 100% sensitive with respect to the gold standard criterion variable against which they were validated, there are different types of misclassification errors. These errors can be compounded in a new sample. Cut-scores, particularly those based on longer scales with a mix of item difficulties including particularly hard items, will result in higher prevalence estimates of disorder because more difficult items may result in more false positives. Even if this is not the case, they will contribute more score points which will result in more individuals crossing over the rather arbitrary threshold established using the development sample. An alternative method is latent class analyses (Clogg, 1979) according to which, in order to be classified in the impaired latent class, one must have a series of incorrect answers such that the probability of class membership is high (see Teresi, Albert, Holmes, & Mayeux, 1999). With cut-scores, it is only necessary to incorrectly answer a sufficient number of hard items to be labeled as positive. It is relatively easy to answer incorrectly on difficult items and therefore easier to be scored as "disordered."

8. Be wary of diagnostic gold standards

Finally, the gold standard diagnostic criterion variable used in assessing sensitivity and specificity of measures may itself be biased. For example, if a diagnosis of dementia is driven by classifications based on cut scores on neuropsychological tests, some of which have themselves been found to be biased for education and ethnic/racial background (see Welsh et al., 1995), the diagnostic classification may be biased, often in the direction of overdiagnosis of people with low education or from minority ethnic/racial groups (see Cobb et al., 1995).

In summary, examination of indices of reliability and validity is critical to accurate assessment across ethnically diverse groups, however, as reviewed above, a cautious approach to their interpretation is warranted.

REFERENCES

Bartko, J. J. (1994). General Methodology II: Measures of agreement: A single procedure. *Statistics in Medicine, 13*, 737-745.

Carmine, E. G., & Zeller, R. A. (1979). *Reliability and validity assessment: Sage University paper on quantitative applications in the social sciences.* Beverly Hills and London: Sage Publications.

Clogg, C. (1979). Some latent structure models for the analysis of Likert-type data. *Social Science Research, 8*, 287-301.

Cobb, J. L., Wolf, P. A., Au, R., White, R., & D'Agostino, R. B. (1995). The effect of education on the incidence of dementia and Alzheimer's disease in the Framingham Study. *Neurology, 45*, 1707-1712.

Cohen J. (1960). A coefficient of agreement for nominal scales. *Educational and Psychological Measurement, 20*, 37-46.

Cronbach, L. J. (1951). Coefficient alpha and the internal structure of tests. *Psychometrika, 16*, 297-334.

DeVellis, R. F. (1991). *Scale development: Theory and applications.* Newbury Park CA: Sage Publications.

Feldt, L. S. (1969). A test of the hypothesis that Cronbach's alpha or Kuder-Richardson coefficient twenty is the same for two tests. *Psychometrika, 45*, 99-105.

Feldt, L. S., & Ankenmann, R. D. (1998). Appropriate sample size for comparing alpha reliabilities. *Applied Psychological Measurement, 22*, 170-178.

Feinstein, A. R., & Cicchetti, D. V. (1990). High agreement but low kappa: I. The problems of two paradoxes. *Journal of Clinical Epidemiology, 43*, 543-549.

Guggenmoos-Holzmann, I., & van Houwelingen, H. C. (2000). The (In) validity of sensitivity and specificity. *Statistics in Medicine, 19*, 1783-1792.

Hambleton, R. K., Swaminathan, H., & Rogers, H. J. (1991). *Fundamentals of item response theory.* Newbury Park, CA: Sage Publications.

Hilden, J. (2000). Prevalence-free utility-respecting summary indices of diagnostic power do not exist. *Statistics in Medicine, 19*, 431-440.

Kraemer, H. C., & Bloch, D. A. (1988). Kappa coefficients in epidemiology: An appraisal of a reappraisal. *Journal of Clinical Epidemiology, 41*, 959-968.

Kraemer, H. C., Moritz, D. J., &Yesavage, J. (1998). Adjusting mini-mental state examination scores for age and educational level to screen for dementia: Correcting bias or reducing validity. *International Psychogeriatrics, 10,* 43-51.

Lindeboom, J., Launer, L. J., Schmand, B. A., Hooyer, C., & Jonker, C. (1996). Effects of adjustment on the case-finding potential of cognitive tests. *Journal of Clinical Epidemiology, 49,* 691-695.

Lord, F. M., & Novick, M. R. (1968). *Statistical theories of mental test scores.* Reading, MA: Addison-Wesley Publishing Co.

McNemar, Q. (1949). *Psychological statistics.* New York: John Wiley & Company.

Muller, R., & Buttner, P. (1994). A critical discussion of intraclass correlation coefficients. *Statistics in Medicine, 13,* 2465-2476.

Sawilowsky, S. S. (2000). Psychometrics versus datametrics: Comment on Vacha-Haase's "Reliability generalization method and some EPM editorial policies." *Educational and Psychological Measurement, 60,* 157-173.

Shrout P., Spitzer R. L., & Fleiss, J. (1987). Quantification of agreement in psychiatric diagnosis revisited. *Archives of General Psychiatry, 44,* 172-177.

Shrout, P., & Fleiss, J. (1981). Reliability and case detection. In J.K. Wing, P. Bebbington & L.N. Robbins (Eds.), *What is a case?* (pp. 117-128). London: Grant Mcintyre.

Teresi, J., & Holmes, D. (1994). Overview of methodological issues in gerontological and geriatric measurement. In P. Lawton & J. Teresi (Eds.), *Annual review of gerontology and geriatrics: Focus on assessment techniques* (vol. 14, pp. 1-22). New York: Springer Publishing.

Teresi, J. A., Albert, S., Holmes, D., & Mayeux, R. (1999). Use of latent class analyses for the estimation of prevalence, of cognitive impairment and signs of stroke and Parkinson's Disease among African-American elderly of Central Harlem: Results of the Harlem Aging Project. *Neuroepidemiology, 18,* 309-321.

Thompson, B., & Vacha-Haase, T. (2000). Psychometrics is datametrics: The test is not reliable. *Educational and Psychological Measurement, 60,* 174-195.

Welsh, K. A., Fillenbaum, G., Wilkinson, W., Heyman, P., Mohs, R. C., Stern, Y., Harrel, L., Edland, S. D., & Beekly D. (1995). Neuropsychological test performance in African-American and white patients with Alzheimer's disease. *Neurology, 45,* 2207-2211.

Acknowledgments. Support for this work was provided in part by the Columbia University Resource Center for Minority Aging Research (RCMAR) and the National Institute on Aging (AG15294). The authors thank Lucja Orzechowska for her valuable editorial assistance on this chapter.

2

Assessing Cross-Cultural Comparability in Mental Health Among Older Adults

Jersey Liang

C ulture is a central dimension underlying differences across various ethnic and racial groups (Markides, Liang, & Jackson, 1990). As the collective programming of the mind, culture plays a key role in shaping individuals' cognitive, emotional, and behavioral functioning. In particular, core cultural ideas together with ecological and socioeconomic factors constitute the collective reality consisting of meanings, practices, norms, and social institutions (Fiske, Kitayama, Markus, & Nisbett, 1998). It has long been recognized that cross-cultural differences in health and illness reflect not only genuine variation in the incidence and prevalence of morbidity, disability, and mortality but also in the social processes by which these data were generated. These processes may be far removed from the biological reality. The conceptualization and measurement of mental health, therefore, can benefit from the adoption of a comparative perspective.

A major assumption underlying the comparative study of health is that beliefs about health, diseases, and medical treatment are products of a particular historical, social, and cultural setting. Thus, culture affects disease manifestation, illness behavior, and diagnostic labeling (Corin, 1994). For instance, Kleinman (1986) was struck by the high prevalence of a diagnosis of "neurasthenia" in China, whereas in the West this diagnosis has almost disappeared and has been replaced by "depression." Chinese patients and their families interpreted the illness primarily in physical terms in spite of the enormous psychosocial stress that was reported and perceived as causing the disorder. According to Kleinman (1986), in Chinese society there is a strong stigma associated with mental illness, which often is viewed as disgraceful. In contrast, physical illness is socially quite acceptable, hence encouraging patients to express and indeed to perceive only the physiological component of their distress.

Baker (1991) called attention to the different symptom patterns among different racial groups in that older African Americans with depression were less likely to complain of dysphoric mood but instead had more somatic complaints. On the other hand, Escobar and colleagues (1986) suggested that the Mini-Mental State Examination (MMSE) contains five items culturally biased against Hispanics. Using item-response theory in a sample of Hispanic, African American, and White elders from New York, Teresi and colleagues (1995) demonstrated that several cognitive screening items including, for example, serial 7's and repetition of "no ifs, ands, or buts" were ethnically biased.

A major research issue in comparative studies has been the equivalence of measures. One must establish that variables measured in different cultures are sufficiently similar as to be treated as the same phenomenon and to warrant a meaningful comparison. Although it may be less complicated when only objective physical measures are employed, the issue of equivalence is particularly serious when self-reported data are involved. Questionnaire items valid and reliable in one language often lose meaning after translation. Furthermore, even with accurate translation, the problem of different connotations and nuances unique to different cultures may not be resolved. In order to make a meaningful comparison, the investigator must understand the similarities and differences between measures of a given variable in different cultures.

It should be noted that there is a strong continuity between cross-national studies and studies of ethnic groups within the same society. Both types of research are concerned with the causes and consequences of cultural differences. Methodologically, cross-national studies and ethnic group studies need to address the issue of comparability in measurement. Accordingly, significant cultural differences frequently exist even among ethnic groups, sharing a common language. Failure to substantiate the equivalence in mental health measures may lead to misleading conclusions in comparing the prevalence of symptoms or disorders across ethnic groups.

In comparative research, there are at least three types of equivalence (Hui & Triandis, 1983; Labouvie, 1980). The first is *conceptual equivalence*, in which research materials or observed behaviors have the same meaning in two or more cultures. The second is measurement equivalence, which guarantees that a given measurement specification can be applied to different cultures; specifically, that the observed indicators have the same relationships with the theoretical constructs across different cultures. The third is structural equivalence, which refers to the fact that the causal linkages between a given construct and its causes and consequences are invariant across different cultures. More important, the three types of equivalence constitute a hierarchy in that metric equivalence assumes conceptual equivalence, whereas both are required for the establishment of structural equivalence.

CONCEPTUAL EQUIVALENCE

To ensure conceptual equivalence, several methods may be employed including back-translation, focus groups, random probe (Schuman, 1966), and in-depth interviews.

These approaches will help to assure cultural meaningfulness and sensitivity. For instance, to develop a quality of life (QOL) questionnaire that is reliable and valid across 15 cultures, the World Health Organization (WHO) established an international panel of experts and 15 centers around the world. All 15 centers contributed to the definition of QOL and items to the questionnaire. Repeated translation and back-translation were used to check the equivalence and meaningfulness of these items (Power, Harper, Bullinger, & WHO QOL Group, 1999). The approach used by the WHO QOL Group is particularly attractive in view of the fact that most of the QOL instruments were developed in one culture and language and then translated into other languages.

As another example, in a comparative study of subjective well-being among American and Japanese elderly people, back-translation, focus groups, and random probes were used to ascertain that items of the Philadelphia Geriatric Center Morale Scale (PGCMS) were understood and interpreted by respondents in both cultures with the same framework as that intended by the investigators (Liang, Bennett, Akiyama, & Maeda, 1992). The PGCMS was subject to a series of translation and back-translation between English and Japanese. In addition, these items were reviewed by several focus groups in Japan. Finally, 23 elderly Japanese were matched by 28 older Americans in terms of age and gender. Each respondent was asked all PGCMS items and a follow-up probe was carried out for a randomly selected subset of the items according to the random probe procedure suggested by Schuman (1966). The probed material was evaluated question by question by coders who first read the follow-up material blind, then used it to predict the respondent's original closed alternative, and finally evaluated the total fit between probe explanation and chosen alternative. These data provided a measure of the respondent's understanding of the questionnaire as a whole.

METRIC EQUIVALENCE

There are two major types of comparability or invariance in measures (Bollen, 1989). One is similarity in model form, and the other is similarity in parameter values. For instance, two models have the same form if they have the same number of factors on which the same items are loaded. The similarity of form thus may range from a low point with a very different number of factors and pattern of factor loadings to a relative minor difference in form where, for example, the models are identical except for the correlations among measurement errors or unique variances. In most applications to date, the same form of the measurement specification or factorial structure is assumed for the groups under study. The focus is placed on the similarities and differences in parameter values or metric equivalence. Some investigators described dissimilarities in model form and those in parameter values, respectively, as qualitative and quantitative differences in factorial structure (Nesselroade & Thompson, 1995; Widaman, 1991).

Metric equivalence can be assessed by comparing the factorial structures that emerge from data obtained in different cultures (Hui & Triandis, 1983; Little, 1997;

Miller, Slomczynski, & Schoenberg, 1981; van DeVijver & Leung, 2000). Exploratory or unrestricted factor analysis as well as confirmatory factor analysis has been used to assess factorial invariance. Exploratory factor analysis (EFA) is useful in a preliminary stage in identifying the number of factors and the underlying pattern of factor loadings within a given group. By contrasting the results from two or more cultural groups, one may obtain some clues as to whether the same factorial structure can apply to different groups.

However, EFA in itself is insufficient for assessing comparability for several reasons. First, comparisons of factor configurations are done by using Pearson correlation matrices. Such comparisons are confounded by variance differences between samples because correlation coefficients are standardized in terms of sample variances. Variance-covariance matrices should be used (Cudeck, 1989; Nesselroade & Thompson, 1995). Second, in EFA no significance tests of the differences in factorial structure can be applied. Given that estimates of structural parameters are random variables, the differences between such estimates from two different samples are also random variables. As a result, significance tests are required to establish the equivalence between the factor structures emerging from two different groups. Third, in exploratory factor analysis, little a priori specification is involved in deriving the factor structure. As suggested by Blalock (1982), an explicit auxiliary measurement model is required to address the issue of comparability of measurement. Such a model is needed to determine the precise nature of potential noncomparability of measures across settings, time periods, or different populations. Without an explicit formulation, the claim of noncomparability is inherently untestable. Accordingly, EFA should always be employed in conjunction with confirmatory procedures such as structural equation modeling.

Covariances among the observable indicators are a function of the underlying parameter matrices including, for example, factor loadings, measurement error variances, and covariances among the factors (Jöreskog & Sörbom, 1979). As a result, various levels of factorial invariance can be defined with reference to equivalence in elements of one or more parameter matrices. In addition, factorial invariance is hierarchical (Bollen, 1989, pp. 355-367; Nesselroade & Thompson, 1995). For instance, the lowest level of factorial invariance is whether the factorial structure has the same form in terms of number of dimensions and the indicators loaded on these dimensions across different groups. A higher level of invariance exists if factor loadings and measurement error variances are equivalent among different groups. Furthermore, invariance can be demonstrated if factor loadings, measurement error (or unique) variances, and factor means do not differ across two or more groups. Other types of equivalence (e.g., those involving higher-order factors) could be evaluated, but the important point is that factorial invariance is not an either-or proposition. It is instead a matter of degree, and the degree of invariance has different implications for data analysis.

Horn (1991) differentiated between configural invariance and metric invariance. Configural invariance implies that all measures marking the factors have their primary nonzero loading on the same construct across groups. They must also have zero loadings on the same measures for all factors. This type of invariance is similar to equivalence in model form as described by Bollen (1989). As observed by Horn (1991), it is questionable whether metric equivalence can be fully established with complex data, and hence, configural invariance is likely to be the best solution that can be obtained.

Although equivalence in factor loadings is not always easy to accomplish, it is probably premature to conclude that metric equivalence is scientifically unreasonable. The degree of metric equivalence required for a given comparison clearly depends on the nature of the research question. Nevertheless, configural invariance remains a minimal requirement, whereas some form of metric invariance across groups is essential before valid comparisons of factor scores can be made. Indeed, all widely used psychosocial measures should be subject to a rigorous analysis in its metric equivalence across different cultural groups. Thus, items suitable for comparison across groups may be distinguished from those unsuitable. Furthermore, metric equivalence should be included routinely as a major criterion in addition to reliability and validity in evaluating psychosocial measures. Without metric equivalence, it is impossible to conclude that a given measure is culturally fair.

Liang and associates (Liang & Bollen, 1985; Liang, Lawrence, & Bollen, 1987) outlined a procedure for analyzing factorial invariance across two or more groups. In particular, basic measurement models are developed separately within each cultural group. Once these models are developed, simultaneous factor analysis involving the explicit comparison of common elements can be undertaken. This entails the examination of changes in goodness of fit by applying equivalence constraints involving factor loadings, measurement error variances, residual error variances and covariances.

This procedure was applied to ascertain racial differences in the factorial structures of two popular instruments of psychological well-being, the Philadelphia Geriatric Center Morale Scale (PGCMS) and Life Satisfaction Index A (LSIA; Liang et al., 1987). In particular, the PGCMS was hypothesized to include 3 first-order factors with 6, 4, and 5 indicators, respectively. A second-order factor was assumed to account for the correlation among the 3 first-order factors. Similarly, LSIA was specified as consisting of 3 first-order factors with 3, 4, and 4 indicators. A second-order factor was assumed to influence the 3 first-order factors. Data for this analysis came from two national probability sample surveys of older Americans. With reference to the PGCMS, the reliabilities associated with two items among the Black respondents were only one-half of the magnitude of those among the White respondents. On the other hand, regarding LSIA, no racial differences were found in terms of measurement specifications (i.e., the relationships between latent variables and their indicators). Accordingly, in making comparisons in mental health between older Black and White Americans, it is advisable to employ LSIA instead of PGCMS. If PGCMS is to be used, one may consider deleting the two items with differential reliabilities.

It should be noted that the observed racial differences may be due to unobserved heterogeneity such as differential compositions in terms of age, gender, and socioeconomic status across the ethnic and racial groups. To test this hypothesis, the measurement specifications may be estimated with the background variables controlled for. In addition, this approach can be justified on the basis of construct validity. As defined by Cronbach and Meehl (1955), construct validity implies that a given measurement specification delineates not only the linkages between a concept and its indicators but also their relationships with relevant exogenous variables. In particular, construct validity presupposes that indicators of a given concept will behave similarly toward relevant external criteria.

As an empirical illustration, Liang and associates (1992) evaluated the metric equivalence in the PGCMS items between American and Japanese elders. Among the 15 PGCMS items, invariance was demonstrated for 11 items in terms of the first- and second-order factor loadings but not in measurement error variances. Because nonequivalence in measurement errors can be easily adjusted, it is reasonable to conclude that for these 11 PGCMS items, cross-cultural comparability exists between the American and Japanese aged. Moreover, when the equivalence in factorial structure of the PGCMS was evaluated, age, gender, education, and physical health were controlled. The results showed that the PGCMS items remained equivalent across the American and Japanese samples, hence suggesting that items' equivalence was not due to population heterogeneity.

Alternatively, a multiple indicators, multiple causes (MIMC) model may be specified for examining item bias associated with specific background characteristics such as age, gender, ethnicity, and education. However, the MIMC model is somewhat limited in testing equivalence constraints which involve parameters other than item factor loadings. In a recent study, Gallo and associates (1998) ascertained racial differences in the reporting of depressive symptoms by examining a latent trait model in which race was hypothesized to have a direct effect on the endorsement of various depressive symptoms. In addition to race, gender, education, MMSE, and marital status were controlled. Elderly African Americans were more likely than their White counterparts to report thoughts of death, but not suicide ideation. Nevertheless, the findings did not support the hypothesis that older African Americans would be more likely than older Whites to report depressive symptoms of a somatic nature and less likely to report symptoms of a psychological nature.

A central issue in cross-cultural comparative research involves the emic-etic distinction (Brislin, 1976; Triandis & Brislin, 1984). An emic analysis seeks to document valid principles within a given cultural system, taking into account what individuals within the culture consider to be meaningful and important. An etic analysis, however, seeks to make valid generalizations across individuals from different cultures. Although in this chapter the primary emphasis has been placed on etic analyses, this does not imply that emic analysis is less important. An emic analysis is particularly useful in understanding the relatively unique features of the manifestation of mental disorders, illness behavior, and diagnosis in a given ethnic group. For example, on the basis of two surveys of Mexican Americans, Miller and his associates (1997) argued strongly for a two-factor model of CES-D among elderly Mexican Americans instead of a four-factor model which was derived from samples of the general American population. This is an example of qualitative differences in factorial structure between two groups, and it raises a serious question as to whether CES-D can be used for analyzing differences in depressive symptoms between elderly Mexican Americans and the general American population.

Studies of mental health are further complicated in that different indicators may be required to measure the same concept. For instance, the instrumental activities of daily living scale (IADL) has been viewed as a proximate measure of cognitive functioning. It includes items such as driving an automobile and balancing a checking account, which are culturally not meaningful to the elderly in countries such as Japan and China. Consequently alternative indicators are required. In general, culture-specific indicators may be used within the same ethnic or cultural group, whereas culture-general items are more appropriate in making comparisons across different groups. Analytically it would be very interesting and challenging to delineate the relationships between culture-specific and culture-general indicators.

STRUCTURAL EQUIVALENCE

Structural equivalence in causal linkages implies that the same causal mechanism extends across different racial, ethnic, and cultural groups. For example, with regard to a depression measure which is metrically equivalent across ethnic groups, one may wish to examine whether its linkage with functional status is the same or different in direction and/or magnitude within various ethnic groups. It should be noted again that the three types of equivalence (i.e., conceptual, metric, and structural) constitute a hierarchy in that metric equivalence assumes conceptual equivalence, whereas both are required for the establishment of structural equivalence. Thus, cross-cultural comparability is viewed as a matter of degree rather than a dichotomy. Accordingly, a mental health measure may be conceptually and metrically equivalent but not structurally equivalent across different ethnic groups.

There are at least three major issues related to the assessment of structural equivalence (Markides, Liang, & Jackson, 1990). The first involves the separation of intragroup differences from intergroup variations. Caution should be exercised when comparisons involving two or more ethnic groups are made without adjusting for differences in other characteristics such as age, sex, and socioeconomic background. Because intergroup differences are likely to be confounded with population heterogeneity, such a simple and gross comparison may result in misleading conclusions. As an illustration of such confounding, in a recent study of the differences in MMSE scores between Black and White elderly women, the crude data showed trends for increased functional difficulty with poorer performance on the MMSE in both groups. However, in comparison with White women, Black women were younger, with lower education and income, and higher rates of certain self-reported diseases. After adjusting for age and education, no association between MMSE and functional status was found among the Black women (Leveille et al., 1998).

The second issue is related to the distinction between main and interaction effects. For instance, when race or ethnicity is introduced into a regression equation as one or more dummy variables, only the main effect is evaluated without testing the interaction effect. That is, only racial differences in intercepts are assessed. Interaction effects imply differences in slopes. To examine interaction effects, significance tests are required for the interaction term involving race and a given independent variable. For instance, one may pose the question of whether the effect of cognitive functioning on functional status is the same or varies across different ethnic groups. In this regard, Leveille and colleagues (1998) observed that the effect of cognitive functioning on disability varied as a function of race. That is, increasing functional difficulty was associated with decreasing MMSE scores among White older women but not in Black elderly women.

The third issue concerns the causal interpretation of the effects of race and ethnicity. In most studies, a single-equation approach is used, and attention is largely focused on direct effects only. Although the interrelationships among race, ethnicity, and other independent variables generally have been recognized, the causal linkages among them have rarely been explicitly specified and examined. Consequently, indirect and noncausal effects are often overlooked, and misleading conclusions may result. As an illustration, in addition to its direct net effect on depression, ethnicity may influence depression through education, income, and health conditions. If one focuses on the net effect only, the total effect of ethnicity is likely to be underestimated and hence misinterpreted. In this regard, models involving multiple equations are required to represent and estimate the various direct and indirect effects.

The three issues related to structural equivalence can all be addressed within the framework of structural equation modeling (SEM) as well as by other techniques. Nevertheless, SEM is probably the most versatile approach to evaluating metric and structural equivalence simultaneously.

CONCLUSIONS

Nearly two decades ago, Palmore (1983) noted that there were relatively few truly comparative cross-cultural studies of social gerontology. Most of the existing studies were primarily descriptive and contained little theory, few generalizations, and few quantitative comparisons with other cultures. Indeed, the majority of social gerontological research published in English dealt only with the dominant White Anglo-Saxon Protestant culture in the United States. Furthermore, Cowgill (1986), observed that much of the empirical research in comparative aging consisted of disparate case studies with no uniformity of definition, method, sample, or range of subject matter. The failure to provide adequate and systematic attention to conceptual and methodological problems undoubtedly contributes to a lack of meaningful and interpretable data, which in turn poses significant risks of misinterpretation. Cowgill (1986) argued eloquently that to further comparative aging research, we should undertake parallel studies by using comparable techniques, covering the same subject matter, and employing comparable concepts in distinct cultures.

Although much progress has been made during the last 20 years, these comments are still applicable to the research on mental health and aging involving different racial and ethnic groups. Most studies have been based on data collected from one ethnic or cultural group, and comparisons are at best implicit. When two or more groups are compared, descriptive and analytical techniques have been applied often without addressing issues concerning conceptual, metric, and causal equivalence. Currently, much more still needs to be learned about the cross-cultural comparability of many widely used mental health instruments.

As a result, an agenda for future work can be outlined. Collecting comparable data and assessing conceptual and metric equivalence of key variables deserves the highest priority. Without resolving these concerns, comparisons across ethnic or racial groups may not be justified. Once equivalence in measurement is demonstrated, equivalence in causal linkages needs to be examined. Only when issues of equivalence have been addressed, can substantive explanations for observed group differences be sought meaningfully.

REFERENCES

Baker, F. M. (1991). A contrast of: Geriatric depression versus depression in younger age groups. *Journal of the National Medical Association, 83,* 340-344.

Blalock, H. M. (1982). *Conceptualization and measurement in the social sciences.* Beverly Hills, CA: Sage.

Bollen, K. A. (1989). *Structural equations with latent variables.* New York: Wiley.

Brislin, R. W. (1976). Comparative research methodology: Cross-cultural studies. *International Journal of Psychology, 11,* 215-229.

Cowgill, D. O. (1986). *Aging around the world.* Belmont, CA: Wadsworth.

Corin, E. (1994). The social and cultural matrix of health and disease. In R. G. Evans, M. L. Barer & T. R. Marmor (Eds.), *Why are some people healthy and others not?* (pp. 93-130). New York: Aldine De Gruyter.

Cronbach, L. J. & Meehl, P. E. (1955). Construct validity in psychological tests. *Psychological Bulletin, 52,* 281-302.

Cudeck, R. (1989). Analysis of correlation matrices using covariance structure models. *Psychological Bulletin, 105,* 317-327.

Escobar, J. L., Burnam, A., Kamo, M., Forsythe, A., Landsverk, J. & Golding, J. M. (1986). Use of the Mini-Mental State Examination (MMSE) in a community population of mixed ethnicity: Cultural and linguistic artifacts. *Journal of Nervous and Mental Disease, 174,* 607-614.

Fiske, A. P., Kitayama, S., Markus, H. R., & Nisbett, R. E. (1998). The cultural matrix of social psychology. In D. T. Gilbert, S. T. Fiske, & G. Lindzy (Eds.), *The handbook of social psychology* (Vol., II, 4th ed., pp. 915-981). New York: McGraw-Hill.

Gallo, J. J., Cooper-Patrick, L., & Lesikar, S. (1998). Depressive symptoms of Whites and African Americans aged 60 years and older. *Journal of Gerontology: Psychological Sciences, 53B*(5), P277-P286.

Horn, J. L. (1991). Comments on issues in factorial invariance. In L. M. Collins & J. L. Horn (Eds.), *Best methods for analysis of change* (pp. 114-125). Washington, DC: American Psychological Association.

Hui, C. H., & Triandis, H. C. (1983). Multi-strategy approach to cross-cultural research: The case of locus of control. *Journal of Cross-Cultural Psychology, 14*(1),65-83.

Kleinman, A. (1986). *Social origins of distress and disease: Depression, neurasthenia and pain in modern China.* New Haven, CT: Yale University Press.

Jöreskog, K. (1979). Simultaneous factor analysis in several populations. In K. Jöreskog & D. Sörbom (Eds.), *Advances in factor analysis and structural equation modeling* (pp. 189-207). Cambridge, MA: ABT Books.

Labouvie, E. W. (1980). Identity versus equivalence of psychological measures and constructs. In L. W. Poon (Ed.), *Aging in the 1980's.* Washington, DC: American Psychological Association.

Leveille, S. G., Guralnik, J. M., Ferrucci, L., Corti, M. C., Kasper, J., & Fried, L. (1998). Black/White differences in the relationship between MMSE scores and disability: The Women's Health and Aging Study. *Journal of Gerontology: Psychological Sciences, 53B*(3), P201-P208.

Liang, J., Asano, H., Bollen, K. A., Kahana, E. F., & Maeda, D. (1987). Cross-cultural comparability of the Philadelphia Geriatric Center Morale Scale: An American-Japanese comparison. *Journal of Gerontology, 42*(1), 37-43.

Liang, J., Bennett, J., Akiyama, H., & Maeda, D. (1992). The structure of PMC Morale Scale in American and Japanese aged: A further note. *Journal of Cross-Cultural Gerontology, 7,* 45-68.

Liang, J. & Bollen, K. A. 1985. Sex differences in the structure of the Philadelphia Geriatric Center Morale Scale. *Journal of Gerontology, 40*(4), 468-477.

Liang, J., Lawrence, R. H., & Bollen, K. A. (1987). Race differences in factorial structure of two measures of subjective well-being. *Journal of Gerontology, 42*(4), 426-428.

Little, T. D. (1997). Mean and covariance structures (MACS) analysis of cross-cultural data: Practical and theoretical issues. *Multivariate Behavioral Research, 32*(1), 53-76.

Markides, K. S., Liang, J., & Jackson, J. S. (1990). Race, ethnicity, and aging: Conceptual and methodological issues. In R. H. Binstock & L. K. George

(Eds.), *Handbook of aging and the social sciences* (3rd ed., pp. 112-129). San Diego, CA: Academic Press.

Miller, J., Slomczynski, K. M., & Scoenberg, R. J. (1981). Assessing comparability of measurement of cross-national research: Authoritarian conservatism in different sociocultural settings. *Social Psychology Quarterly, 3,* 178-191.

Miller, T. Q., Markides, K. S., & Black, S. A. (1997). The factor structure of the CES-D in two surveys of elderly Mexican Americans. *Journal of Gerontology: Social Sciences, 52B*(5), S259-S269.

Nesselroade, J. R., & Thompson, W. W. (1995). Selection and related threats to group comparisons: An example comparing factorial structures of higher and lower ability groups of adult twins. *Psychological Bulletin, 117,* 271-284.

Palmore, E. B. (1983). Cross-cultural research: State of the art. *Research on Aging, 5,* 45-57.

Power, M., Harper, A., Bullinger, M., & The World Health Organization–Quality of Life Group. (1999). The World Health Organization WHOQOL-100: Tests of the universality of quality of life in 15 different cultural groups worldwide. *Health Psychology, 18*(5), 495-505.

Schuman, H. (1966). The random probe: A technique for evaluating the validity of closed questions. *American Sociological Review, 31,* 218-222.

Teresi, J. A., Golden, R. R., Cross, P., Gurland, B., Kleinman, W., & Wilder, D. (1995). Item bias in cognitive screening measures: Comparison of elderly White, African American, Hispanic, and high and low education subgroups. *Journal of Clinical Epidemiology, 48,* 473-483.

Triandis, H. C., & Brislin, R. W. (1984). Cross-cultural psychology. *American Psychologist, 39,* 1006-1016.

van De Vijver, F. J. R. & Leung, K. (2000). Methodological issues in psychological research on culture. *Journal of Cross-Cultural Psychology, 31*(1), 33-51.

Widaman, K. F. (1991). Qualitative transitions amid quantitative development: A challenge for measuring and representing change. In Collins, L. M. & Horn, J. L. (Eds.), *Best methods for analysis of change* (pp. 204-217). Washington, DC: American Psychological Association.

Acknowledgments. Support for this research was provided by the National Institute on Aging grant R37 AG154124 (Jersey Liang, principal investigator). John Skinner, Jeanne Teresi, Doug Holmes, Sid Stahl, and Anita Stewart made useful comments and suggestions on an earlier version of this manuscript. The assistance provided by Joan Bennett is gratefully acknowledged.

3

Statistical Methods for Examination of Differential Item Functioning (DIF) With Applications to Cross-Cultural Measurement of Functional, Physical and Mental Health

Jeanne A. Teresi

D ifferent methodologies for the detection of differential item functioning (DIF) have been used to examine assessment scales in cross-cultural research. The focus of this brief chapter is on methods that have been used to examine measures of health constructs among culturally diverse elderly populations. Other more general reviews can be found in Camilli and Shepard (1994); Holland and Wainer (1993); van de Vijver and Leung (1997).

DIF analysis involves three factors: item response, disability level and subgroup membership; the research question relates to how item response is related to disability for different subgroups. This relationship is usually defined in terms of item parameters so that DIF analysis frequently examines differences in these parameters. DIF analysis is concerned with whether the likelihood of item endorsement is equal across subgroups. A key issue is whether the method used is conditional or nonconditional; only conditional methods that take disability into account are acceptable. An example of early (nonconditional) methods include comparison of differences in item means or proportions, known as item difficulties.

Item response theory (IRT) (Lord, 1980; Lord & Novick, 1968) and confirmatory factor analyses (CFA; Jöreskog, 1979) constitute two general methods of examining item invariance. The latter is reviewed in this book by Liang. The two methods share several features and can produce similar outcomes in the dichotomous case. Both rely on a latent variable; both use model-based goodness-of-fit tests. Both CFA and IRT estimate a parameter similar to the well-known corrected item-total correlation from classical test theory: the factor loading (λ) in CFA and the item discrimination (a_i) in IRT. However, CFA (with the exception of Muthén's model contained in LISCOMP) (Muthén, 1988) does not estimate a difficulty parameter (see also Liang in this book). Moreover, the two models are based on different assumptions, and model different features of the data; the item covariance structure in CFA and the item response pattern in IRT (see also Reise, Widaman, & Pugh, 1993). A brief overview of IRT is presented here, along with other parametric and nonparametric methods for examining DIF.

BRIEF REVIEW OF IRT

IRT provides a method for examining items in terms of relative precision, information, and differential item functioning (DIF) across subgroups. The basic concept is that an item set is being used to measure an underlying attribute such as depression; the concern is the extent to which the item response is related to the trait. For example, the expectation is that depressed respondents would be more likely than nondepressed to respond symptomatically (deviantly) to an item measuring depression. Conversely, a person with little disorder is expected to have a lower probability of responding in a disordered direction to the item. The curve that relates the probability of a deviant item response to the level of the underlying disorder is known as an item characteristic curve (ICC). According to the IRT model, an item shows DIF if people from different subgroups but at the same disability level have unequal probabilities of responding deviantly to a particular item. For example, Latino people who are moderately demented should have the same chance of a correct or an incorrect response to a particular cognitive test item as do African Americans and Whites who are at a similar level of impairment. Put another way, item characteristic curves, which relate the probability of item response to the underlying attribute, should be the same for each group of interest. The model is expressed as follows. The density function of an item response U_i ($i = 1, \ldots n$) conditional on θ, item difficulty b_i, and item slope a_i can be expressed as $P_i = P(U_i = 1 | \theta, a_i, b_i) = [1 + \exp(-1.7a_i(\theta - b_i))]^{-1}$, for the two-parameter logistic binary response model (see Lord, 1980; Lord and Novick, 1968).

Item scores are related to the level of the underlying attribute, theta (θ), for example, depression, by functions that provide an estimate of the probability of occurrence of each possible score on an item for a randomly selected individual of given disorder or disability. In most health applications where guessing is minimal, the item difficulty (b_i) is the point on the disability continuum where the probability of a symptom response is .5. In health applications, a high b means that the item maximally discriminates (separates disability levels or groups) at a higher or more severe level of disability. High b's are characteristic of items that elicit a positive response from individuals with greater disability, so that relative to items with lower b's, individuals have to be at higher levels of disability before they will have a 50% chance of endorsing the item. The item difficulty corresponds to the classical-test theory estimate of the item mean or proportion responding in an impaired direction to health-related items. For example, a high b parameter in the context of a cognitive test (where a wrong response is coded as (1) would correspond to an "easy" item in classical-test theory parlance, with a low proportion answering incorrectly.

In traditional (classical test theory) analyses, the discrimination parameter is estimated by the corrected item-total correlation. In IRT, the discrimination parameter (a_i) is an indicator of how well an item performs at different levels of disability. At any point along the disability continuum, the usefulness of the item for discriminating among the individuals at that point, and those close to that level of disability, is proportional to the slope of the curve at that disability level. Very steep curves are associated with high a_i values.

IRT parameters are relatively distribution-free; that is, ability can be estimated independently of the particular version of a measure and of the population being assessed. Because items have characteristics (e.g., difficulty parameters) which are invariant with respect to prevalence of disorder in the population assessed, item pools of varying item difficulty can be constructed and related to the disability of the individual assessed. The relationship between two scales administered to two different groups will be linear (the parameters will vary but be equivalent within a linear transformation) because they differ only in origin and unit of measurement. A linear transformation of the a and b parameters will not change the probability of a correct response. However, even parameters obtained from IRT and CFA, if collected from independent samples, are not directly comparable. In order for comparisons to be valid, parameters must be rescaled or equated to take into account the different variances of the latent variables in the groups (see Reise, Widaman, & Pugh, 1993). A comparison of item parameters requires that there be a theoretical basis for such comparisons. For CFA, after applying certain constraints, invariance is an hypothesis to be tested— generated from the model. In IRT, invariance is a feature of the model that will apply if assumptions are met. As discussed in the "methods overview" by Teresi and Holmes in this book, this is not true of classical test theory-derived parameters. However, as is true of any method, sample design can be a problem with IRT; if the populations sampled are so different as to imply that underlying constructs differ between the groups, this could invalidate some IRT models. For example, Grayson (1987) used item response theory models to investigate the bimodality versus dimensionality of psychiatric constructs such as schizophrenia and depression. He suggests the use of community samples rather than clinic samples to develop measures of depression, in order to adequately represent all levels of depression by selecting items that discriminate maximally at varying points along the latent continuum.

An illustration of an IRT analysis is provided by Teresi and colleagues (2000) in a study of cognitive test items. In this example, the probability of failing item 15 for a randomly selected Latino of moderate cognitive disability (theta = 1.5) was approximately .68, whereas for African Americans at the same level of disability, the probability of failing the item was only .33. The African American subsample had a relatively lower probability of failure even at the highest level of disability, resulting in a difference in the areas under the curves for the Latino vs. other groups. Thus, this item was not performing in the same manner across the ethnic groups, and model-based significance tests indicated that this item exhibited DIF: it was a harder item for Latinos.

Recent advances in IRT include further development of different response models (see Van der Linden & Hambleton, 1997); and of the methods of Differential Item Functioning (see Camilli & Shepard, 1994; Holland & Wainer, 1993). As reviewed by Teresi and Holmes (1994), a number of features of IRT are useful in evaluating health measures: (a) the capability to estimate the precision of the measure in terms of standard errors computed for different points along the measure of the latent attribute; (b) the ability to examine the fit of individual subjects and raters, and to calculate rater bias; (c) use of the information function (which provides information about how an item performs at various points along the latent attribute continuum) for better selection of items to tailor tests for a specific purpose; (d) the ability to identify items which are sensitive to change and which measure disability or ability across the entire latent attribute spectrum; and (e) the invariance properties of IRT which allow examination of item bias across gender, racial/ethnic, age and education subgroups.

IRT APPLICATIONS TO MENTAL HEALTH ASSESSMENT

IRT methods are being applied more frequently to cognitive and ADL measures than to health and mental health measures. (Studies of cognitive measures using IRT are reviewed by Teresi and colleagues in this book.) However, IRT also has demonstrable utility in the development and evaluation of health and mental health measures. Although some of these studies were reviewed in more detail by Teresi and Holmes (1994), they are worth mentioning here because of their relevance to mental health. For example, Duncan-Jones, Grayson, and Moran (1986) used IRT to examine the gender bias of the 12-item General Health Questionnaire. Two items (feeling constantly under strain and feeling unable to overcome difficulties) are more related to depression for females than they are for males. Gibbons and associates (1985) used IRT to examine the Beck Depression Inventory, comparing medically ill inpatients with psychiatric patients. The vegetative symptoms of weight loss and loss of sexual interest were particularly poor discriminators of depression severity among the medically ill sample. Two items (loss of satisfaction, loss of social interest) were found to maximally assess depression severity. Finally, in an examination of item bias (using IRT) associated with the SHORT-CARE Depression scale used in a study of a probability sample of Latino elderly, Teresi and Golden (1994) found that some of the somatic symptoms (headaches), crying, and lack of interest were relatively less severe indicators of depression for Latinos than for White, non-Latinos. Other recent studies of depression measures are discussed below.

IRT AND NON-IRT-BASED METHODS OF EXAMINING DIF

The general methods for assessing DIF include (a) comparison of parameters across subgroups; (b) examining interactions between subgroup and disability when predicting item response; (c) comparing areas under item response curves; (d) examining (nested) model-based likelihood tests. As discussed in the methods overview by Teresi and Holmes in this book, comparisons of parameters such as corrected item-total correlations or item means or proportions are not acceptable methods for examining DIF because they are nonconditional and do not take into account disability level. Only conditional methods are considered below (for a review of nonconditional methods in the context of health measures, see Teresi, Cross, & Gurland, 1989). Issues related to the adequacy of any DIF detection method is how the method (a) handles nonuniform DIF (the phenomenon occurring, for example, when a subgroup performs better than a comparison group at lower levels of disability, but worse at higher levels), (b) handles polytomous (nondichotomous) responses to items and (c) is affected by sample size.

IRT-based methods for detecting DIF include model-based likelihood ratio tests, IRT-area tests, probability difference tests and parameter comparison methods. Another method which can be used with multidimensional data is the simultaneous item bias test (SIBTEST; Shealy & Stout, 1993). A discussion of these methods is beyond the scope of this chapter (see Teresi, Kleinman, & Ocepek-Welikson, 2000 for a more detailed discussion of these methods as they pertain to assessment of health constructs). Generally, the parameter comparison tests include Lord's chi-square (Lord, 1980) for the two parameter model and a variant of a *t*-test in the special case of the one parameter Rasch model. Lord's chi-square is based on examination of the differences in the variance-covariance matrix of the difficulty and discrimination parameters. The results are equivalent to Raju's signed area test (Raju, 1988), which calculates the differences in the areas between the curves for two groups, and detects uniform DIF. The unsigned area test provides a test of nonuniform DIF. Lord's chi-square is linked theoretically to the likelihood ratio test and has been found to be similar for the two parameter model (Cohen, Kim, & Wollack, 1996). The probability differences, which are summed squared differences in conditional probabilities between comparison groups, provide information about the magnitude of the DIF.

Because of crossing or nonuniform DIF, an item may not show DIF using the signed area test, however, DIF will be observed for the unsigned area test. While the probability difference method focuses on the area of the ICC where there is a greater density of respondents (ICC differences are summed across the actual ability estimates of the individual members of the focal [target] group, and not across the entire range of possible thetas), the other methods examine the entire range of theta. However, this focus may result in too much dependency on a restricted range of theta, and there is no significance test. The unsigned area and probability difference statistics are useful for examining characteristics and magnitude of DIF, and for selecting anchor items for use in further model-based significance tests. A caveat in using IRT-based methods is their requirement for relatively large sample sizes. However, Cohen, Kim and Wollack (1996) found type 1 error rates for the likelihood ratio test for the 2 parameter model to be very close to those expected with n's as small as 250 per group. Another important caveat is that multidimensionality can be mistaken for DIF (Mazor, Hambleton, & Clauser, 1998), so that examining the assumptions of the model are important; the most widely used IRT models assume that the underlying trait is unidimensional, although as previously stated, DIF can be examined in the context of test bias for multidimensional data (see Shealy & Stout, 1993.)

A latent variable approach (based on covariance structure analyses using the normal distribution function) for examining DIF among dichotomous indicators is that of Muthén (1984). The model is linked to IRT as originally proposed by Birnbaum (Lord & Novick, 1968) because the discrimination parameter can be calculated using the factor loadings (lambdas) (see also Thissen, Steinberg, & Wainer, 1993). This model uses equality constraints to test whether the item parameters differ between groups. The test of DIF is whether the likelihood of a positive symptom is different between groups after controlling for disorder as well as other covariates. The estimate of the latent attribute or disorder is based on the covariation among symptoms. Variants of this approach have been applied by Grayson and associates (2000), and earlier by Gallo and colleagues (1998) to the examination of the differential performance of depression items between African Americans and Whites using a multiple indicator-multiple causes (MIMC) analysis, where the direct effects of group status on items serve as DIF indicators, after controlling for the indirect effects of covariates. As previously stated, this approach is a CFA structural equation model that incorporates a threshold (difficulty) value. A major advantage is the inclusion of covariates; possible disadvantages include the restriction that equality constraints can be imposed only on the factor loadings (see Liang, in this book). Other problems are that tests of DIF are less well-developed, and the model's inability to examine polytomous responses.

A contingency table approach, log-linear models, has been used to examine DIF in measures of psychological functioning among ethnic/race groups (e.g., Dancer, Anderson, & Derlin, 1994). Log-linear models can be used to examine whether the term representing the difference in item difficulties between two groups is zero. Certain forms of the log-linear approach to DIF are similar to the Rasch model, which is a log-linear model (see Thissen, Steinberg, & Wainer, 1993). Use of log-linear models for DIF assessment involves examination of cross-tabulations among item response, ability status groupings and demographic subgroup membership. Nested models are tested; an augmented model containing an interaction term for demographic subgroup membership and item response is tested against a null model containing item response and the interaction of item response with ability group. A likelihood ratio test, distributed as a chi-square, is examined in order to determine the difference between models; if the model fit is better with the augmenting interaction term (if the likelihood is smaller and the p value larger), this indicates that DIF occurs because the interaction of item response by ethnic group improves the model fit above and beyond that present with only item response and the interaction of item response and ability status. This method is similar to the likelihood method used to determine DIF for IRT, however in IRT, item discrimination and difficulty are modeled and ability is better measured because log-linear models use categorical ability levels, although with a sufficiently large n to ensure adequate cell sizes, each level of ability could be examined. Unlike IRT, the loglinear approach incorporates the difference in item parameters as part of the model (see Thissen, Steinberg, & Wainer, 1993). A disadvantage of this approach for health applications is the inability to examine nonuniform DIF. An assumption in comparing likelihood ratios is that the log-linear model (which examines how well the estimated, expected and actual observed frequencies agree) fits the data; tests of this assumption are not well developed.

Nonparametric contingency table approaches include the Mantel-Haenszel chi-square method (MH; see Holland & Thayer, 1988). The MH method can be used to examine whether, within each disability score group, the odds of a symptom or incorrect response is the same across groups. This method was used by Bjorner and colleagues (Bjorner, Kreiner, Ware, Damsgaard, & Bech, 1998) to examine the SF-36 Health Survey (Ware & Gandek, 1994). The authors also used a variant of the gamma statistic (Goodman & Kruskal, 1954) to examine polytomous responses. The MH statistic is based on examination of item score by group tables for each score level. DIF is indicated if there is a significant interaction of item by group, controlling for disability level. A common odds ratio, which tests whether the likelihood of item symptom response is the same across ability groups, also can be used to construct a DIF magnitude measure. Because it is a signed test, it is typically used only for detection of uniform DIF, although recently a modification of the method has allowed for detection of nonuniform DIF (Maranon, Barbero-Garcia, & San Luis-Costas, 1997). An advantage of such methods is that model assumptions, for example, unidimensionality, are not required. However, the MH method has been criticized because it focuses on the difference in the intercept, and provides no evidence regarding which part of the underlying distribution is most affected by DIF (see Bock, 1993); similar to the Rasch model, this method is not optimal if the discrimination parameters vary across groups, as is frequently the case with health data. Moreover, the MH method treats ability as a categorical variable. Finally, unlike the log-linear approach, multiple pair-wise comparisons must be performed when comparing multiple groups.

Another non-IRT contingency-table approach to the examination of DIF is based on logistic regression (Swaminathan & Rogers, 1990). Logistic regression examines whether the odds of admitting to a symptom are different between two groups. Item response is predicted from ability scores, group status and the interaction of group by ability. Logistic regression, which has a relationship to the log-linear approach (see Camilli & Shepard 1994), is related to IRT methods by the logistic model. The general logistic cumulative distribution function used for both models is: $\Psi(y) = 1 / 1 + e^{-y}$. Whereas for the two parameter IRT model shown earlier, $y = 1.7a_i(\theta\text{-}b_i)$, where b_i is the item difficulty and a_i is the discrimination parameter as defined earlier; in logistic regression, a dichotomous event or response is modelled as: $P(u = 1) = 1 / 1 + e^{-y}$, where $y = \alpha + \Sigma\beta x$. For the DIF application, the model can be written as follows $y = \alpha + \beta_1 x_1 + \beta_2 x_2 + \beta_3(x_1 x_2)$, where, similar to log-linear models, $\beta_2 x_2$ is the difference in item performance between groups, denoted by x_2, and x_1 is the estimate of ability. Unlike log-linear models, because ability is treated as continuous in the logistic regression model, the interaction term $\beta_3(x_1 x_2)$ can be included, which is an estimate of nonuniform DIF. If β_2 is significant, then there is uniform DIF; if β_3 is significant, then there is nonuniform DIF. Additionally, a likelihood test can be calculated as described above where the test statistic is -2(log likelihood for the null model (with β_2 set to 0)—the log likelihood for the augmented model), distributed as chi-square with 2 *df*. A two-stage procedure is recommended (Camilli & Shepard, 1994), in which a corrected or unbiased estimate of DIF is achieved by removing items with DIF from the total score and repeating the exercise.

Advantages of logistic regression include treating ability as a continuous variable, capability to model multidimensional data and capability to include covariates. However, logistic regression does not allow for the modeling of polytomous response. Additionally, logistic regression assumes that the logit of $P(U = 1|x)$ is linear in the observed score x, which may be violated for the two parameter model (see Camilli & Shepard, 1994). Several recent analyses used logistic regression for the detection of DIF in cognitive tests, for example, Marshall and colleagues (1997) and Woodard and associates (1998).

Model fit, sample size and type of DIF (uniform or nonuniform) can affect the detection rate (Rogers & Swaminathan, 1993; Whitmore & Schumacker, 1999). Recently, logistic regression was compared to analyses of variance using Rasch logits for detection of DIF (Whitmore and Schumacker, 1999); this was an extension of the *t*-test formerly used to examine differences in the difficulty parameter between groups. Generally, it has not been recommended that Rasch models be used for the detection of DIF in health data because of the assumption of equal discrimination parameters; however, some evidence has shown that it either compared favorably or surpassed the performance of the Mantel-Haenszel test (see Whitmore & Schumacker, 1999). The findings indicated that logistic regression was generally favored over use of the Rasch model ANOVA procedure except in the case of uniform DIF; because the discrimination parameters often vary in applications using health data, resulting in nonuniform DIF, it appears as if the logistic regression model would be preferable. Generally, samples of 400 were better in terms of detection rates than those of 200, however, more false positives result in the larger samples. For the smaller sample size of 200, the Rasch ANOVA approach had a lower detection rate for false positives than did the logistic regression approach. The number of items (20 vs. 40 or 60) did not impact on detection rates. Generally, logistic regression and ANOVA using Rasch logits is preferred over the Mantel-Haenszel procedure, although some evidence indicates that the results of logistic regression and the Mantel-Haenszel procedure are comparable in some circumstances (see Mazor, Hambeleton & Clauser, 1998).

SUMMARY

Several methods for examination of item invariance and differential item functioning were reviewed. Differences among methods can be characterized as to whether they: (a) are model-based; (b) assume unidimensionality; (c) are based on latent or observed variables; (d) treat the disability dimension as continuous; (e) assume equal discrimination parameters; (f) can detect both uniform and nonuniform DIF; (g) can examine polytomous responses; (h) can include covariates in the model. IRT, MIMC, log-linear and logistic regression methods can use a model-based likelihood ratio approach to testing for DIF. However, logistic regression is not based on a latent variable model. IRT, MIMC, ANOVA using Rasch logits, and logistic models assume continuous variables. The other methods generally rely on blocking methods to create score groups. Only IRT methods can model polytomous responses. Logistic regression can handle multidimensional DIF by including more than one disability parameter in the model; DIF tests for multidimensional IRT models are also available. Some models, although they do not include a formal discrimination parameter, can still test for nonuniform DIF through the use of item response by ability interactions (logistic regression and Rasch ANOVA.). However, estimation of a discrimination parameter (provided only by IRT and MIMC methods) provides additional information about item performance across subgroups. Several models (MIMC, loglinear, ANOVA using Rasch logits and logistic regression) allow for inclusion of covariates. While the Mantel-Haenszel method has numerous shortcomings, it is frequently used as the first step when analyzing a large pool of items. In the context of IRT, area and probability difference tests are useful in selecting anchor items for further model-based tests and for interpreting the magnitude of DIF. IRT methods are generally preferred in examining health-related scales because of numerous desirable features reviewed above. However, if IRT-based methods are not feasible, approaches that treat disability as continuous, allow detection of nonuniform DIF and inclusion of covariates, for example, logistic regression, are recommended.

REFERENCES

Bjorner, J. B., Kreiner, S., Ware, J. E., Damsgaard, M. T., & Bech, P. (1998). Differential item functioning in the Danish translation of the SF-36. *Journal of Clinical Epidemiology, 51*, 1189-1202.

Bock, D. (1993). Different DIFs: Comment on the papers read by Neil Dorans and

David Thissen. In P. W. Holland & H. Wainer (Eds), *Differential item functioning* (pp. 115-122). Hillsdale, NJ: Lawrence Erlbaum, Inc.

Camilli, G., & Shepard, L. N. (1994). *Methods for identifying biased test items.* Thousand Oaks, CA: Sage Publications.

Cohen, A. S., Kim, S. H., & Wollack, J. A. (1996). An investigation of the likelihood ratio test for detection of differential item functioning. *Applied Psychological Measurement, 20,* 15-26.

Dancer, S. L., Anderson, A. J., & Derlin, R. L. (1994). Use of log-linear models for assessing differential item functioning in a measure of psychological functioning. *Journal of Consulting and Clinical Psychology, 62,* 710-717.

Duncan-Jones, P., Grayson, D. A., & Moran, P. A. P. (1986). The utility of latent trait models in psychiatric epidemiology. *Psychological Medicine, 16,* 391-405.

Gallo, J. L., Cooper-Patrick, L., & Lesikar, S. (1998). Depression symptoms of Whites and African Americans aged 60 years and over. *Journal of Gerontology: Psychological Sciences, 53B,* 277-286.

Gibbons, R. D., Clark, D. C., VonAmmon-Cavanaugh, S., & Davis, J. M. (1985). Application of modern psychometric theory and psychiatric research. *Journal of Psychiatric Research, 19,* 43-55.

Goodman, L. A., & Kruskal, W. H. (1954). Measures of associations for cross classifications. *Journal of the American Statistical Association, 49,* 732-764.

Grayson, D. A. (1987). Can catagorical and dimensional views of psychiatric illness be distinguished? *British Journal of Psychiatry, 151,* 355-361.

Grayson, D. A., Mackinnon, A., Jorm, A. F., Creasey, H., & Broe, G. A. (2000). Item bias in the Center for Epidemiological Studies Depression Scale: Effects of physical disorders and diability in an elderly community sample. *Journal of Gerontology: Psychological Sciences, 55B,* P273-P282.

Holland, P. W., & Thayer, D. T. (1988). Differential item performance and the Mantel-Haenszel procedure. In H. Wainer & J. I. Braun (Eds.), *Test validity.* Hillsdale, NJ: Lawrence Erlbaum.

Holland, P. W., & Wainer, H. (1993). *Differential item functioning.* Hillsdale, NJ: Lawrence Erlbaum.

Jöreskog, K. G. (1979). Basic ideas of factor and component analysis. In K. G. Jöreskog & D. Sörbom, *Advances in factor analysis and structural equation models* (pp. 5-20). Cambridge, MA: ABT Books.

Lord, F. M. (1980). *Applications of item response theory to practical testing problems.* Hillsdale, NJ: Lawrence Erlbaum.

Lord, F. M., & Novick, M.R. (1968). *Statistical theories of mental test scores.* Reading, MA: Addison-Wesley Publishing.

Maranon, P. P., Barbero-Garcia, M. I., & San Luis-Costas, C. (1997). Identification of nonuniform differential item functioning: A comparison of Mantel-Haenszel and item response theory analysis procedures. *Educational and Psychological Measurement, 57,* 559-568.

Marshall, S. C., Mungas, D., Weldon, M., Reed, B., & Haan, M. (1997). Differential item functioning in the Mini-mental State Examination in English and Spanish-speaking older adults. *Psychology and Aging, 12*, 718-725.

Mazer, K. M., Hambleton, R. K., & Clauser, B. E. (1998). Multidimensional DIF analyses: The effects of matching on unidimensional subtest scores. *Applied Psychological Measurement, 22*, 357-367.

Muthén, B. O. (1984). A general structural equation model with dichotomous, ordered categorical, and continuous latent variable indicators. *Psychometrika, 49*, 115-132.

Muthén, B. O. (1988). *LISCOMP: Analysis of linear structural equations with a comprehensive measurement model.* Mooresville, IN: Scientific Software.

Raju, N. S. (1988). The area between two item characteristic curves. *Psychometrika, 53*, 495-502.

Reise, S. P., Widaman, K. F., & Pugh, R. H. (1993). Confirmatory factor analysis and item response theory: Two approaches for exploring measurement invariance. *Psychological Bulletin, 114*, 552-566.

Rogers, H. J., & Swaminathan, H. (1993). A comparison of logistic regression and Mantel-Haenszel procedures for detecting differential item functioning. *Applied Psychological Measurement, 17*, 105-116.

Shealy, R., & Stout, W. (1993). An item response theory model for test bias. In Holland, P.W. & Wainer, H. (Eds.), *Differential item functionin* (pp. 197-239). Hillsdale, NJ: Lawrence Erlbaum.

Swaminathan, H., & Rogers, H. J. (1990). Detecting differential item functioning using logistic regression procedures, *Journal of Educational Measurement, 26*, 361-370.

Teresi, J., Cross, P., & Golden, R. (1989). Some applications of latent trait analysis to the measurement of ADL. *Journal of Gerontology: Social Sciences, 44*, S196-S204.

Teresi, J., Golden, R., Cross, P., Gurland, B., Kleinman, M., & Wilder, D. (1995). Item bias in cognitive screening measures: Comparisons of elderly White, Afro-American, Hispanic, and high and low education subgroups. *Journal of Clinical Epidemiology, 48*, 473-483.

Teresi, J., & Holmes, D. (1994). Overview of methodological issues in gerontological and geriatric measurement. In M. P. Lawton & J. Teresi (Eds.), *Annual review of gerontology and geriatrics: Focus on assessment techniques* (Vol. 14, pp. 1-22). New York: Springer Publishing.

Teresi, J., Kleinman, M., & Ocepek-Welikson, K. (2000). Modern psychometric methods for detection of differential item functioning: Application to cognitive assessment measures. *Statistics in Medicine, 19*, 1651-1683.

Teresi, J., Kleinman, M., Ocepek-Welikson, K., Ramirez, M., Gurland, B., Lantigua, R., & Holmes, D. (2000). Applications of item response theory to the examination of the psychometric properties and differential item functioning of the CARE Dementia Diagnostic Scale among samples of Latino, African American and White non-Latino elderly. *Research on Aging, 22*, 738-773.

Thissen, D., Steinberg, L., & Wainer, H. (1993). Detection of differential item functioning using the parameters of item response models. In Holland, P. W. & Wainer, H. (Eds.), *Differential item functioning* (pp. 123-135). Hillsdale, NJ: Lawrence Erlbaum, Inc.

van de Vijver, F., & Leung, K. (1997). *Methods and data analysis for cross-cultural research*. Thousand Oaks, CA: Sage Publications.

van der Linden, W. J., & Hambleton, R. K. (1996). *Handbook of modern item response theory*. New York: Springer Publishing.

Ware, J. E., & Gandek, B. (1994). The IQOLA Project Group. The SF-36 Health Survey: Development and use in mental health and the IQOLA project. *International Journal of Mental Health, 23*, 49-73.

Whitmore, M. L., & Schumacker, R. E. (1999). A comparison of logistic regression analysis of varience differential item functioning direction methods. *Educational and Psychological Measurement, 59*, 910-927.

Woodard, J. L., Auchus, A. P., Godsall, R. E., & Green, R. C. (1998). An analysis of test bias and differential item functioning due to race on the Mattis Dementia Rating Scale. *Journal of Gerontology: Psychological Sciences, 53B*, P370-P374.

Acknowledgments. Support for this work was provided in part by the National Institute on Aging Coordinating Center for the Collaborative Studies of Special Care Units for Alzheimer's Disease, AG10330, the Columbia University Resource Center for Minority Aging Research (RCMAR), and the National Institute on Aging (AG15294).The author thanks Lucja Orzechowska for her valuable editorial assistance.

Part II

Acculturation, Ethnic Identity, Socioeconomic Status and Social Support

4

Acculturation: Measures of Ethnic Accommodation to the Dominant American Culture

John H. Skinner

Acculturation is a recurrent theme in the literature on minority aging (Krause & Goldenhar, 1992; Silverstein & Chen, 1999; Szapocznik, Scopetta, Kurtines, & Aranalde, 1978; Tran, 1988; Zsembik, 1994). Acculturation is generally viewed as a process that involves adopting or acquiring the language, customs, values, habits, beliefs, attitudes, behaviors, and lifestyles of the host or dominant culture or alternate (nonnative) society (Cortes et al., 1994; Khairullah & Khairullah, 1999; Mendoza, 1989; Szapocznik et al., 1978). Acculturation has also been viewed from the perspective of the predominant culture absorbing other cultures (LaFromboise, Coleman, & Gerton, 1993). Another view suggests that acculturation leads to conflict when individuals from subordinate cultures attempt to adapt to the dominant cultures (Berry, 1980). Berry (1980, p.10) sees acculturation as a result of "contact of at least two autonomous cultural groups" that leads to a change in one or the other of the groups. This process of change is not without conflict or resistance by subordinate cultures when seeking to retain features of their respective culture (Berry, 1980).

Others have viewed acculturation from the perspective of loss of traditional language, customs, values, and habits. Silverstein and Chen (1999, p. 2), for example, define acculturation of Mexican American families as the erosion of traditional Mexican values, language, and practices due to exposure to American culture. Much of the acculturation literature has focused on the ways in which immigrants to the United States have adjusted to the mainstream "White middle-class" culture (Khairullah & Khairullah, 1999; Krause & Goldenhar, 1992; Mendoza, 1989; Silverstein & Chen, 1999; Szapocznik et al., 1978; Tran, 1988; Zsembik, 1994). This has resulted in an emphasis on the ability to speak and read English as an important indicator of acculturation (Cuellar, Harris, & Jasso, 1980; Krause & Goldenhar, 1992; Mendoza, 1989; Silverstein & Chen, 1999; Szapocznik et al., 1978; Tran, 1988; Zsembik, 1994).

Some investigators have focused solely on the command of written and spoken English as the indicator of acculturation (Kamo & Zhou, 1994; Krause & Goldenhar, 1992; Tran, 1988).

Most literature on acculturation addresses the ways in which immigrants speaking languages other than English accommodate to the dominant culture. Some studies involve subjects who already speak English and, in some cases, are native to the United States (Choney, Berryhill-Paapke, & Robbins, 1995; Khairullah & Khairullah, 1999; Landrine & Klonoff, 1994; Parham & Helms, 1981). Choney and colleagues (1995) addressed the issue of acculturation among American Indians. Khairullah and Khairullah (1999) studied the acculturation process of Asian-Indian immigrants who were educated in a system where English is the official language. Landrine and Klonoff (1994) have studied African American acculturation, minimizing the importance of language as a variable in cultural assimilation.

Instruments designed to measure acculturation can be categorized along two axes: the cultural/scaling perspective, and the dimensionality of the measures. The cultural/scaling perspective relates to the focus of the substantive content of the measure, that is, does the measure present statements representing one or more cultural perspectives to which individuals must respond? The cultural perspective of an instrument may focus solely on one cultural perspective such as Mexicans, Greeks, Puerto Ricans, and African Americans or it can contain more than one cultural perspective such as Mexican Americans and Puerto Ricans; or Puerto Rican culture and American Culture.

The methods of scaling can be unipolar or bipolar. Unipolar measures permit only responses in one direction reflecting the degree or frequency with which one agrees, performs, or feels about a particular statement or scale item. Unipolar scales include such responses as none, some, a lot, and many; or agree somewhat, agree, agree a lot, and strongly agree. Bipolar scaling methods permit responses that are anchored at bipolar extremes (e.g., strongly agree/strongly disagree, Mexican/Anglo, only Spanish/only English). Bipolar scales that use an agree/disagree format imply that agreement of disagreement with the cultural perspective represented measures acculturation or the lack thereof. It should be emphasized that the failure to subscribe to a particular cultural perspective in itself does not mean an embracing of another cultural perspective.

Dimensionality reflects the degree of complexity (numbers of conceptual domains) of the concept measured. Unidimensional scales attempt to define acculturation in terms of a single dimension, most often language. Multidimensional scales identify the multifaceted nature of culture and attempt to measure the relevant subcomponents of acculturation. Dimensions identified in the literature reviewed in the chapter are often reported as the result of exploratory factor analyses.

It is noted that the cultural perspective, method of scaling, and dimensionality are not mutually exclusive categories. To the contrary, they necessarily intersect. Any instrument will have a cultural perspective, a method of scaling, and some level of dimensionality.

CULTURAL/SCALING PERSPECTIVE

Acculturation has been conceptualized variously as a monocultural, bicultural, or multicultural phenomenon. The terminology used varies with the instruments reviewed.

Monocultural/Unipolar Scales

Monocultural theorists view acculturation as a one-way, relatively permanent adoption of the dominant culture with the concomitant abandonment of one's native culture. For example, the pioneering work of Szapocznik and colleagues (1978) has viewed acculturation as a linear process affected by time and exposure to a host culture.

Language acculturation has been a focus of some monocultural scales (Krause & Goldenhar, 1992; Tran, 1988; Zsembik, 1988). Others have broadened their conceptualization of acculturation to include ethnic identification, ethnic origin, preference for ethnic group, customs, values, music, television, movies, food, and immigrant history (where born, parents, country of birth, age at immigration, contact with native culture, and time in the United States) (Caetano, Schafer, Clark, Cunradi, & Raspberry, 2000; Cuellar et al., 1980; Kamo & Zhou, 1994). Cortes, Rogler, & Malgady (1994, p. 771) to suggest "acculturation is not equivalent simply to the acquisition of the host society's language."

Tropp, Erkut, Coll, Alarcon, and Garcia (1999) have developed an acculturation scale that focuses on the psychological experience of the individual instead of the behavioral or attitudinal dimension of acculturation.

A number of scales present items on only one cultural perspective, that is, Hispanic, Mexican, African American, and so forth (Harris & Verven, 1996; Landrine & Klonoff, 1996; Resnicow, 1997; Rezentes, 1993; Silverstein & Chen, 1999; Tran, 1988). These scales present ethnically centered statements (reflecting beliefs, customs, behaviors representing one ethnic group) to which respondents are asked their degree of agreement or subscription. Other scales have taken a more neutral position asking respondents their use of, or preference for, one belief, behavior, custom, or language over another (Cuellar et al., 1980; DeLeon & Mendez, 1996; Franco, 1983; Khairullah & Khairullah, 1999; Mendoza, 1989; Padilla, 1980; Suinn et al., 1992; Szapocznik et al., 1978; Tropp et al., 1999; Zsembik, 1988).

An important conceptual issue in measures of acculturation has been the way the items are anchored and the methods of scaling. Respondents to a unipolar scale are generally asked to respond to statements reflecting one cultural perspective. The method of item anchoring refers to the cultural focus represented by the test items, that is, the cultural perspective being assessed.

The assimilation model of acculturation has implied a unidirectional process of adaptation to the dominant culture (a cultural one-way street) (Landrine & Klonoff, 1996). Unipolar scaling typically identifies the extent to which a respondent supports a statement. Scales using unipolar scaling appear to be most often used to ascertain monocultural endorsements of statements. Zsembik (1988) has scaled proficiency in English as one and a person who speaks no English as zero. Tran (1988) has taken a more extensive approach to determining English language acculturation by asking a series of questions about how well the respondent speaks and reads English on a 5-point scale from not at all to very well. Six other items address how well English was used in six situations coded by responses of yes and no. Krause and Goldenhar (1992) have used a scale of language acculturation that summed the extent to which the respondent spoke, read, and wrote English well. Cortes and associates (1994) have determined the frequency or strength of endorsement of a behavior, value, or belief using a 4-point scale.

It should be noted that unipolar scales of monocultural statements leave open to question whether scores that do not support culturally based statements of a native culture reflect acculturation to the host (nonnative) culture. Evidence of weak support for one's native culture does not provide an indication of subscription or assimilation to the host culture.

Multicultural/Bipolar Scales

Some have conceptualized acculturation as a bicultural phenomenon, rejecting the notion that acculturation is a one-way street. They view acculturation as the acquisition of features of a host culture while maintaining aspects of the native culture. Cortes and colleagues (1994, p. 718) argue that "... acculturation does not proceed to a zero-sum process which would imply a linear inverse relationship between the level of involvement in the two cultures." Instead, they suggest that people can be highly immersed in two cultures just as they might be weakly immersed in two cultures. The Psychological Acculturation Scale contains items ". . . pertaining to the individual's sense of psychological attachment to and belonging within the Anglo-American and Latino/Hispanic cultures." (Tropp et al., 1999, p. 351). They suggest that psychological acculturation is a better measure than measures that focus on the amount of contact individuals have with host cultures.

Berry (1980) has made a distinction between a plural society and a multicultural society. In the former many cultural groups are present, in the latter, diversity of cultural groups is valued. Mendoza (1984) has posited that acculturation is more than a monocultural phenomenon. He has referred to the acquisition of customs of an alternate (nonnative) society as a monocultural approach, while the incorporation of customs from the alternate (nonnative) society with those of native societies constitutes a multicultural approach. Mendoza (1984) developed the Cultural Life Style Inventory (CLSI) as a multicultural instrument. The CLSI items were selected using the following item discrimination analysis criteria: the items

1. ". . . produced responses that were typical of 90% or more of the Mexican American sample and

2. were distinct from the types of responses that were typical of at least 90% of the Anglo-American reference group."

DeLeon and Mendez (1996) have tested the CLSI on a Puerto Rican sample. They have concluded that factorial validity of the CLSI supports the scale's ability to measure acculturation as a multicultural and multidimensional phenomenon.

These authors' approach to multicultural measures is the assessment not only of the customs of one culture (the native culture) but of at least one other culture (at minimum the host culture). DeLeon and Mendez (1996) point to the multicultural nature of the CLSI by demonstrating the scale that was first used to assess Mexican American acculturation and could be used with a Puerto Rican sample.

Bipolar scaling of acculturation items permits the measurement of two aspects of a concept, for example, acculturation and traditionalism. Several acculturation scales have taken this approach. Among the earlier scales, most have addressed immigrant assimilation with a key focus on language acculturation, particularly for Hispanic Americans. Szapocznik and colleagues (1978) have used two scaling techniques to establish a range of responses to acculturation. First, Likert 5-point scaling has been used on self-reported behavior items to record the relative frequency of a behavior among Cuban Americans. The second scaling technique provided three value-oriented solutions to problem situations anchored by a traditional cultural solution at one extreme and a host cultural solution at the other extreme. Cuellar and associates (1980) have used a 5-point scale anchored at one extreme with (Mexican/Spanish = 1) and at the other extreme (Anglo/English = 5). The mid-score 3 has been used to represent bicultural/ bilingual responses. Franco (1983) has developed an acculturation scale for Mexican-American children to be completed by an adult informant. He used 5-point rating scales that have different anchors to reflect the content (cultural anchor) of each of the 10 items in the scale. These scales were designed so that low-rated items reflect children who are very "Mexican" and high-rated items reflect children who are very "Anglicized." Mendoza (1989) developed a Cultural Life Style Inventory using a bipolar 5-point scale that anchored Mexican-American and Anglo-American cultures at extremes.

Khairulla and Khairulla (1999) have developed a behavior acculturation scale for Asian-Indian immigrants based on the work of Szapocznik and colleagues (1978). Khairulla and Khairulla (1999, p. 58) have identified this ethnic group as "the fastest growing group of immigrants" in the United States and one that does not encounter the problems of learning the English language that many other immigrant groups experience. However, while Asian-Indians are generally well educated and taught English as one of the official languages for higher education, they still speak their native ethnic languages. Their scale contains 10 items of a 5-point Likert scale using the following values: 1 = Indian all the time, 2 = Indian most of the time, 3 = Indian & American equally, 4 = American most of the time, and 5 = American all the time.

Tropp and colleagues (1999) have employed a 9-point bidirectional Likert-type scale to measure psychological acculturation items that range from 1 (only Hispanic/Latino) to 9 (only Anglo/American). A unique aspect of these scaling techniques is that they permit use of a middle point that reflects equal orientations (bicultural), that is, between Hispanic/Latino and Anglo/American or between Asian Indian and American.

Parham and Helms (1981) have designed a Black Racial Identity Attitudes Scale that included rating scales of 30 items anchored at the extremes with 1 = strongly disagree and 5 = strongly agree. Agreement with the statements reflected high racial identity.

Although the literature provides abundant examples of acculturation scales for Hispanic immigrants to the United States, more recently, acculturation scales have begun to focus on other ethnic groups. Harris and Verven (1996) have used a 7-point agreement scale to study the degree to which respondents supported statements representing traditional Greek culture. Landrine and Klonoff (1996) have also used a 7-point bipolar agreement scale on the African American Acculturation Scale ranging from 1 = "I totally disagree, not true at all" to 7 = "I strongly agree, absolutely true." The mid-point of the scale is 4 = "I sort of agree, sort of true." Resnicow (1997) has developed a racial identity scale for low-income African Americans consisting of 20 items, of which 18 were coded from 1 to 4 with 1 equal to "agree a lot" and 4 equal to "disagree at lot." Two items obtained information on frequencies and were coded from 1 to 5 with 1 equal to "never" and 5 equal to "more than three times." These two items were reverse scored to be consistent with the direction of other items of the scale. The Racial Identity Scale is coded so that low scores reflect stronger racial identity.

DIMENSIONALITY

Unidimensional Scales

Cuellar and colleagues (1980) reported developing a 20-item acculturation rating scale without identifying specific dimensions. The scale items address language, preferences for things Spanish, and time lived in the United States. Mendoza (1989) has suggested that the focus on language distinguishes between unidimensional and multidimensional measures of acculturation. Tran (1988) has focused his unidimensional scale on English language acculturation. Eight items have been incorporated in the scale with two items dealing with a person's ability to speak and read English and six items with the ability to use English in various everyday situations. Krause and Goldenhar (1992) have used an English language measure of acculturation similar to that of Tran (1988). As with Tran the conceptualization of this measure is unidimensional. Rezentes (1993) has developed an Hawaiian acculturation scale consisting of 21 items that address Hawaiian vocabulary, customs, history, culture, and participation in contemporary Hawaiian culture. Rezentes (1993) does not report any attempt to develop dimensions and has treated the items as a unidimensional scale. The items of the scales were, however, selected by their ability to differentiate Hawaiian from Caucasian and Japanese subjects. Kamo and Zhou (1994) have used four items as indicators of acculturation that were used as independent variables in their study of living arrangements of elderly Chinese and Japanese in the United States. These indicators of acculturation are: foreign born, length of stay since immigration, length of stay squared, and non-English spoken at home. Kamo and Zhou (1994) made no attempt to combine these items into a summative scale. Zsembik (1994) has conducted a secondary analysis of data from the National Survey of Hispanic Elderly People, 1988. She has developed a unidimensional acculturation scale of three items: proficiency in English, nativity status and, if foreign born, age at immigration. Tropp and colleagues (1999) focused their scale on an individual's psychological negotiation between two cultures and his/her emotional attachment to an understanding of each culture. Exploratory factor analysis of the 10-item scales has revealed a single factor (dimension) of psychological acculturation. Caetano and associates (2000) have used a unidimensional scale of acculturation that elicits responses on language use, social relationships, opinions about interethnic marriage, preferences for things ethnic, friends, church, neighbors, and parties attended.

Multidimensional Scales

Szapocznik and colleagues (1978) have developed two acculturation scales of self-reported behaviors and relational value orientation to be used among Cuban Americans. They report that although initial factor analysis of the scale resulted in the identification of four factors (one behavioral factor and three value-related factors) only one of the three value factors was retained after testing for discriminant validity between Cuban and "other reference groups," and between low and high acculturated Cubans. The behavioral acculturation scale contains 24 items and the value acculturation scale contains 10 items. Cortes and associates (1994) have developed a 20-item bidimensional acculturation scale by constructing a 10-item scale of Puerto Rican culture and a parallel set of 10 items reflecting American culture. The bidimensionality of the two subscales has been validated by exploratory factor analysis. The final scale has 18 items (nine items for each scale) after dropping the item (and its counterpart) on the importance of friends for one's children.

Silverstein and Chen (1999) have introduced the notion of individual acculturation and intergenerational acculturation. Individual acculturation is identified by the extent to which grandparents and grandchildren endorse traditional beliefs and practices, elicited by a unidimensional 8-item scale. Intergenerational acculturation is determined by the intrafamilial gap between grandchildren and their grandparents' individual acculturation measures, producing a derived score based on the difference between grandchildren and grandparent's acculturation scores.

Padilla (1980) in his study of Mexican Americans has viewed acculturation as consisting of two major components: cultural awareness and ethnic loyalty. Each of these components contains subscales or dimensions. The cultural awareness component consists of four dimensions: respondent's cultural heritage, spouse's cultural heritage and pride, parents' cultural heritage, and perceived discrimination. The ethnic loyalty component consists of four dimensions as well: language preference and use, cultural pride and affiliation, cultural identification and preference, and social behavior orientation. Parham and Helms (1981) have viewed Black racial identity as being measured by four subscales (dimensions): preencounter, encounter, immersion/emersion, and internalization. Franco (1983) has identified three dimensions in his scale of acculturation for Mexican American children: individual's language preference, parental occupations and educational level, and the child's music preferences. Mendoza (1989) has developed a 5-factor scale: Intrafamily language, extra-family language, social affiliation and activities, and cultural familiarity and activities, cultural identification and pride. DeLeon and Mendez (1996) have tested the psychometric properties of the Cultural Life Style Inventory by Mendoza (1989). Their study of a Puerto Rican population confirmed the 5-factor structure of the scale using exploratory factor analysis, although there were some differences in the factor loadings of some items. They found that 9 of the 11 items in Mendoza's cultural familiarity and activities and cultural identification and pride factors are among the 10 items constituting Factor One (cultural definition and identity) of the Puerto Rican sample. All items except one of "marriage partner preferences" in the Mendoza inventory Factor Three (social affiliation and activities) have emerged in Factor Two (ethnicity in social interactions) of the Puerto Rican sample. Further evidence of the migration of items among factors is the finding that the DeLeon and Mendez Factor Three (language used in family and personal interactions) included four of six items from the Mendoza intra-family language Factor One and Two from the extra-family language Factor Two. They conclude that their study "provides strong evidence supporting the factorial validity of the instrument as a measure of acculturation taken as a multicultural and multidimensional phenomenon (DeLeon & Mendez, 1996, p. 163). Suinn and colleagues (1992) have studied Asian self-identity using five dimensions: reading/writing/cultural preference, ethnic interaction, affinity for ethnic identity and pride, generational identity, and food preference. Harris and Verven (1996) have identified six dimensions of acculturation among Greek Americans. They found that Greek acculturation can be measured in terms of the following dimensions: social affiliation and activities, Greek school attendance and language acquisition, traditional Greek values and practices, cultural identification and pride, attitudes about Greeks, and cultural familiarity and comfort. Landrine and Klonoff (1996) have established eight subscales reflective of African American acculturation: traditional African American family structures and practices, preference for things African American, preparation and consumption of traditional foods, interracial attitudes/cultural mistrust, traditional African American health beliefs and practices, traditional African American religious beliefs and practices, traditional African American childhood socialization, and superstitions. Khairullah and Khairullah (1999) have modified the Szapocznik and associates (1978) scale for Asian Indians. The altered scale contains items on, for example, language, music, food, social events, and gestures used.

PSYCHOMETRIC PROPERTIES

Measures of acculturation vary in the amount of information provided on their psychometric attributes. Some authors report reliability coefficients and others report validity studies. Some measures provide no information about psychometric properties (Kamo & Zhou, 1994; Kruse & Goldenhar, 1992; Zsembik, 1988).

Also most all of the measures reviewed in this chapter are, by design, self-administered. The one exception is the Children's Acculturation Scale (Franco, 1983), which requires that teachers or counselors for Mexican American children complete the instrument. Two of these measures contain three items addressing language acculturation (Kruse & Goldenhar, 1992; Zsembik, 1988). Kamo and Zhou (1994) do not attempt to develop a composite score and use four items independently in regression analysis.

The remaining measures in the review provide information reported about their psychometric properties. However, not all measures provide estimates of both reliability and validity. Seven measures provide only reliability estimates (Caetano et al., 2000; Cuellar et al., 1980; Franco, 1983; Padilla, 1980; Parham & Helms, 1981; Resnicow, 1997; Silverstein & Chen, 1999).

Reliability estimates for these measures range from .50 (Parham & Helms, 1981) to .91 (Caetano et al. 2000). Two measures provide no reliability information but do provide validity-related information (Rezentes, 1993; Tran, 1988). Both of these measures provide information on their respective ability to differentiate between cultural groups. Tran (1988) has provided information on gender differences among older Vietnamese on English acculturation. Rezentes (1993) has tested the ability of his 21-item test to differentiate Hawaiian from Japanese and Caucasian subjects.

Eleven reports identified in this review provided both reliability and validity information (Szapocznik et al., 1978; Franco, 1983; Mendoza, 1989; Suinn et al., 1992; Cortes et al., 1994; Landrine & Klonoff, 1995, Landrine & Klonoff, 1996; Harris & Verven, 1996; Tropp et al., 1999, Khairullah & Khairullah, 1999).

Szapocznik and associates (1978) estimated the alpha coefficients for the behavioral acculturation dimension of their scale as .97 and the value acculturation dimension as .77. The correlations of the English and Spanish versions of the behavioral acculturation dimension was .88, $p < .001$. The English-Spanish parallel language forms of the value acculturation dimension was .46, $p < .007$. The four week test-retest correlation for the behavioral dimension was .96, $p < .001$ and for the value dimension was .86, $p < .001$. Criterion validity was estimated using the correlation for males and females between each dimension of the scale and the number of years the subject was in the United States. The correlation for the behavioral dimension for males was .49, $p < .001$ and for females .59, $p < .001$. The correlation for the value dimension for males was .31, $p<$ .005 and for females was .38, $p <$ .005. Construct validity was estimated by testing the effects of inter-generational differences in measured acculturation. The means of the behavioral and value dimensions were tested using five psychosocial [life] stages. Even though no significant difference was observed in the number of years in the United States of subjects in the five psychosocial [life] stages, highly significant differences were found on measured behavioral acculturation F (4,319) 47.01, $p <$ .001. The tests of value acculturation were less clear, perhaps due to the "lack of homogeneity in values within the host culture" (Szapocznik et al.,1978, p. 127).

Franco (1983) has reported three estimates of reliability: coefficient of reliability (.97), alpha (.77) and interrater reliability (r = .93, $p <$ .001). The investigators used three methods of estimating the validity of the instrument. An estimate of concurrent validity between the Children's Acculturation Scale and the Acculturation Rating Scales for Mexican Americans was (r = .76, $p<$ .01). Exploratory factor analysis identified three factors: language preference, parental occupations and educational level of the head of household, and the child's music preference. The third approach was to use criterion validity to determine if students who acquired more education in the United States would score higher on the acculturation measure. The analysis revealed significant differences between the means of students on the acculturation scales and their grade levels.

Mendoza (1989) reported Cronbach's alpha reliability estimates for five scales using factor analysis: intrafamilial language (.87), extrafamilial language (.91), social affiliation and activities (.89), cultural familiarity and activities (.84), and cultural identification and pride (.89). Validity tests of the effects of exposure to mainstream culture were confirmed in the hypothesized directions. Correlations between exposure to Anglo-Americans and scores on the cultural shift and the cultural resistance dimensions were respectively positive r = .656, $p <$ .001 and negative r =-.60, $p <$ .001. In addition, a test of concordant validity, performed examining the correlation between self-assessed acculturation and that based on the assessment of a family member of the subject, was .71, $p <$ .001.

Suinn and colleagues (1992) developed a 21-item scale of Asian self-identity (alpha coefficient of .91). The validity of the scale has been estimated using concurrent validity findings that the scale is highly related to the number of years in the U.S. (r = .56), the years living in a non-Asian neighborhood (r = .41), and the self-rating of acculturation by respondents (r = .62).

The final 18-item bicultural scale of acculturation developed by Cortes and associates (1994) consisted of a 9-item American culture dimension (alpha = .78) and a 9-item Puerto Rican culture dimension (alpha = .73). Criterion validity, tested for both scales, revealed that the American culture scale was negatively correlated with birth in Puerto Rico (-.39) and the age at the time of arrival in the U.S. (-.37). Puerto Rican culture scores are positively correlated with birth in Puerto Rico (.36) and the age arrival in the U.S. (.25).

The split-half reliability of the scale of Greek American Acculturation is .94, and the six factors had alpha coefficients ranging from .82 to .93 (Harris & Verven; 1996).

Concurrent validity studies included tests of the relationship between the level of acculturation and generation category (immigrant, first-generation, second-generation, etc.), finding that the lowest acculturation is related to being a member of the immigrant group ($F = 45.63, p < .001$).

Landrine and Klonoff (1996) developed the African American Acculturation scale consisting of 74 items. They also developed a short-form version of the full scale (Landrine & Klonoff, 1995). The full scale shows a split-half reliability for the total scale of .93. The eight subscales have been found to produce alpha coefficients ranging from .71 to .90. Landrine and Klonoff (1995) reported tests of concurrent validity determined by significant differences between African Americans living in traditional ethnic enclaves and those living in other areas (Hotelling's $T^2 = .568$, F $(8, 42) = 2.98, p = .01$). They report that other tests have confirmed the hypotheses that acculturation scores are not related to social class, education, or other status variables. The short form of the test contains 33 items producing an alpha coefficient $= .88$ and split-half reliability .78. The 10 factors have produced alphas ranging from .40 to .89 with seven of the alphas above .70.

Tropp and colleagues (1999) developed a Psychological Acculturation Scale consisting of 10 attitude items to measure the acculturation of Puerto Rican Americans. A Spanish version of the scale has been developed (alpha = .90) that parallels the English version (alpha = .83). The scale was developed to measure the "psychological negotiation" of individuals between two cultures. Convergent and discriminant validity have been determined by comparing U.S.-born and Puerto Rico-born respondents and their respective language use. The scale effectively discriminates between U.S.-born and Puerto Rico-born respondents ($t(103) = -2.93$, $p < .01$). The ability to detect differences in the use of language is also significant ($t (104) = -4.22, p < .001$).

Khairulla and Khairulla (1999) report that the 20-item instrument, modified from Szapocznik and colleagues (1978), produces a total test alpha coefficient of .96. Inter-item validity was used to determine the construct validity of the scale. Inter-item validity was determined by obtaining the correlation coefficients between responses to each of the 20 items and the mean scores of the total test. These analyses found all correlations to be in the expected direction ranging from ($r = .67$ to $r = .88$) and significant at $p < .001$. The scores from this scale correlate positively with the years of education in the U.S. and the length of stay in the U.S., that is, higher levels of education and longer lengths of stay are positively related to higher level of acculturation.

CONCLUSION

The interest in acculturation as an explanatory and mediating variable in studies of ethnic and minority groups has extended over the last three decades and appears to be of continued interest in the 21st century. As the United States becomes an increasingly multicultural society, there will be increasing interest in understanding how people from different cultures adjust, adapt, or accommodate simultaneously to the demands of their traditional cultures and of their dominant culture. Most models of acculturation either view acculturation as the abandonment of one's traditional culture in favor of adoption of the dominant culture, or as a negotiation between cultures. The latter view approaches the discussion of acculturation more as a bicultural phenomenon where the individuals select aspects of their traditional culture to retain and to adopt selected aspects of the dominant culture. The bicultural approach offers the most promise in a multicultural society.

Some of the shortcomings of the past approaches to the measurement of acculturation should be avoided in future attempts to design cross-cultural instruments. Among these are the use of unidimensional measures and unipolar scales. A number of instruments contain only items that reflect ethnic behaviors, values, beliefs, and practices. In addition, many of these scales measure only the extent to which the respondent endorses ethnically biased statements. One must question if responses to items such as these can be said to measure acculturation. The failure to endorse ethnic statements does not provide us with any indication of the degree to which a respondent endorses statements reflecting the dominant culture. Acculturation to a dominant (nonnative) culture cannot be inferred by the lack of endorsement of the respondent's native culture.

The traditional approach to the development of acculturation measures has been to identify the characteristics of native cultures and the degree of subscription of respondents to these characteristics. This approach arrives at the degree of acculturation indirectly by inferring acculturation from the lack of endorsement of one's native culture. However, the rejection of one's native culture does not directly translate to acceptance of the dominant culture. Perhaps it is time to shift the measurement paradigm from a focus on rejection of native cultures to an emphasis on measures of the extent to which individuals embrace the dominant culture. The immediate value of this approach would be in the development of generic acculturation measures. The longer-range consequence would be that anyone could be placed on a continuum representing acceptance of the dominant culture continuum or his/her immigrant status or nativity.

Another concern in the measurement of acculturation is that the items used should be subject to change over time. If acculturation is perceived as a snapshot of one's degree of acceptance and one's integration into the primary or dominant culture, items and measures must be developed that are sensitive to transitions over time. This is particularly problematic in the scales of Landrine and Klonoff (1995, 1996). The full 74-item and the 33-item scales contain items about the respondent's history that are not likely to change over time. These items become constants in the calculation of scale scores and thus artificially misrepresent the level of acculturation of the respondent and reduce the likelihood of detecting change. Examples of some of these items are:

- When I was young, I shared a bed at night with my sister, brother, or some other relative.
- When I was a child, I used to play tonk.
- When I was young, I was a member of the Black church.

These items constitute examples of items included in the full scale or the short form. Knowing that a respondent engaged in any of the above activities as a child provides no insight into his/her current state of acculturation. These items are not sensitive to the dynamic nature of acculturation, that is, they inflate the scale with items that are not likely to change over time.

Measures of acculturation should attempt to tap the current level of acculturation. To the extent that an individual can actively choose to integrate into or reject completely a host culture, acculturation must be viewed as a dynamic and temporal phenomenon. Any measure of acculturation should be sensitive to detecting these changes over time. We should strive to develop instruments that are capable of detecting movement from traditional cultural behaviors to dominant (host) cultural behaviors and back to traditional cultural behaviors when and if they occur.

REFERENCES

Berry, J. (1980). Acculturation as varieties of adaptation. In Padilla, A. M. (Ed.), *Acculturation: Theory, models and some new findings* (p.165). Washington, DC: American Association for the Advancement of Science Selected Symposium.

Caetano, R., Schafer, J., Clark, C. L., Cunradi, C. B., & Raspberry, K. (2000). Intimate partner violence, acculturation, and alcohol consumption among Hispanic couples in the United States. *Journal of Interpersonal Violence, 15*(1), 30-45.

Choney, S. K., Berryhill-Paapke,E., & Robbins, R. R. (1995). *The acculturation of American Indians: Developing frameworks for research and practice* (p. 679). Thousand Oaks, CA: Sage Publications, Inc.

Cortes, D. E., Rogler, L. H., & Malgady, R. G. (1994). Biculturality among Puerto Rican adults in the United States. *American Journal of Community Psychology, 22*(5), 707-721.

Cuellar, I., Harris, L. C., & Jasso, R. (1980). An acculturation scale for Mexican American normal and clinical populations. *Hispanic Journal of Behavioral Sciences, 2*(3), 199-217.

DeLeon, B., & Mendez, S. (1996). Factorial structure of a measures of acculturation in a Puerto Rican population. *Educational and Psychological Measurement, 56*(1), 155-165.

Franco, J. N. (1983). An acculturation scale for Mexican American children. *Journal of General Psychology, 108*, 175-181.

Harris, A. C., & Verven, R. (1996). The Greek-American acculturation scale development and validity. *Psychological Reports, 78*, 599-610.

Kamo, Y., & Zhou, M. (1994). Living arrangements of elderly Chinese and Japanese in the United States. *Journal of Marriage & the Family, 56*, 544-558.

Khairullah, D. Z., & Khairulla, Z. Y. (1999). Behavioral acculturation and demographic characteristics of Asian-Indian immigrants in the United States of America. *International Journal of Sociology and Social Policy, 19*(1/2).

Krause, N., & Goldenhar, L. M. (1992). Acculturation and psychological distress in three groups of elderly Hispanics. *Journal of Gerontology, 47*(6), S279-S288.

LaFromboise, T., Coleman, H., & Gerton, J. (1993). Psychological impact of biculturalism. *Psychological Bulletin, 114*(3), 395-412.

Landrine, H., & Klinoff, E. A. (1995). The African-American Acculturation Scale 11: Cross-validation and short form. *Journal of Black Psychology, 21*, 124-152.

Mendoza, R. H. (1984). Acculturation and sociocultural variability. In J. L. Martinez, Jr., & R. H. Mendoza (Eds.), *Chicano psychology* (2nd ed., pp. 61-75). Orlando, FL: Academic Press.

Mendoza, R. H. (1989). An empirical scale to measure type and degree of acculturation in Mexican-American adolescents and adults. *Journal of Cross-Cultural Psychology, 20*, 372-385.

Padilla, A. M. (1980). The role of cultural awareness and ethnic loyalty in acculturation. In Padilla, A. M. (Ed.), *Acculturation: Theory, models and some new findings* (pp. 47-84). Washington, DC: American Association for the Advancement of Sciences.

Padilla, A. M. (1980). (Ed.) *Acculturation: Theory, models and some new findings* (p. 165). Washington, DC: American Association for the Advancement of Sciences.

Parham, T. A., & Helms, J. E. (1981). The influence of Black student's racial identity attitudes on preferences for counselor's race. *Journal of Counseling Psychology, 28*, 250-257.

Resnicow, K. (1997, November). Development of a racial identity scale for low-income African Americans. *Journal of Black Studies, 28*, 239-255.

Rezentes, W. C., III. (1993). Na Mea Hamwi'i: A Hawaiian Acculturation Scale. *Psychological Reports, 73*, 383-393.

Silverstein, M., & Chen, X. (1999). The impact of acculturation in Mexican American families on the quality of adult grandchild-grandparent relationships. *Journal of Marriage and the Family, 61*, 188-198.

Szapocznik, J., Scopetta, M. A., Kurtines, W., & Aranalde, M. (1978). Theory and measurement of acculturation. *Interamerican Journal of Psychology, 12*(2), 113-130.

Tran, T. V. (1988). Sex differences in English language acculturation and learning strategies among Vietnamese adults aged 40 and over in the United States. *Sex Roles, 19*(11/12), 747-758.

Tropp, L. R., Erkut, S., Coll, C. G., Alarcon, O., & Garcia, H. A. V. (1999). Psychological acculturation: Development of new measures for Puerto Ricans on the U. S. Mainland. *Educational and Psychological Measurement, 59*(2), 351-367.

Zsembik, B. A. (1988). Ethnic and sociodemographic correlates of the use of proxy respondents: The national survey of Hispanic elderly people. *Research on Aging, 16*(4), 401-414.

5

Measuring the Socioeconomic Status of Elderly People in Health Studies With Special Focus on Minority Elderly

Laura Rudkin, Kyriakos S. Markides

A large and growing body of literature demonstrates a positive association between health and socioeconomic position—the higher an individual's position, the better his or her health. This association generally has been found to hold over time, for most societies, and for a variety of health outcomes. (See reviews by Adler et al., 1994; Feinstein, 1993; Lynch & Kaplan, 2000; Preston & Taubman, 1994; See also, Evans, Barer, & Marmot, 1994). Thus, the concepts of social class and socioeconomic status (SES) are central to public health research. Further, given the marked racial and ethnic differences in both socioeconomic status and health status observed in the U.S., class and SES are particularly important concepts to include in studies focused on minority health.

Measures of class and SES have been treated variously as study population descriptors, confounders or control variables, risk factors or predictors of health, or as factors that modify the relationship between a risk factor and the health outcome. Status measures have been interpreted variously as reflecting access to health-related resources (including medical care), knowledge and attitudes regarding healthy lifestyles, sense of efficacy or control regarding health, exposure to physical or psychosocial stressors, and social prestige and power.

The decision regarding how to incorporate class or SES into a health research project is based on both conceptual and practical considerations. Conceptually, researchers must posit how SES is related to the health outcome and what aspect of SES is relevant for both the research question and the study population. In studies of racial or ethnic differences in health, SES has often been treated as a confounder (i.e., what are the ethnic differences in the health outcome, controlling for SES?).

This approach has been criticized as too simplistic and more attention is being paid to disentangling the independent and joint effects of SES and minority status on health (e.g., Lillie-Blanton & LaVeist, 1996; Lillie-Blanton, Parsons, Gayle, & Dievler, 1996; Williams, 1996; Williams & Rucker, 1996). On the practical side, researchers must take into account the time, expense, and difficulty of collecting data on the various SES measures, as well as considering which measures will show variation in the study population. Research focused on explicating racial and ethnic differences in health outcomes necessarily must include information on multiple dimensions of SES. Studies restricted to a single minority group may need less information on SES, but must give special consideration to how to uncover variation within that population.

In this chapter we review some common indicators of SES in the United States and identify some recent developments influencing SES measurement for elderly populations. In keeping with the theme of this book, we also discuss strengths and weaknesses of the various measures when applied to the health of elderly members of minority groups. We will conclude the chapter with a discussion of issues to consider when selecting the appropriate measure for an analysis.

The examples we use come primarily from two recent panel studies of postretirement aged Americans—the Hispanic Established Populations for the Epidemiologic Study of the Elderly (EPESE) and the Study of Assets and Health Dynamics Among the Oldest Old (AHEAD). We use examples from the first waves of the EPESE and AHEAD data collection to illustrate what types of SES information the study investigators deemed important to gather at baseline. Wave 1 of the Hispanic EPESE was fielded in 1993 and included interviews with a representative sample of 3,050 Mexican Americans aged 65 or older from the southwestern United States (Markides et al., 1999). The first wave of the AHEAD was completed in February 1994 with a nationally representative sample of 7,447 persons aged 70 or older (and their spouses), including oversamples of African Americans, Hispanics, and Florida residents (Juster, 1994). The AHEAD was developed in conjunction with the Health and Retirement Study (HRS) of preretirement age Americans; the two studies were merged in 1998. Thus, the Hispanic EPESE is representative of a survey focused on a single ethnic minority group, whereas the AHEAD is an example of a study with multiple racial/ethnic groups, including oversamples of key minority groups. The primary purpose of the Hispanic EPESE was to obtain epidemiologic information on older Mexican Americans, thus the number of SES questions was limited. In contrast, socioeconomic status was a major focus of the AHEAD and the data gathered on SES were more extensive.

SOCIOECONOMIC STATUS OR SOCIAL CLASS?

The terms socioeconomic status and social class are often used interchangeably, but sociologists regard them as distinct concepts. Although there is no consensus regarding definitions, both concepts are used to refer to possession of or access to material and social resources, most often cast in terms of property, prestige, and/or power. SES indicators, like other status variables (e.g., marital status, nativity status, literacy status) are used to locate individuals' positions in the social structure. Income, education, and occupation are the most common indicators of SES. Social class, in contrast, also draws attention to how economic structures determine distribution of these resources. Further, social class connotes the existence of a group of individuals with similar levels of these resources and with similar lifestyles and political and economic interests. (For example, see discussions by Krieger, Williams, & Moss, 1997; Lynch & Kaplan, 2000.)

THE TRADITIONAL MEASURES: EDUCATION, INCOME, AND OCCUPATION

Education

Education is perhaps the most used measure of SES in adult health studies, both because it is relatively easy to obtain and is potentially measurable for every respondent. Another benefit is that education is typically completed before the onset of health problems. In other words, because education is relatively stable in adulthood, older adults' educational attainment is usually causally prior to the health outcome of interest. This sequencing allows researchers to discount the reverse causation hypothesis that poor health caused low socioeconomic attainment. Education has been interpreted as influencing health through its effect on knowledge and attitudes regarding healthy lifestyles, as well as on the degree of mastery or control individuals feel regarding their own health. Education also has been treated as a proxy for access to social and economic resources that influence health status.

Education may be measured as years of schooling completed (e.g., 0 through 16 or more) or as highest educational degree completed (e.g., high school, associate's, bachelor's, master's, professional or doctorate). The Hispanic EPESE included a single question on "highest grade" completed. The AHEAD followed a similar education question with specific questions about degrees obtained. In both data collection and analyses, the choice of cutpoints for educational groups should bear in mind the experience of the study population. In general, older cohorts are less educated than are younger cohorts. Further, among the older cohorts, women are less educated than are men and older minorities (Hispanics and African Americans) have less schooling than do older non-Hispanic Whites. For example, in the Hispanic EPESE the average level of education was slightly over five years with very few people having completed college or even high school. Thus, the appropriate cutpoints may differ if the study population is restricted to a single demographic subgroup or if the purpose is to make comparisons across groups.

Income

Annual income is a fairly common measure of SES in health studies of older people. In health models, income is interpreted as representing an individual's access to health-related resources, including medical care, and/or exposure to financial stressors. Two factors are of central interest in measuring the income of elderly people—the amount and the sources. Decisions regarding the level of detail needed must balance the research goals with more practical issues in data collection.

Income may be measured at either the individual or household level, although household income is typically a more meaningful indicator of access to resources. Analyses using household income also should take household size and structure into account. For example, a $20,000 annual income goes further in a single person household than in a 6-person multigeneration household. This adjustment may be especially important in studies of minority elderly because they are more likely than non-Hispanic Whites to live in extended family households (Markides, & Black, 1995)

A relatively simple approach to gathering income data was used in the Hispanic EPESE. Respondents were asked "about how much" their annual income was for the past year. They were shown a card with eight income categories ($0-$4,999, $5,000-$9,999, . . . $50,000 & over) and asked to select the appropriate category. Separate questions were included for personal and household income. Data on income sources were gathered with a series of yes/no questions, with the following sources included: Social Security; private pension; Supplemental Security Income; children; railroad or military pension; general assistance; income from stocks, bonds, rent, or other assets. The income categories used should be appropriate for the study population, although if comparability with other studies is sought, researchers may have less flexibility in defining categories. For example, the Hispanic EPESE study is limited to elderly Mexican Americans, predominantly a low-income group. For such populations, it may be important to obtain more detail at the lower ends of the income distribution. The Hispanic EPESE, however, was also intended to be comparable to other EPESE studies which had some influence on income categories obtained. Direct comparisons are further complicated by the fact that the Hispanic EPESE was conducted later than the other EPESE studies.

A more complex approach to measuring income is to obtain actual dollar amounts for each of the sources individually. For example, respondents to the AHEAD were asked a lengthy series of questions about different sources of income. For each type of income received, the survey requested information on frequency, dollar amount in past month, month and year payments began, and more. Much of the data were collected separately for respondent and spouse. At the conclusion of the income section, respondents were asked to report their own (combined with spouse/partner) total before-tax income in past year and before-tax income of others in the household.

Using current or past-year income to assess the influence of socioeconomic status on older adults' health is conceptually problematic. First, household incomes typically are not stable over time due to changes in household structure, source of income, and levels of income by source. More important, income often drops between the preretirement and postretirement periods, with major changes in income sources. Thus, postretirement income may not reflect income during the working years, the years when many chronic diseases begin to develop.

A second problem is the direction of causation in the relationship between contemporaneous measures of health and income. Smith and Kington (1997b) note that income is made up of multiple sources, each of which may bear a unique relationship to health. Using AHEAD data, they examined the association of different sources of income with the presence of functional limitations in old age and find that the relationship does vary by source. Only older people healthy enough to work will report work income, whereas only the sick and disabled will qualify for certain types of income assistance. The authors conclude: "At these older ages, retirement income (from pensions, Social Security, etc.) offers the best hope of estimating an income effect free at least of contemporaneous feedback effects from health to income (p. 166)."

Finally, income is considered a sensitive question and item nonresponse can be a significant problem. One solution to this problem is the use of income bracketing as used in the HRS and AHEAD studies. If a study participant refused to answer or responded "don't know" to the total income question, s/he was asked a series of questions designed to determine an income category for the individual. In the AHEAD, the first bracketing question was whether or not the respondent had received $30,000 or more in the past year. From that point, interviewers moved to higher or lower income levels to identify the income range.

Occupation

Occupation is not as commonly used as are education or income in research on the health of elderly people, due mainly to measurement issues. Most older people are retired and do not have a current occupation. Many members of the current elderly cohorts, primarily women, were never in the paid labor force, or worked intermittently. Further, many people do not remain in just one occupation during their working years. Obtaining a complete occupational history is time consuming and incorporating such extensive information in a model can be difficult.

Nevertheless, occupation may be an important factor to consider. The development of chronic disease is long-term, and information on the SES level as it existed during earlier adulthood may be relevant. Occupation can represent health risks distinct from those associated with education or income, namely, level of social prestige, potential exposures to physical and job-related psychosocial stressors, and access to employer-provided health insurance. Occupation also may be considered a proxy for lifetime earnings, an advantage over current income measures. In fact, participants in an NIH conference on measuring social inequalities in health concluded that occupation should be considered "the core socioeconomic variable" because it reflects educational requirements, income opportunities, and the influence of the economic structure (Moss & Krieger, 1995).

A popular approach for including occupation in studies of elderly people is to ask about the respondent's primary occupation during his or her working years. For example, AHEAD respondents were asked both about their longest-held job ("Thinking about your longest job . . . what kind of work did you do?) and their main occupation ("What kind of work did you do most of your working life?). Subjects in the Hispanic EPESE were asked about the type of work they performed and the kind of business or industry they worked in "most of your working life." Both the EPESE and the AHEAD gathered occupation data for spouses of currently married respondents. Only the AHEAD, however, included occupation questions about the former spouse of widowed or divorced respondents.

There are two main types of occupational measures—nominal measures that simply categorize occupations based on tasks performed and job titles, and interval measures based on occupational prestige scores. Both types of measures begin with a description of the type of work the individual performs in his or her job, such as in the Hispanic EPESE or AHEAD. This information is then used to assign the individual to an occupational group.

Nominal measures of occupation usually employ the categories defined in the Standard Occupational Classification (SOC) used by the U.S. Census Bureau and other federal agencies. (Prior to the development of the 1980 SOC, federal agencies did not use a single standard classification system.) In the most recent revision of this system (the 1998 SOC), occupations were grouped primarily according to the work performed, with "skills-based considerations" being secondary (U.S. Department of Labor, 1999). In this scheme, 820 occupations can be combined to form 23 major groups, 98 minor groups, and 452 broad occupations. Earlier versions of the SOC identified fewer major groups. For example, main occupational categories from the 1990 census include: managerial and professional specialty; technical, sales, and administrative support; service; precision production, craft and repair (skilled labor); operators, fabricators and laborers (unskilled labor); and farming; forestry, and fishing (agricultural) (U.S. Census Bureau, 1999).

Occupational prestige measures have been formed using responses from public opinion polls about the prestige accorded different jobs and information on median education and income for various occupations. Using various algorithms, these scales assign a prestige score to the occupations defined by the Census Bureau. Prestige scales available for U.S. data include the Nam-Powers Occupational Status Scores (Nam & Powers, 1983) and the Nakao and Treas Occupational Prestige Scale (Nakao & Treas, 1994), among others. The latter is an update of earlier scales developed by researchers at the National Opinion Research Center. Both of these prestige scales use the 1980 census occupational classification scheme. A scale appropriate for use with the 1990 census occupation list was developed by Hauser and Warren (1997). (See Haug, 1977, and Liberatos, Link, & Kelsey, 1988, for more detailed discussions of earlier scales.)

Although some recent surveys of elderly people have used the 1980 or 1990 census occupational codes, it may be appropriate to use 1960 or 1970 occupational codes and their associated prestige scales for some postretirement groups. The values in the older scales may reflect more closely occupational status and prestige when these respondents were in their prime working years (i.e., the prestige accorded different jobs may have changed over time).

Occupation measures have been criticized on a number of grounds (Haug, 1977; Hauser & Warren, 1997; Krieger et al., 1993; Smith & Kington, 1997b; Warren, Sheridan, & Hauser, 1998). First, broad occupational groupings fail to capture significant heterogeneity in opportunities and rewards within each group. Second, it is difficult to apply these measures to individuals not in the paid labor force. Third, concern has been expressed that the original prestige scales were formulated for White men and that their use for women or racial/ethnic minority groups is not appropriate. For example, the prestige accorded the same occupation may differ in Black versus White communities. Fourth, focusing on a job title or job prestige ignores other potentially important job characteristics, such as power. Fifth, occupation may not be the most salient indicator of social prestige, particularly when individuals in low prestige jobs hold high prestige positions in alternative social hierarchies (e.g., church leadership).

Composite Indices

Recognizing that all three traditional indicators of SES—education, income, and occupation—are correlated, some researchers have developed composite indices of SES (see reviews by Haug, 1977, and Liberatos, Link, & Kelsey, 1988). Examples for the U.S. include the Nam-Powers Socioeconomic Status Scores (Nam & Powers, 1983) and the Hollingshead Index of Social Position (Hollingshead, 1957, referenced in Haug, 1977), among others. These scales combine information on an individual's occupation with his or her education and/or income to approximate measures of social class. Composite SES scales have been subject to many of the same criticisms as the occupational prestige scales. Regarding studies of SES and health, concern also has been expressed that composite measures mask the unique contribution of each SES component to health (Krieger, Williams, & Moss, 1997; Miech & Hauser, 1998).

EXPANDING THE CONCEPT:
WEALTH, POVERTY, AND NEIGHBORHOOD CONDITIONS

Wealth and Assets

Obtaining information on wealth and assets allows researchers to overcome some of the problems associated with household income. Measures of wealth are preferable to income measures for the elderly population because they represent a longer-term indicator of access to and accumulation of material resources (Carr, Pemmarazu, & Rice, 1996; Smith, 1995, 1997; Smith & Kington, 1997a, 1997b). In measuring wealth, both types of assets and their worth are key factors of interest. Similar to income, the level of detail required should be decided by considering both the study's conceptual model and its population of interest.

In the Hispanic EPESE, levels of respondent wealth were fairly low and questions regarding assets were limited. The older Mexican Americans were asked whether or not they owned any of a series of assets (a home, stocks or bonds, a savings account, or rental property) and the value of their home. Although the majority of respondents reported owning their home, few reported owning any of the other assets.

Information on asset accumulation was much more extensive in the AHEAD survey. Respondents were asked questions regarding ownership and total value of: main home; other real estate; vehicles (cars, boats, motor homes, etc.); business equity; Individual Retirement Accounts (IRA) and Keogh accounts; stocks and mutual funds; checking and savings accounts; certificates of deposit (CD), savings bonds, and Treasury bills; bonds; and any other assets. The bracketing (see income section) was used to probe for value when respondents either said they did not know the value or initially refused to answer.

The importance of considering wealth when assessing racial and ethnic differences in socioeconomic status of older people is dramatically illustrated with data from the AHEAD study. Smith (1997) found that:

1. racial/ethnic inequalities by wealth are markedly greater than are inequalities by income;
2. within-group variation in wealth for Blacks and Whites is greater than within-group variation in income; and
3. older Blacks' and Hispanics' ownership of assets is primarily limited to home equity.

As with income, item nonresponse to questions on wealth can pose difficulties. The bracketing technique employed in the HRS and the AHEAD appears to offer a real solution to this problem (Smith, 1995, 1997). For example, among AHEAD respondents who owned a home, a 22% nonresponse rate for the initial question on home equity was reduced to 2% through the use of the brackets. A 45% initial nonresponse rate on worth was converted to 8% for respondents owning stocks and mutual funds. The value of individual assets owned by bracketed respondents tended to be higher than that for exact answer respondents, suggesting that the technique may be particularly useful and important when working with study populations that include higher-income individuals.

Poverty and Income-to-Needs Ratio

Many health studies of the elderly population, particularly those which examine lower-income minority groups, use measures of poverty to emphasize the lack of resources available to, and the financial stressors facing, some elderly people. Poverty rates differ dramatically by race/ethnicity within the elderly population. In

1998, 8.2% of older non-Hispanic Whites lived below the poverty level, compared to 26.4% of African Americans and 21.0% of Hispanic origin elders (Short et al., 1999).

To assess poverty, researchers have often used a dichotomous measure—above or below the poverty threshold, or alternatively some multiple of the threshold such as 150% or 200%. Using the same information, however, the more informative continuous income-to-needs ratio (also called the income-to-poverty ratio) can be calculated. Given that SES effects on health have been observed throughout the SES hierarchy, the income-to-needs ratio may be the preferred measure.

To determine whether or not a given respondent is living below the poverty threshold, researchers must obtain information on:

1. total family money income before taxes (excluding capital gains and noncash benefits such as food stamps),
2. number of family members, and
3. ages of family members.

The family income can then be compared to the federally defined poverty threshold for a family of that size and composition (Short et al., 1999). The 1998 poverty threshold for an elderly person (aged 65 or over) living alone was $7,818 and for a two-person household headed by an elderly person was $11,193. The income-to-needs ratio is simply taken as family income divided by the defined poverty threshold for the older person's family.

Poverty and related measures, however, use information on current or recent income and therefore face limitations similar to those of income measures in general. First, missing data on income may be problematic. Second, poverty measures fail to consider the dynamic nature of household income. A recent study examining the experience of old age poverty suggests that 40.4% of older Americans will experience a year below the poverty line at some point between the ages of 60 and 90, whereas 47.7% will live below 125% of poverty line at some point (Rank & Hirschl, 1999). These figures are markedly higher than is the cross-sectional poverty rate of 10.5% for the population aged 65 and older in 1998 (Short et al., 1999).

The calculation method for the current poverty measure was developed in 1955 with the poverty line set at three times the cost of a minimum diet, varying by family structure. Since that time the thresholds have been adjusted only for price changes. Major changes in the U.S. economy, increases in living standards, and other factors (e.g., escalating health care costs) have prompted economists to suggest revisions in the method of calculation (Citro & Michael, 1995; Dalaker, 1999). Poverty estimates incorporating the various recommendations show that adoption of one of the "experimental poverty rates" will likely lead to higher poverty rates for the population aged 65 and older (Citro & Michael, 1995; Dalaker, 1999). Having Medicaid and receiving Supplemental Security Income (SSI) can also be used as proxies for poverty among older people.

Community-Level SES

In recent years there has been expanded emphasis on neighborhood conditions and their potential influence on health. Using multilevel analyses, researchers have examined the independent effects on health of individual SES characteristics and neighborhood SES. For example, what are the independent and joint effects on health of living in a household below the poverty line and in a neighborhood with high rates of poverty and unemployment?

Neighborhood measures are typically collected or available at the zip code or census tract level. Community-level measures have focused on such SES characteristics as: education (e.g., percentage of household heads with college degree), income (e.g., median household income), poverty (e.g., percentage of households below the poverty threshold), occupation (e.g., percentage of household heads with White collar job), and home ownership (e.g., percentage of households owning their home). For example, in her study of adult health, Robert (1998) examined the percentage of households receiving public assistance, the percentage of families with $30,000 or more annual income, and the adult unemployment rate. She also combined information on the three measures to form a community disadvantage index.

The bulk of the literature in this area has focused on children or on young and middle-aged adults. Community-level measures, however, may also be useful for examining racial and ethnic group differences in health. Given that many elderly Blacks and Hispanics are living in disadvantaged areas, neighborhood conditions may constitute an important explanatory variable. A potential limitation would again be the ordering of events, that is, did neighborhood residence precede or follow the health event? This issue would be particularly important to consider for elderly people who may have moved following retirement or a major health decline.

WHAT ABOUT POWER? GETTING BACK TO SOCIAL CLASS

The SES measures discussed in this chapter have ignored one potentially important aspect of social class—the issue of power. Although income and occupation may be viewed as proxies for power, they are more often interpreted as indicating resources or prestige. Some researchers have called for more explicit attention to occupational characteristics, such as authority, control, and subordination (Krieger, Williams, & Moss, 1997; Lynch & Kaplan, 2000; Moss & Krieger, 1995).

The occupation classification scheme developed by Wright (1998) offers one possible approach. He suggests differentiating among occupations using four dimensions:

1. relation to means of production (owner, employee);
2. relation to scarce skills (expert, skilled, unskilled);

3. relation to authority (manager, supervisor, nonmanagement); and
4. number of employees (many, few, none).

Obtaining information on each of these dimensions for respondents would allow researchers to assign them to one of the resulting 12 categories and examine the health differences. Wright has developed survey questions for his typology (Krieger, Williams, & Moss, 1997).

The focus on occupational characteristics carries some of the same limitations as other occupational measures, namely, the issues of how to classify retired individuals and those who never worked in the paid labor force. One attempt to relate Wright's typology to health at midlife showed no association (Meich & Hauser, 1998); however, that study used cross-sectional data and a study population with a limited SES distribution.

RECOMMENDATIONS FOR STUDIES OF ETHNIC MINORITY ELDERLY

Studies such as the HRS and AHEAD have highly detailed and elaborate protocols for assessing subjects' SES, especially with respect to income and assets. However, most health studies of older people, such as the Hispanic EPESE (and the previous EPESE), have relatively limited information on income and assets. At a minimum, there is a need to obtain the following information in studies of the health of the elderly from disadvantaged populations.

Education

Actual years of schooling should be obtained, including information as to whether or not a person has completed high school. In the Hispanic EPESE, where educational attainment was very low, questions assessing literacy (e.g., ability to read and write in English and/or in Spanish) have proven useful and are recommended for studies of representative samples of disadvantaged minority elderly. Educational attainment has proved to be the best single indicator of SES in studies of Mexican American elderly, such as in the Hispanic EPESE. A potential complication lies in the issue of whether the schooling took place in the United States or in Mexico. In the Hispanic EPESE this was not a problem in view of the low educational attainment of the population as a whole. Moreover, it is unclear whether the schools attended by elderly Mexican Americans in the United States were of significantly higher quality than were schools in Mexico attended by immigrant Mexican Americans.

Employment Status/Occupation

Very few minority elderly are currently employed, but there is a need to assess whether they are employed full-time or part-time. This information is often collapsed because of small numbers. For retired people, it is important to assess when they retired from their last occupation. Caution is needed in analyzing these data because retirement does not have the same meaning in disadvantaged populations where intermittent employment is common and a gradual exit from the labor force takes place, often because of health problems (Markides & Black, 1995).

The intermittent nature of employment makes it difficult to assess one's main occupation, which is a usual and recommended practice. Generally, this is not a major problem because a subject's many jobs typically fall in the same category, usually in low-income and low-prestige occupational categories. Census-type questions that ask for job titles, nature of duties and type of work, as well as industry type, are important for enabling researchers to assign a Census occupational code or an interval-level prestige score.

Studies tend to ask for information on living spouses, but may not for deceased spouses even though postretirement SES may be substantially determined by deceased husband's career. Thus it is important to assess deceased husbands' occupational status, especially in certain groups, like older Mexican Americans, where very few widowed women ever held a paying job for a significant period of time.

In the Hispanic EPESE, as in previous studies of Mexican American elderly conducted by the second author and his colleagues, occupation generally has not shown an association with health at older ages. One reason for this lack of association may be the limited variation in the types of occupations reported by minority respondents. However, detailed information on the nature of the work may be necessary, especially if there is interest in certain occupational exposures, for example.

Income, Financial Resources, and Assets

It is recommended that a relatively detailed list of sources of current income be presented to subjects of studies of disadvantaged minority, before they are asked about their annual income (usually in previous year). Both personal and household income should be obtained, although typically household income is employed in analyses, with adjustments for number of people living in the household. Bracketing is recommended, as is the use of cards with which subjects can point out the category that represents a particular level of income. Five-thousand-dollar categories up to "$50,000 and above" are appropriate for studies of disadvantaged minority populations. Interviewer assistance is needed in cases of illiterate and/or visually impaired subjects.

In the Hispanic EPESE, income has not proved to be a very useful single indicator of overall SES because income is skewed toward the lower end. An additional complication is the high refusal rate which is typical in all studies of older people.

It is also important to obtain a list of assets, including a home, stocks or bonds, savings and rental property. Most minority elderly own a home, but have no other assets. Thus, obtaining the value of the home is important. This can be done in

$25,000 increments up to "$100,000 and above." Ownership of a home can be important in determining the nature of living arrangements and can clarify the nature of intergenerational dependence in multigeneration households (Markides & Black, 1995).

The above recommendations are for representative studies of disadvantaged populations; when studies include a non-Hispanic White comparison group, there is the need to control for SES differences when interested in examining "ethnic" differences. In practice this turns out to be difficult, if not impossible, because of widely different educational, occupational, and income distributions. As it is becoming common to oversample minority groups to enable meaningful comparative analyses, it is important to also consider oversampling minority elderly from higher SES categories. Conversely, it may be fruitful to also consider oversampling non-Hispanic Whites from lower SES categories. Such data will probably clarify the meaning of high and low SES in both disadvantaged and advantaged populations; differences in meaning also will have implications for understanding how SES may influence health differently in different ethnic groups, something about which we know little.

CONCLUDING REMARKS

Gerontologists studying minority populations have long cautioned that there exists a need to adjust for SES differences among groups to uncover potential "ethnic" differences in health and mental health outcomes (Markides & Mindel, 1987). Ethnic differences often disappear when SES is controlled, leading to the erroneous conclusion that ethnicity or minority status is not as important as SES. Yet we need to remind ourselves that ethnicity and minority status may be viewed as more important than SES because they are the primary determinant of SES differences between groups. Thus eliminating socioeconomic inequalities in health will ultimately involve dealing with racial and ethnic factors that are associated with low SES in ethnic minority populations.

As indicated above, in studies of older people, socioeconomic disparities among groups are often so large that adequate statistical control for them is not possible. Oversampling of higher SES minority elderly and of lower SES majority elderly will enable us to examine potential differences in the meaning and influence of SES within socioeconomically different populations. For example, one might speculate that low socioeconomic status is more likely to be associated with poor health and mental health among Non-Hispanic Whites than among African Americans and other disadvantaged minority populations. Adequate numbers of low SES Non-Hispanic Whites as well as higher SES minority subjects would enable testing this and other related hypotheses.

In the meantime, studies of minority elderly need to assess the main dimensions of SES with the nature and extensiveness of the assessment depending on the purpose of each study. At a minimum educational attainment, occupational status, and income and financial assets must be assessed. Assessment of financial strain can add another dimension that has proven to be predictive of mental health outcomes.

Which one (or which combination) of the above measures will be employed in the data analyses will depend on the purpose of the analysis. Education appears to be the most convenient and useful predictor of health status in studies of minority elderly (and of elderly in general), partly because it precedes the health outcome temporally.

Finally, any knowledge that might help society eliminate SES and ethnic disparities in the health of older people must come from studies conducted earlier in life. Health disparities at any age cannot be eliminated without eliminating socioeconomic disparities among ethnic groups earlier in life.

REFERENCES

Adler, N. E., Boyce, T., Chesney, M. A., Cohen, S. Folkman, S. Kahn, R. L., & Syme, S.L. (1993). Socioeconomic status and health:The challenge of the gradient. *American Psychologist, 49*, 15-24.

Carr, D., Pemmarazu, A., & Rice, D. P. (Eds.). (1996). *Improving data on America's aging population: Summary of a workshop.* Washington, DC: National Academy Press.

Citro, C. F., & Michael, R. T. (Eds.). (1995). *Measuring poverty: A new approach.* Washington, DC: National Academy Press.

Dalaker, J. (1999). Poverty in the United States: 1998. *Current Population Reports* (Series P60-207). U.S. Census Bureau.

Evans, R. G., Barer, M. L., & Marmor T. R. (Eds.). (1994). *Why are some people healthy and others not?* New York: Aldine de Gruyter.

Feinstein, J.S. (1993). The relationship between socioeconomic status and health: A review of the literature. *Milbank Quarterly, 71*, 279-322.

Hauser, R. M., & Warren, J. R. (1997). Socioeconomic indexes for occupations: A review, update, and critique. *Sociological Methodology, 27*, 177-298.

Haug, M. (1977). Measurement in social stratification. *Annual Review of Sociology, 3*, 51-77.

Hollingshead, A. B. (1957). *Two factor index of social position* [mimeograph]. New Haven, CT: Yale University.

Juster, T. (1994). *Codebook: Assets and health dynamics of the oldest old (AHEAD).* Ann Arbor, MI: University of Michigan.

Krieger, N., Rowley, D. L., Herman, A. A., Avery, B., & Philips, M. T. (1993). Racism, sexism, and social class: Implications for studies of health, disease, and well-being. *American Journal of Preventive Medicine, 9* (Suppl. 2), 82-122.

Krieger, N., Williams, D. R., & Moss, N. E. (1997). Measuring social class in U.S. public health research: Concepts, methodologies, and guidelines. *Annual Review of Public Health, 18*, 341-378.

Liberatos, P., Link, B. G., & Kelsey, J. L. (1988). The measurement of social class in epidemiology. *Epidemiologic Reviews, 10*, 87-121.

Lillie-Blanton, M., & Laveist, T. (1996) Race/ethnicity, the social environment, and health. *Social Science and Medicine, 43*, 83-91.

Lillie-Blanton, M, Parsons, P. E., Gayle, H.,& Dievler, A. (1996) Racial differences in health: Not just Black and White, but shades of gray. *Annual Review of Public Health , 17*, 411-448.

Lynch, J., & Kaplan, G. (2000). Socioeconomic position. In L.F. Berkman & I. Kawachi (Eds.), *Social epidemiology* (pp. 13-35). New York: Oxford University Press.

Markides, K. S., & Black, S. A. (1995). Race, ethnicity, and aging: The impact of inequality. In R. H. Binstock & L. K. George (Eds.), *Handbook of aging and the social sciences* (pp. 153-170). San Diego, Academic Press.

Markides, K. S., & Mindel, C. H. (1987). *Aging and ethnicity.* Newbury Park, CA: Sage.

Markides, K. S., Stroup-Benham, C. A., Black, S. A., Satish, S., Perkowski, L. C., & Ostir, G. (1999). The health of Mexican American elderly. Selected findings from the Hispanic EPESE. In M. Wykle & A. B. Ford (Eds.), *Serving minority elders in the 21st century* (pp. 72-90). New York: Springer Publishing.

Miech, R. A., & Hauser, R. M. (1998). *Social class indicators and health at midlife* (Center for Demography and Ecology Working Paper No. 98-06). University of Wisconsin-Madison.

Moss, N., & Krieger, N. (1995). Measuring social inequalities in health: Report on the conference of the National Institutes of Health. *Public Health Reports, 110*, 302-305.

Nakao, K., & Treas, J. (1994). Updating occupational and socioeconomic scores: How the new measures measure up. *Sociological Methodology, 24*, 1-72.

Nam, C. B., & Powers, M. G. (1983). *The socioeconomic approach to status measurements (with a guide to occupational and socioeconomic status scores).* Houston,TX: Cap & Gown Press.

Preston, S. H., & Taubman, P. (1994). Socioeconomic differences in adult mortality and health status. In L. G. Martin & S. H. Preston (Eds.), *Demography of aging* (pp. 279-318). Washington, DC: National Academy Press.

Rank, M. R., & Hirschl, T. A. (1999). Estimating the proportion of Americans ever experiencing poverty during their elderly years. *Journals of Gerontology: Social Sciences, 54B*, S184-S193.

Robert, S. A. (1998). Community-level socioeconomic status effects on adult health. *Journal of Health and Social Behavior, 39*, 18-37.

Short, K., Garner, T., Johnson, D., & Doyle, P. (1999). Experimental poverty measures: 1990 to 1997. *Current Population Reports* (Series P60-205). U.S. Bureau of the Census.

Smith, J. P. (1995). Racial and ethnic differences in wealth in the Health and Retirement Study. *The Journal of Human Resources, XXX*, (Suppl.) S158-S183.

Smith, J. P. (1997). Wealth inequality among older Americans. *The Journals of Gerontology, 52B*, (Special Issue), 74-81.

Smith, J. P., & Kington, R. S. (1997a). Race, socioeconomic status, and health in late life. In L. G. Martin & B. J. Soldo (Eds.), *Racial and ethnic differences in the health of older Americans* (pp. 105-162). Washington, DC: National Academy Press.

Smith, J. P. & Kington, R. S. (1997b). Demographic and economic correlates of health in old age. *Demography, 34*(1), 159-170.

U.S. Bureau of the Census. (1999). Statistical abstract of the United States: 1999. Washington, DC: Government Printing Office.

U.S. Department of Labor. (1999). Revising the standard occupational classification system (Report 929). Author.

Warren, J. R., Sheridan, J. T., & Hauser, R. M. (1998). *Choosing a measure of occupational standing: How useful are composite measures in analyses of gender inequality in occupational attainment?* (Center for Demography and Ecology Working Paper No. 96-10). University of Wisconsin-Madison.

Williams, D. R. (1996). Race/ethnicity and socioeconomic status: Measurement and methodological issues. *International Journal of Health Services, 26*(3), 483-505.

Williams, D.R., & Rucker, T. (1996). Socioeconomic status and the health of racial mino rity populations. In P. M. Kato & T. Mann (Eds.), *Handbook of diversity issues in health psychology* (Vol. 21, pp. 407-423). New York: Plenum Press.

Wright, E.O. (1998). Class analysis. In R.F. Levine (Ed.), *Social class and stratification: Classic statements and theoretical debates* (pp. 141-165). Lanham, MA: Rowman & Littlefied Publishers.

Acknowledgments. The authors wish to thank the reviewers and editors for their helpful comments on an earlier draft of this chapter.

6

Social Support: Clarifying the Construct With Applications for Minority Populations

Elizabeth J. Mutran, Peter S. Reed, S. Sudha

T he literature on social support abounds. In 1988, House, Umberson, and Landis showed the phenomenal growth of research interest in the area of social support by the increase in articles in the Social Science Citation Index containing the words "social support" in the title. Replicating their approach in the medical and health research by using Medline, a computerized database of health literature, the continued growth can be documented. During the 1970s an average of slightly more than three articles per year included "social support" in the title; in the '80s, the average was over 52; and in the '90s, over 100 articles per year focused on social support. The measures of social support in these articles are quite varied and only a subset focuses on social support among older minority populations. In this chapter, we propose to survey and document several of the more widely used instruments and what they purport to measure in terms of social support. Only a few scales will be presented, focusing on those for whom some psychometric properties have been reported. In most instances the scale has yet to be validated in minority populations. The chapter will emphasize that, though much has been done using the construct of social support, little has been done to ensure that the construct is appropriately assessed across ethnic and racial subgroups.

Not only has the number of studies grown, but there is also a parallel growth in the theoretical discussions of social support and attempts to document how the beneficial effects of social support are conveyed. Researchers in the field have noted (Barrera, 1986; Berkman, 1984; House et al., 1988b; Krause & Markides, 1990), that this growth has not been linear, and social support has proven to be a difficult construct to define. In many ways, it is the crux of belonging to a society, of being incorporated into a family, and being part of a community; yet it must include something more than interpersonal contact. Social support implies that something is given to another who receives it. There is either a cognitive or an affective response, assumedly positive, from the individual receiving support, and an intent on the part of the support provider to express empathy with another or to be helpful in some fashion.

There is a wide range of outcomes partially attributed to social support. Research finds social support to be related to stress (Krause, 1987a; Russell, & Cutrona, 1991), to emotional distress (Bazargan & Hamm-Baugh, 1995; Dilworth-Anderson, Williams, & Cooper, 1999), and to a reduction of mortality (Berkman & Breslow, 1983; Berkman & Syme, 1979; Blazer, 1982; House, Robbins, & Metzner, 1982). Social affiliation reduces the risk of coronary heart disease (Reed, McGee, Yano, & Feinleib, 1983), assists sufferers of hip fracture to recover their walking ability (Mutran, Reitzes, Mossey, & Fernandez, 1995), and promotes compliance in the management of diabetes (Ford, Tilley, & McDonald, 1998). While there is increasing research on the outcomes and the theoretical definitions of social support, researchers have been slow to move toward a consensus of the term "social support," or the mechanism by which it achieves positive outcomes (Berkman, 1984; House et al., 1988a; Russell & Cutrona, 1991). As described by Stahl and Potts (1985), in order to discover the mechanisms of the influence of social support, appropriate attention should be paid to "interaction of source, content, and scope of socially supportive behaviors" (p. 323), which maintains relevance in moving toward evaluating social support across diverse populations.

This chapter will first, examine definitions of social support; second, review measures of social integration/isolation; third, review measures of social support; and fourth, selectively present some uses of social support in analyses of health in minority populations.

DEFINING SOCIAL SUPPORT

While there is no one definition of the term "social support," there is recognition of common components. Several researchers define the term in a conceptual way, such as Hobfall and Vaux (1993) who define social support as a grand meta-construct with three social support constructs within it: support network resources, supportive behavior, and the subjective appraisals of support. House and colleagues (1988b) also speak of three general classes of phenomena or variables, each with multiple components and indicators. The three classes are social integration/isolation, social network structure, and relational content. They define each as follows:

1. Social integration refers to the existence or quantity of social ties, which includes type and frequency of contact.
2. Social network refers to the characteristics of a web of social ties, such as density of the network, its homogeneity, its dispersion, and its multiplexity (House et al., 1988b).

3. Relational content refers to the functional nature or quality of social relation-ships, which has three content areas, with social support as one area (House et al., 1988b, p. 302). The other two include relational demands or conflicts and social regulation or control. Social support is the positive component, referring to instrumental aid, emotional caring or concern, and information.

In a similar fashion, Berkman (1984) has pointed out that social networks and social support are distinct concepts. Social networks are the webs of social ties that surround an individual, while social support, on the other hand, is the emotional, instrumental, and financial aid that is offered by one's social network. A distinction between House and Berkman is that House divides the construct of social networks into two categories, social integration/isolation and network structure.

Other theorists, such as Kaplan, Cassel, and Gore (1977), Thoits (1982), and Wellman (1981), have all contributed to defining social support, and these many variations have converged in the distinction of social networks/social integration and social support. However, as House and colleagues (1988b) and Berkman (1984) point out, the empirical research on physical and mental health often has blurred these two distinctions. Berkman emphasizes that the measures used for both social networks and social support often lack sophistication, and that there has been more rigorous assessment of the health outcome measures, the dependent variables, than on the independent variable of social support. House and his colleagues argue that distinc-tions should be made on the basis of structure and process. They point out that there are two structural issues, integration/isolation and network structures, and three social processes, social regulation or control, relational demands and conflicts, and social support.

The review of measures in this chapter will focus primarily on one structural issue, integration/isolation as defined by House and associates (1988b), and one social process, social support. The review of measures of social support will be followed by examples of research where the social support scale is included in analyses as the dependent variable. Examples relating social support to outcomes will also be presented. The reader should distinguish between studies in which social support is the predicted variable and those in which it is the predictor.

MEASURES OF SOCIAL INTEGRATION/ISOLATION

The most common way of measuring the social integration of older persons, including older minority persons, is to ask a set of questions assessing marital status, number of family members, kin and friends, and the amount and type of contact with family, kin, and friends. The items described above might be called social network measures or social functioning measures, but regardless of the terminology, they clearly show whether the individual is isolated from or integrated into social relationships, while leaving unanswered whether the family, kin, and friends know or relate to each other.

Studies which use social integration items often sum the frequency of contact that the individual has with various others and use this as an index of social integration, such as Berkman and Syme's Social Network Index (1979). The Social Network Index is constructed from assessments of four types of social ties: marital status, number of close relatives and friends, church participation, and participation in other organizations. While clearly named a network index, this measure is used as a measure of social support in some studies (e.g., Kang and Bloom, 1993). Other studies (e.g., Schoenbach, Kaplan, Fredman, & Kleinbaum, 1986) retain the concept as one of social ties modeling their measures after that of Berkman and Syme. A network index might be used by itself or in conjunction with other dichotomous measures. For example, marital status might be used separately and coded married versus nonmarried, as may presence or absence of children, as well as a measure for living alone or with others (e.g., Lubben & Becerra, 1987).

The caregiving literature often emphasizes social integration variables as resources for social support. One example is the study of Biegel, Magaziner, and Baum (1991), which concludes from the literature that the kinship system of elderly African Americans serves as a source of support more often than the kinship system of Whites. Still, other studies argue that the evidence is unclear whether the social networks of African Americans are more supportive than that of others (Silverstein & Waite, 1993). Also, there are several studies which caution against the assumption that families and churches are able to support the most vulnerable elderly (Bowles et al., 2000). Cantor, Brennan, and Sainz (1994) conclude that, while ethnicity is important, it is only one indicator of the nature of informal networks. Measures of gender, health, and social class, or income, must also be considered.

A second measure of social integration was developed for the Piedmont site of the Established Populations for Epidemiologic Studies of the Elderly (EPESE), which contains an oversampling of African Americans (Cornoni-Huntley et al., 1990). A social support scale, the Duke Social Support Index (Landerman, George, Campbell, & Blazer, 1989), was designed for this EPESE site. It comprises 35 items, addressing the social network of the respondent and the support provided by the social network. At this point in the article, only the social network components will be discussed. In the Piedmont EPESE, African American women were more likely to live with others than were White women, and African American men were less likely to live with a spouse than were White men. The Piedmont survey also showed racial differences in the number of children seen monthly or more often. African Americans were more likely than Whites both to see no children and to see six or more children (Cornoni-Huntley et al., 1990). Similar questions regarding one's social network were asked in the National Survey of Black Americans (1979), with questions concerning the frequency of contact with and proximity of friends and relatives. It is important to point out that both surveys also asked about helping behavior, or items more in line with a conceptualization of social support that is distinct from social integration.

There are a number of studies that relate social integration to outcome measures like well-being and depression, but many of these studies concern merely one ethnic/racial group. Some researchers have also extended the research on networks to include characteristics that go beyond the scope of this chapter. For example, using a measure of social networks emphasizing various network characteristics, such as interactional, structural, member, and environmental attributes, Cohen, Teresi, and Holmes (1985) found that among a group of inner-city older persons, social networks did influence ability to adapt and meet one's own needs. This study, along with most studies that emphasize scale development, incorporates a predominately White sample. When more than one ethnic/racial group is considered, race is often used as an independent variable in a regression equation. Race is then assessed as a predictor of an outcome (e.g., depression) after social support is controlled.

In terms of psychometric properties, many measures of social integration versus isolation are mere indices or count measures. Thus, issues of internal reliability are not relevant. As Hays, Saunders, Flint, Kaplan, and Blazer (1997) point out, the use of internal consistency measures as reliability coefficients is inappropriate because there is no reason to expect high interitem correlations. For example, there is no reason to expect that someone with few siblings would have more or fewer friends than someone with many siblings. In terms of construct validity, one might argue that measures counting friends or relatives have relatively low validity as measures of social support, if support is defined as emotional, instrumental, and financial aid. In fact, these measures of integration may be indicators of social control or relational demands, which as previously stated, are two other social processes described by House and colleagues (1988b).

MEASURES OF SOCIAL SUPPORT

House and associates (1988b), Berkman (1984), Barrera, Sandler, and Ramsay (1981), Krause and Markides (1990), to name but a few, focus on social support as a process involving instrumental and affective components. Though there are numerous measures of social support throughout the literature, as authors tend to construct their own measures or modify existing ones, most incorporate similar conceptualizations of social support as instrumental and/or affective. The affective component comprises emotional support, involving the provision of caring, empathy, love, and trust (Barrera, 1986; House, 1981; Langford, Bowsher, Maloney, & Lillis, 1997; Tilden & Weinert, 1987). Instrumental support is defined as the provision of tangible goods, services, and aid (Barrera, 1986; Cohen & McKay, 1984; Cutrona & Russell, 1990; Krause, 1986). Informational support and appraisal support are also considered (House, 1981; Krause, 1986), with informational support aiding in problem solving, and appraisal support relaying information that relates to self-evaluation. These instrumental and affective components are each measured by several indicators or question items. In this case, the interitem correlations are important as each indicator or item is supposed to measure the same underlying construct, whether it is the emotional component, the informational component or the instrumental component.

Many studies examining the construct of social support (as distinct from network size or attributes) often assume that the relationships are positive and support is given.

For example, some studies use marital status as an indicator of social support (Bland, Krogh, & Winkelstein, 1991), while others use this variable to indicate social network or living status (Chappell, 1991). The distinction is between the importance of the existence of a relationship and that of relationship content.

A search of the literature found a few primary scales that address the issue of social support content. Though, except for a few measures of instrumental support (caregiving) most have not been used in minority populations, these scales are reviewed below. First, the original scale is described along with its psychometric properties. Second, modifications of the original scale are presented, as there has been a drive toward revising and shortening scales with known psychometric properties. Lengthy scales are purported to be less effective and more tedious for older people to complete, with an extended interview placing unrealistic demands on the subject (Goodger, Byles, Higgabotham, & Mishra, 1999; Koenig, Westlund, George, Blazer, & Hybels, 1993). The success of these attempts in maintaining the psychometric properties of the original measures will be reviewed following a description of the scale. Third, the use of the scales in research will be documented, showing that with all the work that has been done on scale construction and attention to psychometric properties, there is little that examines the scale across population groups. Measures that exhibit ease of administration, maintain validity and reliability, are appropriate for diverse populations, and are based on a consensus of the conceptual components of social support are yet to be developed.

The Social Support Questionnaire (SSQ), developed by Sarason, Levine, Basham, and Sarason (1983), is a 27-item questionnaire that addresses social network, social support (primarily emotional support), and support satisfaction. The measure was created through factor analysis of many items intended to measure functions of social networks and ultimately incorporated two factors: number or perceived availability of support and satisfaction with the support (Sarason, Sarason, Shearing, & Pierce, 1987). Sarason and his colleagues did find that the measure holds together well, and that the psychometric properties are good, with both factors in the 27-item SSQ having reliabilities of alpha = 0.97 (Sarason et al., 1987). Sarason and his colleagues (1983, 1987) have shown the measure to have good test-retest reliability, as well as good factor and predictive validities (Furukawa, Harai, Kitamura, & Takahashi, 1999).

Sarason and colleagues (1987) condensed the original 27-item version, consisting of two factors (number of social supports and satisfaction with perceived support available), into a six-item version loading on the same two factors. The Abbreviated Social Support Questionnaire has been evaluated to determine its reliability and validity relative to the longer version (Sarason and et al., 1987). Sarason and associates (1987) found that the good test-retest reliability, factor reliability, and internal consistency of the longer version is replicated in the 6-item version (alpha = 0.90 - 0.93), which does exhibit concurrent validity with the original 27-item version (Furukawa et al., 1999). Sarason and associates (1987) contend that the 6-item version is highly similar to the 27-item version, both in terms of correlation with the original SSQ and with satisfactory test-retest reliability and internal reliability.

The 6-item version of the Social Support Questionnaire has recently been tested in Japan among a group of psychiatric patients in comparison with controls of nonpsychiatric patients to measure its applicability across various groups (Furukawa et al., 1999). While there is little research that explicitly examines the effectiveness of social support scales among older minority populations, this study at least provides insight into the usefulness of the short version of the SSQ across another population. Looking at the group of Japanese psychiatric patients, the items loaded clearly on the two expected factors, and expressed high reliability coefficients for each of the factors, alpha = 0.91 and 0.94 (Furukawa et al., 1999).

The Inventory of Socially Supportive Behavior (ISSB), a 40-item scale developed by Barrera and colleagues (1981) is a measure of assessing help received from a natural support system. The authors drew from a range of social support transactions that occurred in a wide range of populations, as found in the literature. The items were seen as representative of supportive behavior and not as an exhaustive list. The internal consistency of the ISSB was approximately 0.93 as measured by the coefficient alpha.

The ISSB has been used with a number of modifications. A Spanish version of the scale (ISSB28) was used to examine the relationship between social support, activity level, and physical health in a sample of 96 Puerto Rican elderly persons (Velez-Pastrana, Rodriguez, & Martinez, 1997). However, no information on the reliability or validity of the modified scale as used in this population was reported.

Krause and Markides (1990) modified the scale as developed by Barrera and associates (1981) in several ways to make it more appropriate for an older population. First, they added a dimension of integration. These new items asked if older adults provided informational, tangible, and emotional support to persons in their social environment. Second, they changed the response format to extend beyond a month to the last year. Third, the authors added items to assess satisfaction with support. Twelve of the original items less pertinent to Krause and Markides's interest in stress were deleted. The final scale consisted of 41 items in contrast to the original 40.

Krause and Markides completed a number of exploratory analyses with 3-5 factors using both orthogonal and oblique rotation, and settled on a 4-factor solution: informational, tangible, emotional, and integration. They then assessed whether the 4 factors adequately represented the correlations in the observed data. This question was tested in a second-order factor analysis, where the higher-order construct of social support was indicated by the 4 components listed above. This analysis resulted in an acceptable fit of the model to the data. The data showed that the 4 dimensions of social support were all strongly related to the higher-order factor; however, the strongest indicator of social support was emotional support.

Krause has used the modified version of the scale to examine whether social support buffers the effects of stressful life events on depressive symptoms (Krause, 1987a, 1988). He has also found that satisfaction with support was an important determinant of self-perceived health (Krause, 1987b).

The Duke Social Support Index (DSSI; Landerman et al., 1989), in addition to its measures of social integration discussed above, has three factors that are clearly indicative of social support: satisfaction with social support, perceived social support, and instrumental support (Landerman et al., 1989). The subjective support, or perceived social support subscale comprises items which focus on emotional content, such as "how often do you feel lonely?" Instrumental support items ask whether friends or family help the respondent in any of 13 ways, such as transportation, chores, gifts of money, providing advice and companionship, and so forth (Landerman et al., 1989).

This measure has been abbreviated to create two shorter measures, a 23-item, 3-factor scale (Social Interaction, Subjective Support, Instrumental Support) and an 11-item, 2-factor scale (Social Interaction, Subjective Support) (Koenig et al., 1993). Of the two shorter versions of the DSSI, the only difference is that the 23-item version incorporates instrumental support items that the 11-item version does not (Koenig et al., 1993). Koenig and associates felt that the longer, 23-item version, would be better than the 11-item version among older people because of the inclusion of the instrumental support, as older persons are expected to need more assistance with such support due to physical limitations. However, an analysis of the 11-item version of the Duke Social Support Index among chronically ill elderly (Koenig et al., 1993) found that the 11-item version performed at a level comparable to the original 35-item version in spite of its being one-third the length. The analysis revealed one factor while acknowledging the two major dimensions of social interaction and satisfaction with support received.

In analysis by Goodger and colleagues (1999) among community dwelling older people (ages 70+), the 11-item version also performed quite well. The items loaded on two factors as expected from the two major dimensions incorporated by Koenig and associates, (1993) providing information on social interaction and satisfaction with support received. Overall, the two subscales explained 46% of the variance in the DSSI, and the 11-item version as a whole had an internal consistency reliability of alpha = 0.77.

The MOS Social Support Survey (Sherbourne & Stewart, 1991), is a 20-item measure that evaluates several major dimensions of social support. While there is a single-item structural support component eliciting a number of close ties, the main focus is the perceived availability of functional support (Sherbourne & Stewart, 1991). Four subscales (19 items) measure components similar to those found in other social support scales, which are theorized to be the major dimensions of functional support, including tangible support, affectionate support, positive social interaction, and emotional/informational support. In the developmental form of the MOS Social Support Survey, emotional and informational support comprised two separate components, but through analyses exhibited significant overlap, and thus the final version combines them into a single factor. Each of the 19 functional support items lists a particular type of support, for example, someone to help you if you were confined to bed, and asks how often the support is available on a 5-point scale.

The previously described trend of reducing scale length was present in the initial development of the MOS Social Support Survey. It intentionally was designed to be brief both in the number of items and each item was stated succinctly in order to reduce the burden placed on the respondent (Sherbourne & Stewart, 1991). While this brevity was achieved, it was not at the expense of utility. In an evaluation conducted among chronically ill patients by Sherbourne and Stewart (1991) the 19-item functional support scale exhibited strong psychometric properties, adequately measuring overall social support, as well as the 4 intended dimensions of social support, with both high convergent and discriminant validity. They found high reliability, with alpha = 0.91-0.96 for the 4 subscales and alpha = 0.97 for the overall social support measure. Their analyses also showed all of the items to load clearly onto the expected factors, with an overall range of factor loadings from 0.76 to 0.93 across all 4 factors.

Summarizing, two trends are clear in terms of the current state of social support measures, and several questions remain to be answered. First, in order to make the measures more applicable to diverse groups of people, there has been a move toward shortening the scales. It is believed that the shorter versions will be more accessible, in particular to older people, and the usefulness of these shorter scales relative to their longer versions has been established (Furukawa et al., 1999; Goodger et al., 1999; Koenig et al., 1993; Sarason et al., 1987). In addition, with the Abbreviated Duke Social Support Index and the 6-item Social Support Questionnaire, there appears to be a move toward incorporating both the structural component, social integration/isolation (number of potential contacts), and the process component of support adequacy, or satisfaction with support. Essentially, social network and subjective support seem to be commonly used among these newer, shorter versions. While this work in measurement is laudable, efforts must be forthcoming to assess the psychometric property of these scales on older minority populations.

MEASURES OF SOCIAL SUPPORT IN STUDIES OF MINORITY GROUP MEMBERS

An examination of articles relating social support to health or disease management among minority group members showed that several authors did not report the psychometric property of the scales, and that each appeared to have a unique way of measuring the construct. Most studies used either measures of integration/isolation or instrumental helping behavior. Ford, Tilley, and McDonald (1998) reviewed a number of studies on social support among African American adults with diabetes. Their review lists a variety of measures, ranging from support groups, to social networks, to family helping behavior. Their review concluded that African Americans tend to rely more heavily than Whites on informal social networks in managing diabetes, but also pointed out the need to increase the research on minority populations.

Strogatz and associates (1997) defined social support to include emotional support and instrumental assistance, and used this in their research on social support, stress, and blood pressure in African American adults. They used a set of questions on the likelihood of receiving help for different kinds of problems such as repairs around the house, need to borrow money, and advice. They report scale reliabilities of 0.69-0.79 for African American women and 0.65-0.74 for African American men. They found all associations to be in the expected direction. That is, social support was associated with lower blood pressure, while stress was associated with higher blood pressure.

Lubben and Becerra (1987) examined social support among African American, Mexican, and Chinese elderly persons using a measure of support that incorporated source of social ties, closeness of ties, frequency of contact, and perceived quality of the network. They found ethnic differences in the structural and interactional aspects of the networks, but after controlling for age and marital status, found few differences in social support. However, Lubben and Becerra also pointed out the need for larger samples of minority group members.

Biegel, Magaziner, and Baum's (1991) research emphasized the need to have a sample size large enough to examine interaction effects. In their study they found that White older persons, with greater social support and a larger social network, had a weaker association between stress and depressive symptoms than African American elderly persons. For African American elderly, having a larger network and receiving support resulted in a stronger relationship between stress and depressive symptomatology. The measure of social support in this study emphasized respondents' embeddedness. Respondents were asked to name up to eight people with whom they had close ties and from this a measure of network size was computed. Social support was measured by focusing on the three closest network members and asking about the quality and content of the relationship. Their measure of social support had a standardized alpha of 0.97 for the sample as a whole, 0.96 for Whites, and 0.97 for African American respondents.

A study by Haley and colleagues (1996) used the Social Support Questionnaire Short Form (Sarason et al., 1987) with a sample of 123 White and 74 African American family caregivers. This article addressed the well-being of African American and White family caregivers of patients with Alzheimer's disease. The researchers found that African American and White caregivers differed somewhat in the covariance structure of these measures. However, they concluded that in terms of social support, White and African American caregivers did not differ in total number of social supports, total satisfaction with social support or in the total number of visits with relatives and friends. The alpha coefficients for satisfaction with social support were 0.87 for African American caregivers and 0.88 for White caregivers.

CONCLUSION

This area of research clearly requires consistency in definitions and in use of terms. With all the research evaluating social support, and with all the various attempts at conceptualizing and measuring social support, there is no clear and effective standard for its definition or its measurement. The resolution to this question may lie in conducting more research that utilizes consistent measures of social support and confirming the scales or indices on minority populations. There is a need for extensive evaluations of the existing measures both in terms of their structural efficacy and in terms of their predictive capacity. Clearly defining the components of efficient measures would lend itself to moving the field toward increased consideration of social support as a dependent variable, as urged by House and colleagues (1988a) and Berkman (1984).

Still, in order for measures to be of a caliber warranting their widespread use, the measures need to be widely applicable across a range of population subgroups. As of now, the minority older population is underrepresented in social support research. There is a need to evaluate the effectiveness of existing social support measures among older minority groups to establish their relevance and the equivalence of their properties among these populations. Regardless of the measure used, there is a need to begin to reach consensus on the definitions and constructs that are most appropriate, which could be accomplished by evaluating existing measures. Studies could be designed with control trials by administering the social support scales to randomly selected samples of older minorities and older Whites for comparison. In a less rigorous manner, researchers could administer the scales to a group of older minorities and compare the properties that emerge to published reports of the scale properties among majority populations. Irrespective of the methods by which it is conducted, the need now exists to move toward widely accepted measures that are consistently utilized and shown to be effective across diverse groups of people.

REFERENCES

Barrera, M., Sandler, I. N., & Ramsay, T. B. (1981). Preliminary development of a scale of social support: Studies on college students. *American Journal of Community Psychology, 9*(4), 435-447.

Barrera, M. (1986). Distinctions between social support concepts, measures and models. *American Journal of Community Psychology, 14*(4), 413-445.

Bazargan, M., & Hamm-Baugh, V. P. (1995). The relationship between chronic illness and depression in a community of urban Black elderly persons. *Journal of Gerontology: Social Sciences, 50B*(2), S119-S127.

Berkman, L. F. (1984). Assessing the physical health effects of social networks and social support. *Annual Review of Public Health, 5*, 413-432.

Berkman, L., & Breslow, L. (1983). *Health and ways of living: Findings from the Alameda County Study.* New York: Oxford University. Press

Berkman, L., & Syme, S. L. (1979). Social networks, host resistance, and mortality: A nine-year follow-up study of Alameda County residents. *American Journal of Epidemiology, 109*, 186-204.

Biegel, D. E., Magaziner, J., & Baum, M. (1991). Social support networks of White and Black elderly people at risk for institutionalization. *Health and Social Work, 16*(4), 245-257.

Bland, S. H., Krogh, V., & Winkelstein, T. (1991). Social network and blood pressure: A population study. *Psychosomatic Medicine, 53*(6), 598-607.

Blazer, D. G. (1982). Social support and mortality in an elderly community population. *American Journal of Epidemiology, 115*(5), 684-694.

Bowles, J., Brooks, T., Hayes-Reams, P., Butts, T., Myers, H., Allen W., & Kington, R. S. (2000). Frailty, family, and church support among urban African American elderly. *Journal of Health Care for the Poor and Underserved, 11*(1), 87-99.

Cantor, M. H., Brennan, M., & Sainz, A. (1994). The importance of ethnicity in the social support systems of older New Yorkers: A longitudinal perspective (1970 to 1990). *Journal of Gerontological Social Work, 22* (3/4), 95-128.

Chappell, N. L. (1991). Living arrangements and sources of caregiving. *Journal of Gerontology, 46*, S1-S8.

Cohen, C. I., Teresi, J., & Holmes, D. (1985). Social networks and adaptation. *The Gerontologist, 25*(3), 297-304.

Cohen, S., & McKay. (1984). Social support, stress and the buffering hypothesis. In A. Baum, J. E. Singer, & S. E. Taylor (Eds.), *Handbook of psychology and health* (Vol. 4). Hillsdale, NJ: Lawrence Erlbaum.

Cornoni-Huntley, J., Blazer, D. G., Lafferty, M. E., Everett, D. F., Brock, D. B., & Farmer, M. E. (Eds.). (1990). *Established populations for epidemiologic studies of the elderly. Volume II: Resource data book.* NIH Publication #90-495. Washington, DC: National Institute on Aging.

Cutrona, C. E., & Russell, D. W. (1990). Type of social support and specific stress: Toward a theory of optimal matching. In B. R. Sarason, I. G. Sarason, & G. R. Pierce (Eds.), *Social support: An interactional view* (pp. 319-366). New York: John Wiley and Sons.

Dilworth-Anderson, P., Williams, S. W., & Cooper, T. (1999). The contexts of experiencing emotional distress among family caregivers to elderly African Americans. *Family Relations, 48*, 391-396.

Ford, M. E., Tilley, B. C., & McDonald, P. E. (1998). Social support among African American adults with diabetes, Part 2: A review. *Journal of the National Medical Association, 90*(7), 425-432.

Furukawa, T. A., Harai, H., Kitamura, T., & Takahashi, K. (1999). Social support questionnaire among psychiatric patients with various diagnoses and normal controls. *Social Psychiatric Epidemiology, 34*, 216-222.

Goodger, B., Byles, J., Higganbotham, N., & Mishra, G. (1999). Assessment of a short scale to measure social support among older people. *Australian and New Zealand Journal of Public Health, 23*(3), 260-265.

Haley, W. E., Roth, D. L., Coleton, M. I., Ford, G. R., West, C. A. C., Collins, R. P., & Isobe, T. L. (1996). Appraisal, coping, and social support as mediators of well-being in Black and White family caregivers of patients with Alzheimer's Disease. *Journal of Consulting and Clinical Psychology, 64*(1), 121-129.

Hays, J. C., Saunders, W. B., Flint, H. P., Kaplan, B. H., & Blazer, D. G. (1997). Social support and depression as risk factors for loss of physical function in late life. *Aging and Mental Health, 1*(3), 209-220.

Hobfoll, S. E., & Vaux, A. (1993). Social support: Social resources and social context. In L. Goldberger & S. Breznitz (Ed.), *Handbook of stress: Theoretical and clinical aspects* (pp. 685-705). New York: The Free Press.

House, J. S. (1981). *Work stress and social support.* Reading, MA: Addison-Wesley.

House, J. S., Landis, K. R., & Umberson, D. (1988a). Social relationships and health. *Science, 241,* 540-545.

House, J. S., Umberson, D., & Landis, K. R. (1988b). Structures and processes of social support. *Annual Review of Sociology, 14,* 293-318.

House, J., Robbins, C., & Metzner, H. (1982). The association of social relationships and activities with mortality: Prospective evidence from the Tecumseh Community Health Study. *American Journal of Epidemiology, 116*(1), 123-140.

Kang, S. H., & Bloom, J. R. (1993). Social support and cancer screening among older Black Americans. *Journal of the National Cancer Institute, 85*(9), 737-742.

Kaplan, B. H., Cassel, J.C., & Gore, S. (1977). Social support and health. *Medical Care, 15*(5 Suppl.), 47-58.

Koenig, H. G., Westlund, R. E., George, L. K., Blazer, D., & Hybels, C. (1993). Abbreviating the Duke Social Support Index for use in chronically ill elderly individuals. *Psychosomatics, 34*(1), 61-69.

Krause, N. (1986). Social support, stress, and well-being among older adults. *Journal of Gerontology, 41*(4), 512-519.

Krause, N. (1987a). Life stress, social support, and self-esteem in an elderly population. *Psychology and Aging, 2*(4), 349-356.

Krause, N. (1987b). Satisfaction with social support and self-rated health in older adults. *The Gerontologist, 27*(3), 301-308.

Krause, N. (1988). Social support, stress, and well-being among older adults. *Journal of Gerontology, 41*(4), 512-519.

Krause, N., & Markides, K. (1990). Measuring social support among older adults. *International Journal on Aging and Human Development, 30*(1), 37-53.

Landerman, R., George, L. K., Campbell, R. T., & Blazer, D. G. (1989). Alternative models of the stress-buffering hypothesis. *American Journal of Community Psychology, 17*(5), 625-642.

Langford, C. P., Bowsher, J., Maloney, J. P., & Lillis, P. P. (1997). Social support: A conceptual analysis. *Journal of Advanced Nursing, 25*(1), 95-100.

Lubben, J. E., & Becerra, R. M. (1987). Social support among Black, Mexican, and Chinese elderly. In D. E. Gefland & C. M. Barresi (Eds.), *Ethnic dimensions of aging.* New York: Springer Publishing.

Mutran, E. J., Reitzes, D. C., Mossey, J. & Fernandez, ME. (1995) Social support, depression, and recovery of walking ability following hip fracture surgery. *Journal of Gerontology, 50B*(6), S354-S361.

National Survey of Black Americans: A Study of Black American Life. (1979). Survey Research Center, Institute for Social Research, Ann Arbor, MI.

Reed, D., McGee, D., Yano, K., & Feinleib, M. (1983) Social networks and coronary heart disease among Japanese men in Hawaii. *American Journal of Epidemiology, 117*(6), 384-96.

Russell, D. W., & Cutrona, C. E. (1991). Social support, stress, and depressive symptoms among the elderly: Test of a process model. *Psychology and Aging, 6*(2), 190-201.

Sarason, I. G., Levine, H. M., Basham, R. B., & Sarason, B. R. (1983) Assessing social support: The social support questionnaire. *Journal of Personality and Social Psychology, 44*, 127-139.

Sarason, I. G., Sarason, B. R., Shearing, E. N., & Pierce G. R. (1987). A brief measure of social support: Practical and theoretical implications. *Journal of Social and Personal Relationships, 4,* 497-510.

Schoenbach, V. J., Kaplan, B. H., Fredman, L., & Kleinbaum, D. G. (1986). Social ties and mortality in Evans County, Georgia. *American Journal of Epidemiology, 123*(4), 577-591.

Sherbourne, C. D., & Stewart, A. L. (1991). The MOS social support survey. *Social Science Medicine, 32*(6), 705-714.

Silverstein, M., & Waite, L. J. (1993). Are Blacks more likely than Whites to receive and provide social support in middle and old age? Yes, no, and maybe so. *Journal of Gerontology, 48*, S212-S222.

Stahl, S. M., & Potts, M. K. (1985). Social support and chronic disease: A propositional inventory. In W. A. Peterson, & J. Quadagno (Eds.), *Social bonds in later life: Aging and interdependence.* Beverly Hills, CA: Sage.

Strogatz, D. S., Croft, J. B., James, S. A., Keenan, N. L., Browning, S. R., Garrett, J. M., & Curtis, A. B. (1997). Social support, stress, and blood pressure in Black adults. *Epidemiology, 8*(5), 482-487.

Thoits, P. (1982). Conceptual, methodological, and theoretical problems in studying social supports as a buffer against life stress. *Journal of Health & Social Behavior, 23*(2), 145-59.

Tilden, V. P., & Weinert, S. C. (1987). Social support and the chronically ill individual. *Nursing Clinics of North America, 22*(3), 613-620.

Velez-Pastrana, M. C., Rodriguez, G., & Martinez, L. M. (1997). Social support, activity, and health among the elderly (Spanish). *Boletin-Asociacion Medica de Puerto Rico, 89*(10-12), 174 - 183.

Wellman, B. (1981). Applying network analysis to the study of support. In B. H. Gottlieb (Ed.), *Social networks and social support* (pp. 171-200). Beverly Hills, CA: Sage.

Acknowledgments. This research was supported by the National Institute on Nursing Research grant R01 NR 03406. The authors thank Kevin Harrell and Jeff Rurka for assistance with chapter preparation.

Part III

Cognitive Function Measures and Cross-Cultural Variation

7

Performance of Cognitive Tests Among Different Racial/Ethnic and Education Groups: Findings of Differential Item Functioning and Possible Item Bias

Jeanne A. Teresi, Douglas Holmes, Mildred Ramírez,
Barry J. Gurland, Rafael Lantigua

E valuation of cognitive assessment measures across elderly subgroups can be cast in terms of both item and test bias. Test bias can include examination of the relationship of demographic factors to test performance, or examination of the performance of a test in relation to diagnosis. While the chapter by Ramírez and colleagues (in this book) focuses on the test bias of cognitive screening measures in relation to diagnosis, the focus of this chapter is on studies of differential item functioning and of item bias of direct cognitive assessment measures with respect to race/ethnicity and education.

SCOPE OF THE PROBLEM

Differences in Prevalence

Different prevalence ratios (defined as the proportion of persons with the disorder at a specified point in time) and incidence rates (defined as disease occurrence over the cumulative amount of observation time) of cognitive impairment observed for different minority subgroups have led to examination of cross-cultural bias. Are the estimated ratios and rates reflective of the true cognitive impairment and dementia, or are they a reflection of cultural bias inherent in the measures used to assess cognitive impairment and to diagnose dementia?

Prevalence estimates for dementia and cognitive impairment are generally higher for African Americans and Latinos than for White non-Latinos and Asians. Previous estimates of cognitive impairment among probability samples of African American elderly have yielded point prevalences as high as 56%, depending upon the definition, sample and method of estimation (Fillenbaum, Hughes, Heyman, George, & Blazer, 1988). A latent class methodology using five screening measures yielded more stable estimates of cognitive impairment indicative of latent dementia of 8% to 12% among African Americans of Central Harlem (Teresi, Albert, Holmes, & Mayeux, 1999). Prevalence of diagnosed dementia ranged from 5% to 16% (Fillenbaum, Heyman, Williams, Prosnitz, & Burchett, 1990; Heyman, Fillenbaum Prosnitz, Raiford, Burchett, & Clark, 1991; Fillenbaum et al., 1998; Hendrie et al., 1995).

Few studies have examined rates of dementia among Latino respondents. Typically, prevalence ratios of cognitive impairment (Mulgrew et al., 1999) or dementia (Gurland et al., 1999; Perkins et al., 1995) have been higher for Latinos than for White non-Latinos. For example, Gurland and colleagues (1999) developed a stratified probability sample of residents of North Manhattan, New York; using a two-stage screening process they estimated that 7.5% of Caribbean Latinos 65-74, 27.9% of those 75 to 84 and 62.9% of those 85 and over met DSM/ADRDA-NINCD criteria for dementia. These estimates were higher than for White non-Latinos across age strata (2.9%, 10.9% and 30.2%, respectively); the estimates for the White non-Latinos were similar to numerous other European and United States studies of Whites.

Finally, studies of Japanese have yielded prevalence ratios of about 6% (see Graves et al., 1996), while studies of samples of Chinese have yielded somewhat lower estimates, that is, 1.8% (3.2% after age standardization to a U.S. population) to 4.6% (Liu et al., 1995; Li et al., 1989; Zhang et al., 1990). Most studies have found higher prevalence estimates among persons with low education or of low literacy levels. A recent metanalysis (General Accounting Office, 1998) of rates of dementia included only studies of predominantly White populations, concluding that "it is not known whether blacks or other minorities have different prevalence rates than do Whites or Europeans." The GAO called for more study among minority groups.

Differences in Cognitive Scale Distributions

Differences in cognitive scale distributions have been observed between different ethnic groups after controlling for factors such as disease severity (Hohl et al., 1999), or for demographic characteristics such as education, age and gender (Manly et al., 1998; Mulgrew et al., 1999). Do these differences reflect biased measures or are they indicative of true differences in the population distributions?

Correlation of Demographic Factors With Screening and Diagnostic Scales

The role of education as it relates to cognitive assessment has been debated (Berkman, 1986; Cobb, et al., 1995; Cummings, 1993; Kittner, et al., 1986; Lindeboom, et al.,

1996; Stern, et al., 1994; Welsh, et al., 1995). Does a lower educational level constitute a risk factor for dementia or is the association between dementia and education due to the failure to control for confounding variables which are correlated with education (Callahan et al., 1996), or to measures and diagnostic procedures which are educationally biased?

Several factors may contribute to item bias; these include lower levels of literacy and education (including noncomparable levels across ethnic subgroups), lack of test-taking experience, varying degrees of acculturation and poor item translation (Mahurin, Espino, & Holifield, 1992). The Advisory Panel on Alzheimer's Disease (1993) specifically calls for the development and validation of "screening and diagnostic methods that will work effectively and fairly across ethnocultural variations. . . ." An examination of differential item functioning (DIF), which may be indicative of bias, is crucial in determining whether or not items are operating in a culture-fair manner. Such analyses have been the cornerstone for evaluating the performance of educational tests. (See the methods overview chapter by Teresi, in this book, for a discussion of DIF and bias.)

SCREENING SCALES

Mini-Mental Status Examination (MMSE)

Numerous studies have examined the MMSE (Folstein, Folstein, & McHugh (1975), arguably the most widely used cognitive assessment screen. Escobar and associates, (1986), using the Los Angeles ECA data on 1244 Mexican Americans and 1310 non-Hispanic Whites, examined the effects of age, education ($0 = 8, 9\text{-}12$, $13+$ years), ethnicity and language on MMSE items using log-linear analyses for proportional data (dichotomous items) and ANCOVA for continuous items. The authors identified several items that elicited a deviant response more frequently among the Hispanic subsample: "recall of state"; "recall of season"; "recall of county"; "performance of serial 7's"; and "spelling WORLD backwards." The item, "repeating no if's, and's, or but's" was easier for Latinos. Several of these items were also possibly biased for low education groups in the direction of more errors: "season"; "county"; "serial 7's"; and "world backwards." Additionally, other items were more difficult for those with low education: "reading and following the command, close your eyes" "writing a sentence"; "copying the intersecting pentagons."

Valle and colleagues, (1991) studied 72 Hispanics of Mexican descent from San Diego; all had been diagnosed for dementia. They compared the false positive rates of traditional MMSE, Blessed and other mental status tests to alternative items, designed to increase the accuracy of assessment. Several items were identified as problematic, using this criterion: "repeat no if's and's or but's"; "read the phrase (close your eyes) and do what it says"; "what is the name of this place"; "how long have you been here"; "what is the season"; and various components of the address, such as the state.

Teresi and colleagues (1995) examined the MMSE for cultural and educational bias using item response theory (IRT) (Lord, 1981) to evaluate items from six well-known screening scales for cognitive impairment in samples of 182 African Americans, 184 Latino (Dominican, Puerto Rican and Cuban) and 184 non-Hispanic Whites from the Transcultural and North Manhattan Aging Projects. About half of the scale points were contributed by items biased either for ethnic/ race group (Latino, African American and White non-Latino), education (0 to 8 years vs. 9 and above) or both. They found the following items to show DIF for ethnic/race group: "state location"; "no ifs, ands, or buts"; "serial 7's"; and "sentence completion." Additionally the command, "close your eyes" was a poorly discriminating item for those with low education. In addition the items: "state location"; "close eyes" and "sentence writing"; "repeating apple, table, penny"; and "folding paper" were biased for education groups, and "world backwards"; "serial 7's"; and "no ifs, ands, or buts" were poorly discriminating items. The "state location" item was more difficult for Latinos than for Whites and for the lower education group. "No if's, ands, or buts" was easier, while "serial 7's" was more difficult for Latinos. "Sentence completion" was harder for African Americans and was a poorly discriminating item for most racial/ethnic and education subgroups. "Close your eyes" was a poorly discriminating item for lower education, Latinos and African Americans.

Using logistic regression, Marshall and associates, (1997) examined the Mini-Mental Status Exam (Folstein, Folstein, & McHugh, 1975) for DIF among 988 English-speaking non-Latino, 138 Latinos interviewed in English and 227 Latinos interviewed in Spanish. Four items differed between Latinos 60 and over and their non-Latino counterparts: "season"; "date"; "penny repetition"; and "apple recall." "Season" was easier, but evidenced poor discrimination for non-Latinos; "apple" and "date" were easier for Latinos, but better discriminating for non-Latinos. "Repeating no ifs, ands, or buts" was easier for the group tested in Spanish.

Finally, a study by Hohl and colleagues (1999) examined 21 Spanish-speaking Latinos and 21 non-Latinos diagnosed with possible or probable Alzheimer's Disease and who were similar on education, duration of disease and functional impairment, matched for overall MMSE score. The Latino group performed significantly worse than did non-Latinos on "serial 7's" and on "spelling world backwards". However, the sample size was too small to insure that other items might not also have performed differently.

Short Portable Mental Status

Teresi and colleagues (1995) examined items from three popular short screening measures: the Short Portable Mental Status Questionnaire (SPMSQ; Pfeiffer, 1975), the Kahn-Goldfarb MSQ (KSMQ; Kahn, Goldfarb, Pollack, & Peck, 1960), and the CARE MSQ (CMSQ; Golden, Teresi, & Gurland, 1984). Two items from the 10-item SPMSQ showed DIF: "recall of exact day, month and year" was a harder item for White, non-Latinos than for Latinos and African

Americans. The item: "phone number or address if no phone number" was easier for Whites than for Latinos. The "phone number" item was less discriminating for Whites. One item from the 10-item Kahn-Goldfarb Mental Status Exam: "naming the past president" was harder for the White sample. Two of the eleven items in the Care MSQ evidenced DIF; they were: "street address," which was easier for Whites and hardest for Latinos and "name of the past president," as stated above, a harder item for Whites. Additionally, the "hand-ear test" was a poorly discriminating item for the low education group.

Blessed Information, Memory and Concentration

Five items out of 26 (15% of points) on the Blessed IMC (Blessed, Tomlinson, & Roth, 1968) were found to show DIF. Recall of occupation showed DIF for both education and racial/ethnic group. The item was harder for African Americans and easier for Latinos. "Name spelling" was more difficult for Latinos and least difficult for African Americans. "Recall date of World War I" was more difficult for Latinos, while "recall of place of birth" was easier for African Americans than for Whites and Latinos. Finally, "recall of the past president" was harder for Whites. Additionally "name spelling" and "school attended" were poorly discriminating for Latinos and for those with low education groups.

Care Diagnostic Scale

The CARE Diagnostic Scale (Golden, Teresi, & Gurland, 1983) was developed with the goals of being (a) culturally-fair across education subgroups and (b) maximally associated with diagnosis. It was used as the screening scale in two large epidemiological studies of dementia among Latinos, African Americans and non-Latino Whites in North Manhattan (Gurland et al., 1992; Gurland et al., 1999). The scale was subjected to item response theory analyses using both the one and the two-parameter model; three of fifteen items were found to show DIF: these were "current address," which was harder for Latinos, "recall the past president," which was harder for Whites and "recall of the phone number," harder for Latinos and less discriminating for Whites (Teresi et al., 1995). Finally, the "hand-ear-test" was poorly discriminating for those with low education. In a second study using IRT (Teresi et al., in press) among a random sample of persons from Northern Manhattan, stratified by age (65-74 and 75+) and racial/ethnic group (African American, Latino (Dominican, Puerto Rican and Cuban) and White, non-Latino), the following CARE Diagnostic Scale items showed significant, albeit low magnitude DIF: "recall of rater's name on first trial," an item which was harder for Latinos, "recall of telephone number," harder for Latinos and those with low education, and difficulty with "shopping" and "personal business," both harder (more severe indicators) for Whites. Additionally, difficulty "recalling names and words due to memory problems" was a poorly discriminating and fitting item. Only two of these items were found to evidence DIF in a cross-validation study "recall of telephone number" and "personal business," The scale includes items which measured well at low and mid-level ability ranges, although fewer items discriminated and provided information at the highest ability levels. IRT-based reliability (precision) estimates were good for all groups, although less precision was observed among the higher ranges of ability, and somewhat lower reliability was observed for White non-Latinos and for those with the highest education.

NEUROPSYCHOLOGICAL TESTS

Mattis Dementia Rating Scale (DRS)

Woodard and associates, (1998) used the logistic (or multiple) regression approach to examine the DRS (Mattis, 1976) among Caucasians and among African American elderly matched on age, education and gender. Item response was predicted from DRS severity ratings, group status and the interaction of group by severity. An interaction of group by severity indicates nonuniform DIF (see the DIF Methods chapter by Teresi in this book). Uniform DIF was indicated by a significant group effect, while a significant interaction indicates nonuniform DIF. The authors followed the two-stage procedure, in which a corrected or unbiased estimate of DIF is achieved by removing offending items from the total score and repeating the exercise. Using this method, four items evidenced DIF: "palm up/palm down"; "fist clenched/fist extended"; "point out and count the A's"; and "visual recognition."

Another study used the two-parameter IRT model (Teresi, Kleinman, & Ocepek-Welikson, 2000), and found relatively little DIF across educational subgroups in the Attention subscale of the Mattis DRS (Mattis, 1976). There was slight DIF associated with several items, "raise your hand" and "second round of four designs"; lesser DIF was observed for "imitation" and "first counting distraction." Most items performed in a similar fashion across education groups; the ICC's were almost identical across groups, indicating little or no differential item functioning. "Digit span backwards" was a malfitting item which evidenced DIF; those with high education had a greater probability of a correct response to the item for most levels of θ. This item had a large error term when subjected to confirmatory factor analysis, and a low discrimination parameter for all education subgroups. In general, the Attention subscale of the Mattis performed in an education-fair manner and is, therefore, a good measure of severe impairment. It includes items that measured well at low and mid-level ability ranges, although fewer items discriminated and provided information at the highest ability levels. Reliability estimates were good for all groups, although less precision was observed among the higher ability group.

DISCUSSION

Because most DIF studies of cognitive scales have focused on the MMSE, items found consistently across studies of the MMSE to show DIF are discussed first. The

MMSE item, "does not close eyes," which requires that the subject close his/her eyes in response to a written command, showed DIF for all group comparisons in the study by Teresi and colleagues (1995). The item was a poor discriminator for African Americans, for Latinos and for those with little education. This finding is similar to that of Escobar and associates (1986) and of Valle and colleagues (1991), who found this item to perform differently for high and low education groups.

Both Escobar (1986) and Teresi and colleagues (1995) found the MMSE "sentence completion" item to be biased for education, and that it was easier for Whites than for African Americans. Marshall and colleagues (1997) also found this item to be less discriminating for Latinos interviewed in Spanish versus those interviewed in English. The "state recall" item was more difficult for Latinos than for non-Latinos in both the Escobar (1986) and Teresi (1995) studies. The item was also more difficult and discriminated poorly for the low education group. This is similar to the findings of Valle and associates, (1991) of fewer false positives for the city item, and more for the state item. Teresi and colleagues (1995) also found the "city" and the "two nearby streets" items to show the least DIF among such items.

Several investigators have found the "serial 7's" task from the MMSE to be biased (see Escobar et al., 1986). Teresi and colleagues (1995) found that the item was not a good discriminator for Whites and Latinos and was an easier item for the White subsample than for the African American and Latino subsamples. Hohl and colleagues (1999) also found the item to be more difficult for Latinos than for non-Latinos, and Valle and colleagues (1991) found this item to perform poorly. Teresi and colleagues (1995) found that "serial 7's," as well as the substitute, "spelling WORLD backwards," were poor discriminators for those with low education.

Every study of the MMSE reviewed here has found the item "no if's, and's, or but's," to be problematic. The item has been found to be easier for Latinos interviewed in Spanish. Valle and associates (1991) and Escobar (1986) and colleagues discuss the reasons: there is no strict Spanish translation for the item and the alternatives do not measure adequately the intended construct, language. The item: "season" was found to perform differently for Latinos than for non-Latinos by both Escobar and colleagues (1986) and by Marshall and colleagues (1997). Valle and colleagues (1991) found more false positives among Latinos. Escobar also found "season" to be harder for those with low education.

Turning to the items which were investigated from scales other than the MMSE, Teresi and colleagues found that several items showed DIF or were poorly discriminating: "spelling own name"; "school attended"; "occupation"; "correct street address"; and "recall telephone number." Of interest is that asking elements of the date separately, such as the month or the year was more culture and education fair than was asking for the exact date all at once. "Recall of the date of World War I" and "Recall of the past president" were also problematic.

Several of the items found to perform differently across education or racial/ethnic groups require literacy (e.g., "writing a sentence") or skills practiced in school (e.g., spelling tasks, calculation, "naming a school attended"). Some of the poorly performing items relate to language: repeating phrases ("repeating a name and address"; "repeating names of objects"; "repeating the phrase no ifs, ands, or buts") or following commands ("closing eyes upon command"; "folding paper"; "touching right or left hand to right or left ear").

Turning to the Mattis DRS, Woodard and colleagues identified four items of the total DRS that evidenced DIF in a comparison of African Americans and Whites: "palm up/palm down"; "fist clenched/fist extended"; "point out and count the A's"; and "visual recognition." Teresi and colleagues, examining the Attention subscale, found slight DIF associated with several items, "raise your hand" and "second round of four designs"; lesser DIF was observed for "imitation" and "first counting distraction." Most items performed in a similar fashion across education groups; the ICC's were almost identical across groups, indicating little or no differential item functioning, however, "Digit span backwards" was a malfitting item across several analyses.

The results reviewed here represent a beginning step in the use of modern psychometric methods to confirm and supplement the results of earlier analyses identifying biased items, using statistical techniques which are not invariant across samples varying in prevalence of disorder. These convergent findings are suggestive of the need to develop more socioculturally fair cognitive screening scales.

Methods used to develop more culturally fair measures include (a) starting with a large item pool, examining previous findings from the literature and deleting those items dependent on culture or literacy (e.g., Hall et al., 1993), (b) replacing or modifying items influenced by setting, translation or time (e.g., Teng et al., 1994; Valle et al., 1991) or (c) constructing a new test (e.g., Fuld et al., 1998; Gurland et al., 1992). For example, the Cognitive Abilities Screening Instrument (Teng et al., 1994), used in several studies of Asian samples, contains 19 items taken from several screening measures, including the MMSE. Because most items have multiple points, the range of possible scores is from 0 to 100. The Community Screening Instrument for Dementia (CSI-D) (Hall et al., 1993) contains 33 items measuring cognitive performance and 24 items obtained from a relative. The measure is derivative from several well-known measures including the CARE, MMSE and DRS. The Fuld Object-Memory Evaluation is a selective reminding task, requiring respondents to identify ten items (e.g., key, cup, bottle) by touch; those missed are shown visually. Objects are removed, a distractor is administered and the respondent is asked to recall the items. Five trials are conducted. While some evidence has been provided regarding the relative promise of these procedures, no differential item functioning has been performed on these measures, with the exception of the Care Diagnostic Scale.

It has been suggested that overlearned and well-practiced tasks may be more culture-fair (Loewenstein, Argüelles, Argüelles, & Linn-Fuentes (1994). Generally, the results presented here suggest that (a) shorter tests (e.g., the Care MSQ, the Short-Portable MSQ, the Kahn-Goldfarb MSQ, the Care Diagnostic scale), (b) measures comprised of easier items and (c) those that rely more on memory (recall) rather than on performance related to language and literacy, including reading, writing and repeating, perform better. However, recall items that may have variability due to cultural relevance, such as recall of the date of World War I may be problematic. More work on differential item functioning is needed, examining the new versions of widely used scales as well as other screening and neuropsychological measures.

REFERENCES

Advisory Panel on Alzheimer's Disease. (1993). *Fourth report of the advisory panel on Alzheimer's Disease* (NIH Publication No 93-3520). Washington, DC: U.S. Government Printing Office.

Berkman, L. F. (1986). The association between educational attainment and Mental Status Examinations: Of etiologic significance for senile dementia or not? *Journal of Chronic Diseases, 39*, 171-175.

Blessed, G., Tomlinson, B. E., & Roth, M. (1968). The association between qualitative measures of dementia and senile change with cerebral matter of elderly subjects. *British Journal of Psychiatry, 114*, 792-811.

Callahan, C. M., Hall, K. S., Hui, S. L., Musick, B. S., Unverzagt, F. W., & Hendrie, H. C. (1996). Relationship of age, education and occupation with dementia among a community-based sample of African Americans. *Archives of Neurology, 53*, 134-140.

Cobb, J. L., Wolf, P. A, Au, R., White, R., & D'Agostino, R. B. (1995). The effect of education on the incidence of dementia and Alzheimer's Disease in the Framingham study. *Neurology, 45*, 1707-1712.

Cummings, J. A. (1993). Mini-Mental State Examination: Norms, normals, and numbers. *Journal of the American Medical Association, 269*, 2420-2421.

Escobar, J. L., Burnam, A., Karno, M., Forsythe, A., Landsverk, J., & Golding, J. M. (1986). Use of the Mini-Mental State Examination (MMSE) in a community population of mixed ethnicity. *Journal of Nervous and Mental Disease, 174*, 607-614.

Fillenbaum, G. G., Hughes, D. C., Heyman, A., George, L. K., & Blazer, D. G. (1988). Relationship of health and demographic characteristics to Mini-Mental State Examination score among community residents. *Psychological Medicine, 18*, 719-726.

Fillenbaum, G. G., Heyman, A., Williams, K., Prosnitz, B., & Burchett, B. (1990). Sensitivity and specificity of standardized screens of cognitive impairment and dementia among elderly Black and White community residents. *Journal of Clinical Epidemiology, 43*, 650-660.

Fillenbaum, G. G., Heyman, A., Hubert, M. S., Woodbury, M. A., Leiss, J., Schmader, K. E., Bohannon, A., & Trapp-Moen, B. (1998). The prevalence and 3-year incidence of dementia in older Black and White community residents. *Journal of Clinical Epidemiology, 51*, 587-595.

Folstein, M. F., Folstein, S. E., & McHugh, P. R. (1975). Mini-Mental State: A practical guide for grading the cognitive state of patients for the clinician. *Journal of Psychiatric Research, 12*, 189-198.

Fuld, P. A., Muramoto, O., Blau, A. D. et al. (1988). Cross-cultural and multi-ethnic dementia evaluation by mental status and memory testing. *Cortex, 24*, 511-519.

General Accounting Office. (1998). Alzheimer's Disease: Estimates of prevalence in the United States (GAO/HEHS-98-6). Author.

Golden, R. R., Teresi, J. A., & Gurland, B. J. (1984). Development of indicator scales for the Comprehensive Assessment and Referral Evaluation (CARE) interview schedule. *Journal of Gerontology, 39*, 138-146.

Golden, R. R., Teresi, J. A., & Gurland, B. J. (1983). Detection of dementia and depression cases with the Comprehensive Assessment and Referral Evaluation interview schedule. *International Journal of Aging and Human Development, 16*, 242-254.

Graves, A. B., Larson, E. B., Edland, S. D., Bowen, J. D., McCormick, W. C., McCurry, S. M., Rice, M. M., Wenzlow, A., & Uomoto, J. M. (1996). Prevalence of dementia and its subtypes in the Japanese American population of King County, Washington State. *American Journal of Epidemiology, 144*, 760-771.

Gurland, B. J., Wilder, D. E., Cross, P. E., Teresi, J. A., & Barrett, V. W. (1992). Screening scales for dementia: Toward reconciliation of conflicting cross-cultural findings. *International Journal of Geriatric Psychiatry, 7*, 105-113.

Gurland, B. J., Wilder, D. E., Lantigua, R., Stern, Y., Chen, J., Killeffer, E. H. P., & Mayeux, R. (1999). Rates of dementia in three ethnoracial groups. *International Journal of Geriatric Psychiatry, 14*, 481-493.

Hall, K. S., Hendrie, H. C., Brittain, H. M., Norton, J. A., Rodgers, D. D., & Prince, C. S. (1993). The development of a dementia screening interview in two distinct languages. *International Journal of Methods in Psychiatric Research, 3*, 1-28.

Hendrie, H. C., Osuntokun, B. O., Hall, K. S., Ogunniyi, A. O., Hui, S. L., & Unverzagt, F. W. (1995). Prevalence of Alzheimer's Disease and dementia in two communities: Nigerian Africans and African Americans. *American Journal of Psychiatry, 152*, 1485-1492.

Heyman, A., Fillenbaum, G., Prosnitz, B., Raiford, K., Burchett, B., & Clark, C. (1991). Estimated prevalence of dementia among elderly Black and White community residents. *Archives of Neurology, 48*, 594-598.

Hohl, U., Grundman, M., Salmon, D. P., Thomas, R. G., & Thal, L. J. (1999). Mini-Mental Status Examination and Mattis Dementia Rating Scale performance differs in Hispanic and non-Hispanic Alzheimer's disease patients. *Journal of Neuropsychological Society, 5*, 301-307.

Kahn, R. L., Goldfarb, A. I., Pollack, M., & Peck, A. (1960). Brief objective measure for the determination of mental status in the aged. *American Journal of Psychiatry, 117*, 326-328.

Kittner, S. J., White, L. R., Farmer, M. E., Wolz, M., Kaplan, E., Moes, E., & Brody, J. (1986). Methodological issues in screening for dementia: The problem of education adjustment. *Journal of Chronic Disease, 39*, 163-170.

Li, G., Shen, Y. C., Chen, C. H., Zhao, Y. W., Li, S. R., & Lu, M. (1989). An epidemiological survey of age-related dementia in an urban area of Beijing. *Acta Psychiahica Scandinavica*,79, 557-563.

Lindeboom, J., Launer, L. J., Schmand, B. A., Hooyer, C., & Jonker, C. (1996). Effects of adjustment on the case-finding potential of cognitive tests. *Journal of Clinical Epidemiology, 49*, 691-695.

Liu, H.-C., Lin, K.-N., Teng, E.-L, Wang, S.-J., Fuh, J.-L., Guo, N.-W., Chou, P., Hu, H.-H., & Chiang, B. N. (1995). Prevalence and subtypes of dementia in Taiwan: A community survey of 5297 individuals. *Journal of the American Geriatrics Society, 43*, 144-149.

Lord, F. M. (1980). *Applications of item response theory to practical test problems.* Hillsdale, NJ: Lawrence Erlbaum.

Loewenstein, D. A., Argüelles, T., Argüelles, S., & Linn-Fuentes, P. (1994). Potential cultural bias in the neuropsychological assessment of the older adult. *Journal of Clinical and Experimental Neuropsychology, 16*, 623-629.

Mahurin, R. K., Espino, D.V., & Holifield, E. B. (1992). Mental status testing in elderly Hispanic populations: Special concerns. *Psychopharmacology Bulletin, 28*, 391-399.

Manly, J. J., Jacobs, D. M., Sano, M., Bell, K., Merchant, C. A., Small S. A., & Stern. Y. (1998). Cognitive test performance among non-demented elderly African-Americans and Whites. *Neurology, 50*,1238-1245.

Marshall, S. C., Mungas, D., Weldon, M., Reed, B., & Haan, M. (1997). Differential item functioning in the Mini-Mental State Examination in English- and Spanish-speaking older adults. *Psychology and Aging, 12*, 718-725.

Mattis, S. (1976). Mental status examination for organic mental syndrome in the elderly patient. In L. Bellak & T. B. Karasu (Eds.), *Geriatric psychiatry: A handbook for psychiatrists and primary care physicians* (pp. 77-121). New York: Grune and Stratton.

Mulgrew, C. L., Morgenstern, N., Shetterly, S. M., Baxter, J., Baron, A. E., & Hamman, R. F. (1999). Cognitive functioning and impairment among rural elderly Hispanics and non-Hispanic Whites as assessed by the Mini-Mental State Examination. *Journal of Gerontology: Psychological Sciences, 54B*, P223-P230.

Perkins, P., Annegers, J. F., Doody, R. S., Cooke, N., Aday, L., & Vernon, S. W. (1997). Incidence and prevalence of dementia in a multiethnic cohort of municipal retirees. *Neurology, 49*, 44-50.

Pfeiffer, E. (1975). A short portable mental status questionnaire for the assessment of organic brain deficit in elderly patients. *Journal of the American Geriatrics Society, 22*, 433-444.

Stern, Y., Gurland, B., Tatemichi, T. K. Xin Tan, M., Wilder, D., & Mayeux, R. (1994). Influence of education and occupation on the incidence of Alzheimer's disease. *Journal of the American Medical Association, 271*, 1004-1010.

Teng, E. L., Hasegasa, K., Homma, A., Imai, Y., Larson, E., Graves, A., Sugimoto,

(1994). The Cognitive Abilities Screening Instrument (CASI): A practical test for cross-cultural epidemiological studies of dementia. *International Psychogeriatrics, 6*, 45-62.

Teresi, J., Kleinman, M., Ocepek-Welikson, K., Ramirez, M., Gurland, B., Lantigua, R., & Holmes, D. (2000) Applications of item response theory to the examination of the psychometric properties and differential item functioning of the CARE dementia diagnostic scale among samples of Latino, African American and White, non-Latino elderly. *Research on Aging, 22,* 738-773.

Teresi, J., Golden, R., Cross, P., Gurland, B., Kleinman, M., & Wilder, D. (1995). Item bias in cognitive screening measures: Comparisons of elderly White, Afro-American, Hispanic, and high and low education subgroups. *Journal of Clinical Epidemiology, 48*, 473-483.

Teresi, J. A., Albert, S. M., Holmes, D., & Mayeux, R. (1999). Use of Latent Class Analyses for the estimation of prevalence of cognitive impairment, and signs of Stroke and Parkinson's Disease among African American elderly of Central Harlem: Results of the Harlem Aging Project. *Neuroepidemiology, 18,* 309-321.

Teresi, J. A., Kleinman, M., & Ocepek-Welikson, K. (2000). Modern psychometric methods for detection of differential item functioning: Application to cognitive assessment measures. *Statistics in Medicine, 19,* 1651-1683.

Valle, R., Hough, R., Kolody, B., Cook-Gait, H., Velazquez, G. F., & Jimenez, R. (1991). The validation of the Blessed Mental Status Test and the Mini-Mental Status Examination with an Hispanic population. In *Final Report to the National Institute of Mental Health,* The Hispanic Alzheimer's Research Project (HARP). San Diego, CA: San Diego State University.

Welsh, K. A., Fillenbaum, G., Wilkinson, W., Heyman, P., Mohs, R. C., & Stern, Y. (1995). Neuropsychological test performance in African American and White patients with Alzheimer's Disease. *Neurology, 45*, 2207-2211.

Woodard, J. L., Auchus, A. P., Godsall, R. E., & Green, R. C. (1998). An analysis of test bias and differential item functioning due to race on the Mattis Dementia Rating Scale. *Journal of Gerontology: Psychological Sciences, 53B*, P370-P374.

Zhang, M., Katzman, R., Salmon, D., Jin, H., Cai, G., Wang, Z. (1990). The prevalence of dementia and Alzheimer's Disease in Shanghai, China: Impact of age, gender and education. *Annals of Neurology, 27*, 428-437.

Acknowledgments. Support for this work was provided in part by the Columbia University Resource Center for Minority Aging Research (RCMAR), the National Institute on Aging (AG15294), and by the Hebrew Home for the Aged at Riverdale. The authors thank Lucja Orzechouska for editorial assistance on this book.

8

Cognitive Assessment Among Minority Elderly: Possible Test Bias

Mildred Ramírez, Jeanne A. Teresi, Stephanie Silver, Douglas Holmes, Barry Gurland, Rafael Lantigua

The confounding effects of education, socioeconomic status and race ethnicity, as well as factors such as language and literacy, must be considered when conducting cognitive assessments. The purpose of this chapter is to examine the performance of cognitive screening measures across samples from ethnically diverse populations, in terms of sensitivity and specificity with respect to a clinical diagnosis. While the relative strengths and weaknesses of the selected measures are presented, the aim is not to make definitive recommendations in terms of the best performing and/or the most "culture-fair" screening measures, but to summarize and to review issues relevant to interpretation of results.

Most investigations have reported racial/ethnic and education subgroup differences in classification rates (lower specificities with higher false positives) among commonly used cognitive screening measures when examined in relation to clinical diagnosis (Anthony, LeResche, Niaz, Von Korff, & Folstein, 1982; Fillenbaum, Heyman, Williams, Prosnitz, & Burchett, 1990; Gurland, Wilder, Cross, Teresi, & Barrett, 1992; Wilder et al., 1995). An important caveat is that diagnoses are often based in part on neuropsychological tests; to the extent that these tests are themselves biased, the diagnoses also will be biased.

METHODOLOGICAL CAVEATS

Before reviewing briefly the findings from these studies, several methodological caveats must be considered. Comparisons of sensitivities and specificities across studies must be undertaken with caution for several reasons. First, variation in

97

sensitivities and specifities may be due to actual differences in prevalence and severity of disorder across the groups studied (Kraemer, 1982), so that the differences in sensitivity and specificity may or may not be an indicator of the invariance of the measure (Kraemer, Moritz, & Yesavage, 1998). Second, cut-scores typically are derived by examining the sensitivity, the specificity, and the positive and negative predictive values of a scale against a criterion; these statistics are variously affected by the base (case) rates or marginal distribution and the reliability of the measure in the normative population. Thus, such summary statistics do not necessarily cross-validate with samples that differ in base rates (see the Methods Overview chapter by Teresi & Holmes in this book). Finally, sensitivities will be inflated in two-stage screening studies if the majority of cases referred for diagnosis scores positive on the screening test, or if the cognitive screening test was also part of the clinical evaluation. Additional methodological issues relevant to interpretation of results are: (a) how nonresponses and missing data are treated; (b) how interrater reliability is established; and (c) whether sensitivity and specificity are examined in relation to one cut-point or across all scale points using Receiver Operating Characteristic (ROC) curves (Hanley & McNeil, 1982) (the latter producing the strongest evidence regarding scale performance).

Cognitive Performance and Demographics

There is a growing literature relating to the effects of demographic variables such as education and race/ethnicity on cognitive assessment instruments. The role of education, in particular, has been debated in the literature (e.g., Berkman, 1986; Kittner et al., 1986). This issue, reviewed earlier by Teresi & Holmes (1997) remains salient. That is, does a lower educational level constitute a risk factor for dementia or is the association between dementia and education due to biased measures and diagnostic procedures, or to the failure to control for confounding variables that are associated with education (Callahan et al., 1996)? For example, differences in cognitive scale distributions have been observed among different ethnic groups even after controlling for factors such as disease severity (Hohl, Grundman, Salmon, Thomas, & Thal, 1999) or demographic characteristics such as education, age and gender (Manly et al., 1998; Mulgrew et al., 1999; Welsh et al., 1995). Despite controlling for numerous confounding variables, exercising careful control for selection bias and using a new measure which contained items found in previous research to be unrelated to education, a recent study conducted among community-resident African Americans (Callahan et al., 1996) documented the inverse association of education with cognitive impairment and diagnosed dementia. Literacy, found to be positively related to neuropsychological test performance among nondemented community-residing elders after controlling for education and administration language (Manly, et al. 1999), also could explain discrepancies between White and African Americans (Manly et al., 2000) in neuropsychological test performance. For example, Albert and Teresi (1999) found that literacy and education each made a unique explanatory contribution to cognitive test scores among a probability sample of African American community resident elderly.

The 18 studies reviewed and summarized in Table 1 were the product of a four-database search (MEDLINE, CINAHL, HealthGate, PsycINFO) for studies examining the performance of cognitive screening measures across samples from ethnically diverse populations in terms of sensitivity and specificity of clinical diagnosis. The studies varied in terms of: (a) sample design, (b) severity of dementing illness among subjects, (c) method of classification of cases, (d) method of diagnosis, for example, whether or not clinicians were blinded to screening scale status. Although the majority of the articles compare test performance among ethnically diverse subgroups, usually Whites and Blacks, some articles focus exclusively on one group, for example, Chinese (Fuh et al., 1995; Hill et al., 1993; Li et al., 1989; Tsai & Gao, 1989). Multisite designs were employed when the aim was to screen samples of similar ethnic/racial background but from differing environments (see, Hall et al., 1996; Hendrie et al., 1995; Teng et al., 1994). Some investigators examined the performance of cognitive screens in languages other than English, for example, Spanish (Lowenstein, Duara, Arguelles, & Arguelles, 1995), and Cree versus English-speaking (Hall et al., 1993). Designs varied across studies, and included convenience samples comprised of clinic patients or community samples, as well as multistage probability samples. Samples often were stratified by age and sex, or by age, sex and race/ethnicity.

Positive classification of cases based on their screening scale was generally determined using "standard" (previously published) cut-scores although some, for example Hall and associates (1993), classified "possibly demented cases" based on discriminant function-derived cut-scores, and Pittman and colleagues (1992) classified cases using an algorithmically driven diagnostic paradigm. Investigators such as Anthony and colleagues (1982), Bohnstedt, Fox and Kohatsu (1994) and Li and associates (1989) lowered or recommended lowering "standard" cut-scores for minority samples, and/or adjusting for education (Murden, McRae, Kaner, & Bucknam, 1991). Gurland and associates (1992) established sensitivity at 90% or above, with the intent of partially resolving the issue of variant summary statistics associated with cut-scores when applied to different samples. Hall and colleagues (1993) established sensitivity at 100% (based on a discriminant function) for testing CSI'D' performance with two distinct cultural and linguistic groups.

Criteria presented in the *Diagnostic and Statistical Manual of Mental Disorders-III-Revised* (DSM-III-R; and in fewer studies the DSM-III or DSM-IV) constituted the modal standard in determining "caseness." When not the only factor, DSM-III-R-derived criteria, used in combination with other elements such as direct neurological assessments, reviews of medical history and level of functioning (usually involving informant-provided information), were part of a complex multistep procedure used to develop a clinical diagnosis. That is, the clinical diagnosis was determined through review of clinical criteria conducted by either a physician (e.g., a neurologist) or an evaluation team which usually reflected an interdisciplinary effort. In most studies, both individuals with a diagnosis of "potential dementia" and "normal" individuals were referred for clinical evaluations. However, this varied across studies. In some instances all subjects (regardless of the screen scores) were referred for clinical evaluations, whereas in others only cases and a proportionate number of noncases comprised the clinically evaluated subsample.

The various screening measures included the Mini-Mental State Exam (MMSE; Folstein, Folstein, & McHugh, 1975); the Chinese-Mini Mental State (CMMS; Katzman, Zhang et al., 1988); the Cognitive Abilities Screening Instrument (CASI; Teng et al., 1994) (which includes the Hasegawa Dementia Screening Scale [HDSS] the MMSE and the Modified MMSE (3MS); the Hasegawa Dementia Screening Scale (HDSS; Hasegawa, 1974); the Blessed Memory-Information-Concentration test (MIC Blessed, Tomlinson, & Roth, 1968); the Katzman Orientation-Memory-Concentration Test (OMC; Katzman, Brown et al., 1983); the Mental Status Questionnaire (MSQ; Kahn, Goldfarb, Polack, & Peck, 1960); the Short Portable Mental Status Questionnaire (SPMSQ; Pfeiffer, 1975); the Comprehensive Assessment and Referral Evaluation (CARE)-Diagnostic Scale (Gurland et al., 1977; Gurland, Golden & Challop, 1982); the Community Screening Interview for Dementia (CSI'D'; Hall et al. 1993), (which includes items from several widely used dementia instruments); the Crichton Royal Behavioural Rating Scale (CRBRS; Wilkin, Mashiah, & Jolley, 1976-1977); the Fuld-Object-Memory-Evaluation (Fuld-OME; Fuld, 1981); the Storandt Battery (Storandt, Botwinick, Danziger, Berg, & Hughes, 1984); the Iowa Screening Battery for Mental Decline (Eslinger, Damasio, Benton, & Van Allen, 1985); the Kendrick Cognitive Tests (Kendrick, 1985); the Informant Questionnaire on Cognitive Decline in the Elderly (IQCODE; Jorm & Korten, 1988); the Spanish-IQCODE, the Shortened Spanish IQCODE; and the Diagnostic Paradigm (Stern et al., 1992). Shown in Table 8.1 (begins on page 102) are sensitivities and specificities associated with measures across studies.

False Positives Among African Americans and Latinos

Several of the screens (e.g., the MMSE, OMC, MSQ, and SPMSQ) yielded relatively higher false positive ratios for Blacks and/or Latinos than they did for Whites, and for those with lower education levels (see Anthony et al., 1982; Fillenbaum et al., 1990, Gurland et al., 1992). Bohnstedt and associates (1994) found that the sensitivity and specificity of the MMSE among Black and Latino Alzheimer's Disease Diagnostic Treatment Centers' patients differed from those of Whites. Using a logistic regression model predicting MMSE scores (dichotomized at a cut of 23), the authors found that the scores were not accounted for by education, occupation and/or age, but by race/ethnicity status; results suggest that the MMSE underestimated the cognitive capacities of Blacks and Latinos (as compared to Whites). The authors suggest lowering the cut-score to 19 for members of both Black and Latino populations. On the other hand, Murden and associates (1991) found education, not race (White vs. Black) to be associated with MMSE scores when used in screening for dementia in primary care geriatric clinics, and suggested modification of education-related MMSE items, or adjusting the cut-point according to level of education; (in this particular study, clinicians were not blinded to MMSE scores when performing evaluations, which may have inflated the sensitivity estimates.) Among members of a community sample of Black and White elderly, Fillenbaum and colleagues (1990) found that the SPMSQ and the Kendrick Test, in contrast with the MMSE, MSQ, OMC, Storandt Battery, and the Iowa Screening Battery, yielded more culture-fair results, based on the specificity estimated for standard cut-points across the groups. On the other hand, Heyman and associates (1991) found the SPMSQ to discriminate differently between White and Blacks in a community sample, although the diagnostic evaluations may have been contaminated for this comparison by the inclusion of SPMSQ scores. Wilder et al. (1995), examining the Area Under the Curve (AUC) of ROC curves for various cognitive screens, found discrepancies in terms of the screens' performance across the three (African American, Latino & White) groups in the sample, as well as across educational groups. Results indicated that in general, the MMSE and the SPMSQ yielded the highest proportions of false positives.

The CSI'D', adapted for and applied to a sample of Yorubas in Nigeria, was also applied to an African American sample in Indianapolis. Although sensitivity/ specificity estimates were for the combined sample, results might have been inflated because referrals for clinical assessments were based on screens cut-scores. That is, individuals with reported "low performance" as contrasted with intermediate or good performance were disproportionately represented in the clinical assessment group (see Hendrie et al., 1995). Similarly, the CSI'D' was reported to perform well for community samples of African Americans in Indianapolis and of blacks in Nigeria, as evidenced by improvement in the prediction of clinicians' diagnosis of dementia based on logistic regression (after entering age, gender, education and cognitive score), with the introduction of the informant- activities of daily living score (Hall and colleagues, 1996). Hall et al. (1993) reported the informant interview of the CSI'D', in particular, to be applicable to Cree-speaking natives in Manitoba and to English-speaking persons in Winnipeg; the investigators, however, acknowledged the likelihood of inflated sensitivity and specificity rates, given that these estimates as well as the discriminant function were derived from the same data.

Language and Screening Scale Performance

Several studies identified individuals sampled both from the community and from memory disorder clinics, and compared emergent groups that were based on dominant language (English vs. Spanish). In one study, the MMSE yielded lower sensitivity coefficients than did the Fuld-OME for both the English- and the Spanish-speaking groups; the latter showed better sensitivity and comparable specificity (to the MMSE) for the two language groups (see Loewenstein et al., 1995). The authors suggest that the Fuld OME is preferable also because of its

TABLE 8.1 Summary of Studies: Methods, Sample, Analyses and Recommendations of Investigators

Reference/ Instrument	Method of data collection/ Clinical criteria	Sampling method/ Sample characteristics/ Response rate	Method of analysis: Results by group/Validity (Criterion)	Recommendations of investigators
Anthony et al., 1982 MMSE	Non-psychiatrist investigators administered the MMSE, obtained social and demographic information within 24 hours of admission; psychiatrist (blinded to MMSE score) tested for dementia and delirium using Folstein and McHugh (1976) criteria (based on DSM-III). MMSE was independent of clinical evaluation. Those with discrepant MMSE and clinical evaluations, were re-examined on day 2 by psychiatrists blinded to group. Cut-score of 23/24 used because recommended in most publications (0–23 impaired).	Consecutively admitted patients to the general medical ward of Johns Hopkins Hospital, Baltimore, Md. n = 97; 23% White, 77% Black, 63% female. age range/%: 20–29/16; 30–39/13; 40–49/18 50–59/13; 60–69/12; 70–79/23; 80+/6 Education: ≤ 8 years: 47%; Response rate: Initial: 98%	Comparison of sensitivity/specificity at the standard cut-score. At 23 cut-score: 87% sensitivity; 82% specificity Subgroup specificities: Blacks vs Whites: 78.2% vs 94.7% women vs men: 76.6% vs 92.6% ≤ 8 years education vs 9 or more years: 63.3% vs. 100% ≥ 60 years old vs < 60 years old: 65.2% vs. 92.0%	Sensitivity levels support the MMSE as a screen for dementia and delirium. It should not be used as the sole criterion for diagnosis due to the high false-positive ratio, especially for the elderly and poorly educated. Modifications in scoring to improve sensitivity and specificity were tested (lower cut-score, eliminate difficult items): these not satisfactory due to the decreases in sensitivity that accompany increases in specificity.
Bohnstedt et al., 1994 MMSE	Subjects diagnosed by interdisciplinary teams. Staff completed neuropsychologic tests on a variety of patients and collected clinical diagnostic, neuroimaging, demographic, and neuropathologic data. DSM-III-R criteria for clinical dementia; NINCDS-ADRDA criteria for AD.	8 Alzheimer's Disease Diagnostic and Treatment Centers throughout CA. N = 1888; 83% White (W), 10% Black, 7% Latino; 67% Female; median sample patient age at enrollment into the centers = 76 years	Comparison of sensitivity/specificity/PPV/ NPV at standard and adjusted cut-scores. % demented according to MMSE (≤ 23) / clinically: White: 72/93; Black: 90/96; Latino: 88/96; MMSE: $p < .001$ between groups; Clinically: $p > .10$ between groups	Consider lowering the cut-score for Blacks and Latinos to 19 (from 23) in order to provide a more accurate estimate of cognitive functioning compared to a diagnosis of dementia.

TABLE 8.1 *(Continued)*

Reference/ Instrument	Method of data collection/ Clinical criteria	Sampling method/ Sample characteristics/ Response rate	Method of analysis: Results by group/Validity (Criterion)	Recommendations of investigators
	Standard cut-score of ≤ 23 used. By reducing the cut score to ≤ 19 for Blacks (B) and Latinos (L), sensitivity and specificity values are closer to those for Whites. Diagnoses were NOT made independent of MMSE.		MMSE vs. Clinical diagnosis., at cut points 23/19 for subgroups: Sensitivity- B: 93.0/78.0%; L: 90.0/75.4%; W: 76.6% Specificity- B: ($n = 8$) 87.5/100%; L: ($n = 5$) 60.0/100%; W: 93.6% PPV- B: 99.4/100%; L: 98.3/100%; W: 99.4% NPV- B: 35.0/16.3%; L: 18.8/13.5%; W: 23.1%	
Fillenbaum, et al., 1990 Katzman OMC, MSQ, MMSE, Storandt, Iowa, Kendrick, SPMSQ	SPMSQ score used as the sampling screen, and to aid in the diagnosis of dementia. Administered to Duke EPESE cohort, and sample classified by score (impaired, marginal, unimpaired). Cut-score determined so that 10% of an older community population would be impaired (Pfeiffer, 1975). Clinical diagnosis: semi-structured interview by a neurologist using DSM-III and NINCDS/ADRDA criteria to determine dementia status, battery administered by 2 middle-aged, White college graduates, mental status information from close family member. 22 of 26 dementia cases confirmed through reevaluation at Duke Memory Disorder Clinic using MRI and lab tests.	Used random sampling with replacement, matched for race, age, SPMSQ score, & sex. Numbers weighted to allow generalization to entire sample. Duke EPESE, 5 counties in North Carolina; N = 164; Black: $n = 83$, White: $n = 81$; 57.9% female; demented: $n = 26$, non-demented: $n = 132$; 1 person untestable, 5 with unclear diagnoses; minimum age = 65 Response rate: 67% (33% refusal)	Comparison of sensitivity/specificity at the standard cut-scores. Sensitivity/specificity by race (weighted to represent all community Black & White residents): Black White Overall (Total) OMC: 100/38.2% 100/8.5% 100/58.1% MSQ: 100/70.5% 100/96.0% 100/83.1% MMSE: 100/26.4% 100/69.1% 100/48.8% (uncodable) 5.1% 3.5% 4.4% Storandt: 100/42.0% 100/69.2% 100/56.6% (uncodable) 4.0% 3.1% 3.6% Iowa: 100/26.4% 100/69.1% 100/48.8% (uncodable) 5.1% 3.5% 4.4% Kendrick 64.8/92.4% 77.6/97.2% 66.6/94.7% SPMSQ 89.6/89.9% 100/90.0% 91.1/90.0% Follow-up study of Fillenbaum (1998) used ROC curve: cut-score at the posterior probability of .465. 69% sensitivity; 92% specificity.	Most tests showed a high 'false-positive' rate, particularly for Blacks. This limits the usefulness of these tests for large-scale screening for prevalence. Briefest measures with the easiest scoring systems were the most accurate- SPMSQ one of the best. SPMSQ and Storandt least biased for race and education. Storandt and Iowa valuable in clinical settings.

TABLE 8.1 (*Continued*)

Reference/ Instrument	Method of data collection/ Clinical criteria	Sampling method/ Sample characteristics/ Response rate	Method of analysis: Results by group/Validity (Criterion)	Recommendations of investigators
Fuh et al., 1995 IQCODE, MMSE-CE	IQCODE administered to an informant by trained research assistants who were medical or nursing students blinded to dementia status. Dementia status determined by a physician according to DSM-III-R criteria based on semi-structured interview and testing, neurologic exam, and standardized assessment. Clinical Dementia Rating (CDR) level measured. Family member interviewed for history, daily activities, and social functioning when dementia was suspected.	Community sampling frame: all those aged 50 and over according to 1990 housing registration records in the township of Kin-Hu (Kinmet, west of Taiwan); demented: outpatients at a Veterans General Hospital, or those identified from community sample ($n = 16$). Random sample stratified by age and sex. $N = 460$; overall: 49% female, demented population: 36% female ($n = 22$), control population: 51% female ($n = 203$); $n = 399$ non-demented community elderly (control), $n = 61$ demented patients. 0 age: control-68.1 ± 11.1; demented-73.3 ± 8.3; 0 education: control-1.6 ± 3.0; demented-6.6 ± 6.3. (63% had 0 years of formal education) Response rate: Non-demented community residents: 49.1%.	IQCODE: area under ROC curve (AUC) = 91.3% (SE = 2.4%); at cutscore ≥ 3.4: 88% specificity; 89% sensitivity; PPV = 45%; NPV = 99%. 17 item IQCODE: AUC = 91.1% (SE = 3.1%) MMSE: AUC = 84.0% (SE = 3.1%); at cutscore 20: 72% sensitivity; 81% specificity; PPV = 30%; NPV = 96%. {$p = .01$ ($z = 2.57$) between measures}.	IQCODE has high internal consistency, score has little to no association with education, age or gender, high association with cognitive abilities. It effectively discriminates between those with and without dementia. IQCODE better in terms of AUC than MMSE in detecting dementia among a sample of individuals with low education. IQCODE can be shortened from 26 to 17 items for predominantly illiterate Chinese elders.
Gurland, et al. (1992)	Cases initially identified based on physician classification of possibly, probably, or defi-	Subjects recruited from outpatient primary care clinics (AIM) at Columbia Presby-	Sensitivity set at 90% or better. Positive classification using cut-scores without adjustments (%):	Conflicts between scales can be partially resolved through adjustments of the

TABLE 8.1 (*Continued*)

Reference/ Instrument	Method of data collection/ Clinical criteria	Sampling method/ Sample characteristics/ Response rate	Method of analysis: Results by group/Validity (Criterion)	Recommendations of investigators

Kahn Golfarb MSQ; Short Portable MSQ; CARE-Diagnostic; Blessed MIC; MMSE	nitely organic brain syndrome. Most subjects were referred to a clinical evaluation team who used a structured medical and neurological examination, assessment of extrapyramidal signs and other involuntary movements, a history, functional evaluation, psychiatric evaluation, and a battery of neuropsychological tests. Diagnoses were assigned at a conference attended by the examining research neurologist, and physician. A case was defined by criterion diagnosis of dementia according to DSM-III-R criteria (Gurland 1995).	terian & two local senior centers, and a local nursing home. $N = 550$; Black: $n = 182$, Latino: $n = 184$, White: $n = 184$.
		
		 age range (%): education: (%):
		 65-74 75-84 85+ 0-6 7-11 12+
		 B: 41.8 39.6 15.9 22.5 45.6 26.4
		 L: 50 34.8 13.6 55.4 30.6 11.4
		 W: 17.4 41.3 36.4 12.0 33.9 43.7
		
		 Response rate: 90%.
			B L W T
			 CARE Diagn
			 [cut-score 0–6/7+]: 11.5 15.2 24.5 17
			 KG- MSQ
			 [cut-score 0–2/3+]: 20.3 28.8 37.0 28.6
			 SP MSQ
			 [cut-score 0–2/3+]: 28 38 36.4 34.2
			 Blessed MIC
			 [cut-score 0–7/8+]: 34.1 55.4 41.8 43.8
			 MMSE
			 [cut-score 0–6/7+]: 57.1 64.7 52.2 58.1
			
			 No. of false positives using criterion diagnosis:
			 CARE Diagn
			   [cut-score 3+]: 5 20 2 27
			 KG- MSQ
			   [cut-score 1+]: 12 32 10 57
			 SPMSQ
			   [cut-score 2+]: 8 24 5 37
			 Blessed MIC
			   [cut-score 7+]: 7 34 2 43
			 MMSE
			   [cut-score 7+]: 11 36 7 54
				cut-scores for determination of a possible case. Efforts should be made to reduce discrepancies between methods introduced by varying sensitivities (and specificities).

TABLE 8.1 *(Continued)*

Reference/ Instrument	Method of data collection/ Clinical criteria	Sampling method/ Sample characteristics/ Response rate	Method of analysis: Results by group/Validity (Criterion)	Recommendations of investigators
Hall et al., 1996 CSI 'D'	Pilot study conducted to determine cut-score. Cut-score was selected at 100% sensitivity, and 89% specificity for dementia (Hall 1993). Sampling: Indiana- simple random sample of 60% of homes in 29 contiguous tracts in Indianapolis, IN with an avg of 80% Black residents; Ibadan- a census to enumerate all households with residents aged 65 and over (total population survey), door to door screen. All of poor performance, 50% of intermediate performance, & 5% of good performance (75% aged ≥75) offered clinical assessment. Clinical assessment of selected subjects by senior neurologists, & psychiatrists for DSM-III-R & ICD10 criteria, CDR for severity. Clinical exam includes CERAD-NB, CAMCOG, CT scans, relative interview, neurological assessment, lab tests. Consensus diagnosis.	Indiana (IN): $n = 2212$; Ibadan (Ib): $n = 2494$; Idakan area of Ibadan, mainly Yoruba. IN: 65% female; Ib: 65% female; $\bar{x}$ age: IN: 74 ± 7; Ib: 72.3 ± 7.5. Literacy: IN: 97.9%; Ib: 15.2%. $\bar{x}$ education: IN: 9.6 ± 3.1; Ib: 8 ± 2.3. Subjects with clinical assess: IN demented: $n = 65$; Ib demented: $n = 28$; Ib non-demented: $n = 395$. Response rate: IN: 85.6%; Ib: 98.4% Relative interview: IN: 67.8% Ib: 100%.	Combined sites: 87.02% sensitivity: 83.12% specificity (Standard errors: 6.76%, .57%) if applied to population age ≥ 65, with typical dementia prevalence of 8%: PPV = .31; NPV = .99 area under ROC for discriminant function: IN: .98; Ib: .90 area under ROC for cognition only: IN: .94; Ib: .84.	The screening instrument shows minimal cultural bias, and performed well in both cultures. The authors do not adjust screen scores for education because it is a significant risk factor for Alzheimer's Disease (AD).
Hall et al., 1993	Sampling: English (Eng) sample taken from the database for	Cree: $N = 198$; community: $n = 192$; nursing home: $n = 6$;	Using cut-score obtained in pretest:	Construction of comparative cognitive

TABLE 8.1 (*Continued*)

Reference/ Instrument	Method of data collection/ Clinical criteria	Sampling method/ Sample characteristics/ Response rate	Method of analysis: Results by group/Validity (Criterion)	Recommendations of investigators
CSI 'D'	Manitoba's health insurance system, stratified by age to over-sample older age groups. The proportion of each age group was based on prevalence rates of dementia- the sampling fractions were roughly proportional to these rates. Stratified by sex to reflect the distribution in Winnipeg. Random selection within age/sex strata. All Cree aged 65 and older were eligible for participation. Pre-test to determine cut-score at 100% sensitivity. One week interviewer training; interviewers for Cree originate from Nelson and Norway Houses, interviewers for English were Winnipeg residents; clinical evaluations for Cree and English speakers made by same neurologists & psychiatrists (at least 2 saw each subject); diagnosis made at consensus conference by 4 physicians blind to screen results; dementia status based on DSM-III-R criteria, mild dementia criteria of Roth, AD diagnosis by NINCDS/ADRDA criteria.	clinical assessment subset: $N = 91$; cognitive and informant sections complete: $N = 171$; non-demented: $n = 165$; demented: $n = 6$. Eng: $N = 252$; community: $n = 227$; nursing home: $n = 25$; clinical assessment subset: $N = 67$; cognitive and informant sections complete: $N = 16$; non-demented: $n = 200$; demented: $n = 16$; two geographically remote Cree reserves, Manitoba & Eng-speaking, non-Indian residents of Winnipeg; Cree: older subjects oversampled; Cree: 52% female; Eng: 56% female. Age range: 65–69: $n = 68$; 70–74: $n = 52$; 75–79: n-32; 80+: $n = 46$. Eng: 65–69: $n = 21$; 70–74: $n = 35$; 75–79: $n = 55$; 80+: $n = 141$. Years of education: Cree: 0: 47%; 7–11: 7%; 12: 1%; Eng: 0: 8%; 7–11: 45%; 12: 13%. Response rate: Cree: screening: 92%, clinical: 94%. Eng: screening: 70%, clinical: 86%.	discriminant function: 100% sensitivity, 79% specificity, no false negatives. Total cognitive score had the lowest specificity: 60% specificity (95%CI: 55–65%) combining cognition without calculation+ informant score+education, best specificity: 89% (86–92%). Area under ROC curve (using cognitive score without calculation and informant score) = .976. Note: For more specificity data see cited article Table 5, has cognitive score with & without calculation items & education & informant score- for several combinations of variables.	scales proved more difficult than construction of an informant interview. This new instrument exhibits evidence of validity and reliability. It may be useful in other cross-cultural studies.

TABLE 8.1 (*Continued*)

Reference/ Instrument	Method of data collection/ Clinical criteria	Sampling method/ Sample characteristics/ Response rate	Method of analysis: Results by group/Validity (Criterion)	Recommendations of investigators
Hendrie et al., 1995 CSI 'D'	In Indiana, battery administered by trained technicians, and in Ibadan by faculty members; 40% of clinical evaluations done in home; median time between screen and evaluation: IN: 5 months, Ibadan: 10 months. Sampling, cut-score determination, case definition: see Hall 1996. 60% simple random sample.	Nursing home: $n = 106$ screen & clinical evaluation; IN community: $n = 2212$ screen, $n = 351$ clinical evaluation; Ibadan (Ib): $n = 2494$ screen, $n = 423$ clinical evaluation. Community and nursing home dwellers in 29 census tracts in Indianapolis, IN and community residents (mainly Yoruban) in Ibadan, Nigeria. Nursing home: 66% female; IN community & Ib: 65% female. x̄ age: nursing home: 80.7 ± 9.0; IN community: 73.9 ± 7.0; Ib: 72.3 ± 7.5; x̄ education: IN: 9.6 ± 3.1; Ib: $.8 \pm 2.3$; Literacy rate: IN: 97.9%; Ib: 15.2%. Response rate: IN: 85.7%; Ibadan: 98.4%.	Dementia: good screen performance: IN: 1.0%; Ibadan: 1.7%; intermediate screen performance: IN: 6.4%; Ibadan: 2.1%; poor screen performance: IN: 33.9%, Ibadan: 11.2%. good/intermediate&poor performance (2 groups): 87% sensitivity; 83.1% specificity.	
Heyman et al., 1991 SPMSQ	Four-stage sampling design for $N = 164$; Duke EPESE; minimal sample, here: random selection by trichotomized SPMSQ score, race (Black or White), sex, and 5-year age group. Tried selecting the same number of Black men as White men, and as many Black	mum age: 65. Response rate: 74%.	27% of White subjects with impaired SPMSQ were diagnosed as demented by neurologist; 44% of Black subjects with impaired SPMSQ found demented by neurologist; of the 26 found impaired by neurologist: 19 scored as impaired on SPMSQ (73%), 4 marginal (11 point above cutoff; 15%), 3 unimpaired (12%). Of these	

TABLE 8.1 *(Continued)*

Reference/ Instrument	Method of data collection/ Clinical criteria	Sampling method/ Sample characteristics/ Response rate	Method of analysis: Results by group/Validity (Criterion)	Recommendations of investigators
	women as White women. Demographics, health charac-teristics, & SPMSQ collected at baseline; semistructured interview administered by a neurologist; diagnosis based on DSM-III, and NINDS/ ADRDA, severity based on CDR; medical, and psychiatric history obtained; brief physical and neurologic exam; SPMSQ screen included in diagnosis.		26: according to medical records, 13 (50%) had prior diagnosis of dementia, 7 had been referred to a memory disorders clinic for a second evaluation.	

TABLE 8.1 *(Continued)*

Reference/ Instrument	Method of data collection/ Clinical criteria	Sampling method/ Sample characteristics/ Response rate	Method of analysis: Results by group/Validity (Criterion)	Recommendations of investigators
Hill et al., 1993 CMMS	Investigators from the Shanghai Mental Health Center screened in subject homes; clinical examination for those below the cut-score, and 5% of those above; single-stage cluster sampling, random probability sample: in 1/3 of all neighborhoods all those aged 55 and over were included, in 1/3 all those aged 65 and over were included, and in 1/3 all those aged 75 and over were included; age and education adjusted cut-scores used (per Kittner et al. 1986); a cut-score for the predictive equation with approximately equal sensitivity and specificity chosen, operating characteristics as described by Vecchio (1966); presurvey cutoff of ≤ 20 to determine direct or proxy interview; dementia determined by history, NINCDS-ADRDA criteria, Hachinski score, DSM-III criteria & neuropsychological instruments; clinical diagnosis	N = 643; Jing-An district of Shanghai; 159 cases of dementia according to DSM-III, approximately 2/3 of these met AD criteria. Response rate: 85.6%.	CMMS: 69.5% sensitivity, 90.2% specificity, PPV = 62.4%, NPV = 92.7%; CMMS+ function measures: 92.4% sensitivity, 93.3% specificity, PPV = 76.4%, NPV 98.1%; Education adjusted CMMS + function measures: 92.4% sensitivity, 92.0% specificity, PPV = 72.9%, NPV = 98.1%. * predictive value estimates do not have the usual meaning since there was no attempt to have this sample emulate the population prevalence rate for dementia. Note: For other results see cited article Table 3. Different combinations of variables (e.g., history, IADL, POD).	Findings suggest the possible usefulness of combining the CMMS, functional scales, and history in determining dementia status. Using DSM-III criteria, subjects with no education or 6 years or less have a significantly greater risk of being diagnosed with dementia than those with more than 6 years of education.

TABLE 8.1 *(Continued)*

Reference/ Instrument	Method of data collection/ Clinical criteria	Sampling method/ Sample characteristics/ Response rate	Method of analysis: Results by group/Validity (Criterion)	Recommendations of investigators
	made independently by 3 psychiatrists blind to CMMS score and reviewed by a US clinician and neuropsychologist.			
Li et al., 1989 MMSE, CRBRS	All persons aged 60 and older in all households in 4 geographically representative residents' committees in the West District of Beijing were contacted for the survey. Pretest to determine cut-score for MMSE. All those who scored ≤ 17 on the MMSE, and a random sample of 5.5% of those who scored above 17 received clinical evaluation from a psychiatrist; final diagnosis was made according to operating diagnostic criteria, a restricted DSM-III definition of dementia. The clinical exam consisted of the Geriatric Mental State Exam, the Dementia Differential Diagnostic Schedule. All those who scored ≤ 2 on CRBRS received clinical evaluation from a psychiatrist, information received from informant.	Pretest: *N* = 137; age range: 50–89; 44% female; in- or out-patients of the Institute of Mental Health or nursing home residents. Tested on 17 demented, 47 other mental disorders, & 73 normal patients; study N = 1090; 53.7% female; age groups: 60–64: 34.4%, 65– 69: 27.3%, 70–74: 21.4%, 75– 79: 10.0%, 80–84: 5.2%, 85+: 1.7%; 33.7% illiterate. Response rate: 81.9%.	Pretest to determine cut-score, at 100% sensitivity, 89% specificity. 98.3% took the MMSE. *N* = 42 scored ≤ 17, 6 (14% of the 42) clinical diagnosis of moderate or severe dementia, 4 (9.5% of 42) diagnosed with potential dementia, 1 (2.4% of 42) refused exam, 31 (73.8% of 42) non- dementia cases; for 57 subjects scoring ≥ 17 with clinical evaluation: no cases of dementia were found; CRBRS: 8 (44.4% of 18) clinical diagnosis of moderate or severe dementia, 1 (5.5% of 18) diagnosed with possible dementia.	MMSE is simple to use and acceptable to the Chinese population. MMSE score was significantly correlated with age, education level, and level of physical ability, perhaps different cut-scores for different education levels should be developed.

TABLE 8.1 (*Continued*)

Reference/ Instrument	Method of data collection/ Clinical criteria	Sampling method/ Sample characteristics/ Response rate	Method of analysis: Results by group/Validity (Criterion)	Recommendations of investigators
Loewenstein et al., 1995 OME, MMSE	Normal subjects (MMSE ≥ 23) recruited from the community as part of an ongoing longitudinal study. Entire OME 5 trials takes 20 minutes to administer; first trial alone takes 5 minutes. Complete neurological, medical, psychiatric, and neuropsychological evaluation, MRI, NINCDS/ADRDA criteria for AD. MMSE cut-scores derived on the basis of normal control scores applied to those with a clinical diagnosis of AD but with an MMSE score of 18 or above, equivalent to cut-scores derived in the ECA investigation.	$N = 191$; control (MMSE ≥ 23) no reported memory deficit): $n = 53$ recruited from the community, English (Eng) speakers: $n = 30$, Spanish (Sp) speakers: $n = 23$; AD: $n = 138$, Eng speakers: $n = 111$, Sp speakers: $n = 27$; recruited from Memory Disorders Clinic. Virtually all Spanish speakers of Cuban descent. $\bar{x}$ age: Sp AD: 72.0 ± 7.7; Eng AD:77.81 ± 6.8; Sp control: 71.91 ± 4.4; Eng control: 75.59 ± 5.6. $\bar{x}$ education: Sp AD: 10.25 ± 4.8, Eng AD: 12.03 ± 3.8, Sp control: 13.43 ± 5.2, Eng control: 14.37 ± 2.8.	The terms sensitivity and specificity apply to well-defined AD and normal control groups. OME: (29 cut-score): Sensitivity-Spanish AD: 95.9%, English AD: 95.5% (for those age ≤ 79 sensitivity: 94.1%); Specificity- Spanish control: 100%, English control: 96.7%; Sensitivity trial 1 (< 5)-English: 92.8% (for those age ≤ 79 sensitivity: 91%), Spanish: 100%; Specificity trial 1–total: 91.6%, Spanish only: 87%.: MMSE: (23 cut-score): Sensitivity-English: 77.8%, Spanish: 73.1%; at 24 cut-score: Sensitivity-English: 81.0%, Spanish: 88.9%.	OME sensitivities greater than MMSE, and has several advantages: easy to administer, uses common items, easily translated, limits confounding due to poor auditory or visual perception. Cut-scores of 29 for total OME, and 5 for the first trial are culturally appropriate.
Morales et al., 1995 S-IQCODE, SS-IQCODE, MMSE	Sample stratified by age and sex randomly selected from the census of three districts in Madrid, Spain. Door-to-door screening, including MMSE. Interview with informant who lived with subject. Dementia diagnosed in the study sample by a neurologist using neurological and neuropsychological	Whole sample: $N = 352$; study sample (those who participated in phase 2 of the study without those excluded): $N = 68$ (no significant differences between whole and study samples in sex, age, # of chronic diseases, # of drugs, GDS Scale. MMSE higher). Demented: $n = 7$; non-demented: $n = 61$.	S-IQCODE: 86% sensitivity, 92% specificity, PPV = .54; NPV = .98; accuracy = .91. Item score and total score correlation using ROC curves: r ranges from .4120 (remember present date)-.8558 (has his/her intelligence changed) for items selected for SS-IQCODE (some items with r in range not selected). SS-IQCODE: 86% sensitivity, 91% specificity; PPV = .50; NPV = .98; accuracy = .90.	S-IQCODE valid for detection of mild dementia. It is not affected by the most frequent confounding variables.

TABLE 8.1 *(Continued)*

Reference/ Instrument	Method of data collection/ Clinical criteria	Sampling method/ Sample characteristics/ Response rate	Method of analysis: Results by group/Validity (Criterion)	Recommendations of investigators
	assessment, CAT scan, lab tests, diagnosis according to DSM-III-R criteria. Takes approximately 10 minutes to administer. Refusals were assessed by mailed questionnaires and/or medical records.	Madrid, Spain. Study sample: 51.5% female; x̄ age: total population: 73.1 ± 5.2, demented: 74.8 ± 5.5, non-demented: 72.9 ± 5.2. education: 7.4% illiterate; 92.6% had at least primary schooling.

Response rate: 73% (whole sample for initial interview). All screened invited for clinical evaluation: 52.5% response rate. | MMSE: 57% sensitivity; 84% specificity; PPV = .29; NPV = .94; accuracy = .81. | |
| Murden et al., 1991

MMSE | Administered to subject by a geriatrician or physician's assistant trained in geriatrics with the collaboration of a geriatrician. Dementia diagnosed using 4 criteria: history of memory decline & other cognitive function, no impaired consciousness, abnormal MMSE (≤ 23), dementia presence according to examiner. Those with uncertain diagnoses followed up with MMSE and clinical exams a minimum of 6 months later in order to determine certain diagnoses. MMSE performed by initial clinical examiner. | $N = 358$; Demented: $n = 110$ (100% Black): Non-demented: Black: $n = 148$, White: $n = 100$; Kings County Hospital outpatient clinic and geriatric clinic at Bellevue Hospital (NY). 76% female; age range: 60–99; Black: $n = 258$, White (Non-Latino): $n = 100$; Nondemented patients- ≥ 9 years ed: White: $n = 74$, Black: $n = 38$; < 9 years ed: White: $n = 26$, Black: $n = 110$.

Response rate: (Follow up) 84.1%. | MMSE sensitivity and specificity lowering cut-score to 17 from 23 for Black subjects: $(23 \rightarrow 17)$: ≥ 9 years education: sensitivity- $93\% \rightarrow 52\%$, specificity- $100 \rightarrow 100\%$; <9 years education: sensitivity- $98\% \rightarrow 81\%$, specificity-$75\% \rightarrow 100\%$. | Reduce the cut-score to 17 to reduce false labeling of dementia in Blacks with less than a 9th grade education. The authors are working on a revised MMSE that may be more appropriate for people of all education levels. |

TABLE 8.1 (*Continued*)

Reference/ Instrument	Method of data collection/ Clinical criteria	Sampling method/ Sample characteristics/ Response rate	Method of analysis: Results by group/Validity (Criterion)	Recommendations of investigators
Pittman et al., 1992 Diagnostic paradigm (battery of neuro-psychological tests)	Subjects selected from volunteers who met inclusion criteria for a study that aims to attain a high degree of accuracy and consistency in the diagnosis of dementia in heterogenous populations (Stern, 1992). Cut-scores based on performance of 172 previously studied subjects (Stern, 1992). Physician diagnosis based on semi-structured medical and psychiatric history, physical & neurological exam, short Blessed, and 3 ADL measures. Diagnostic paradigm diagnosis based on DSM-III-R criteria (poor performance on 2 of 3 areas assessed).	$N = 430$; 37.5% White (W), 29.1% Black (B), 33.4% Latino (L); Washington Heights & Inwood (northern Manhattan); 0 education: W: 13 years, B: 9.9 years, L 7.2 years; < 6 years education: 23.5%, college education: 25.6%. Response rate: 6.4% of subjects refused to complete one or more of the tests, 14.6% unable to complete one or more of the tests (Stern, 1992). Note: partial information included.	Categories for each method: 0 = normal; 1 = cognitively disordered; 2 = demented. 9 subjects (2%) with maximum disagreement between methods (7 cases physician found normal, paradigm found demented); Physician found: %(n): 0 = 68.6% (295), 1 = 21.6% (93), 2 = 9.8% (42) battery found: 0 = 60.5% (260), 1 = 29.1% (125), 2 = 10.5% (45) 71.8% ($n = 309$) agreement between physician & battery: 0 = 53.5% (230), 1 = 12.3% (53), 2 = 6.0% (26). among cases of disagreement: 63.6% (77 of 121) more impaired by battery- 71% (86 of 121) of these in 0 vs. 1 categories, 67.4% (58 of the 86) rated 0 by physician, & 1 by battery, 21.5% (26 of 121) 1 vs. 2, 46% (of 26) 2 by battery & 1 by physician; 54% (14) 2 by physician and 1 by battery.	Further refinement of the paradigm could raise reliability to an acceptable level (reliability probably underestimated since those who did not represent a challenge for the diagnostician were excluded from the sample). A composite diagnosis (paradigm and diagnostic) is most reliable.
Teng et al., 1994 Cognitive Abilities Screening Instrument	CASI-E & CASW-J were simultaneously tested in LA and in Seattle & in Osaka and Tokyo. No match on age and education done for patients and controls. All patients met the DSM-III-R criteria for dementia; the diagnosis was	LA: patients: $n = 62$, control: $n = 50$; Osaka: patients: $n = 23$, control: $n = 61$; Seattle: patients: $n = 71$, control: $n = 86$; Tokyo: patients: $n = 52$, control: $n = 38$. % Female/Age: $\bar{x}$, sd:	USA samples: (see table below)	In assessing dementia, care should be taken to consider the "ecological validity" of the test for the study population; test items, cutoff points, and even cognitive domains may need to be adjusted accordingly.

USA samples:

	[LA]			[Seattle]		
	Cut-score	sens	spec	Cut-score	sens	spec
CASI	78	.91	.91	86	.94	.94
CASI-Short	23	.95	.94	25	.94	.94
HDSS-CE	26	.84	.85	28	.86	.88
MMSE-CE	22	.86	.86	24	.91	.93
3MS-CE	76	.92	.92	83	.94	.94

TABLE 8.1 *(Continued)*

Reference/ Instrument	Method of data collection/ Clinical criteria	Sampling method/ Sample characteristics/ Response rate	Method of analysis: Results by group/Validity (Criterion)						Recommendations of investigators
			Japan samples:	[Osaka]			[Tokyo]		
				Cut-score/	sens/	spec	Cut-score/	sens/ spec	
(CASI). (It includes: HDSS-CE; MMSE-CE; 3MS-CE)	made by physicians based on history, functional assessment, clinical examinations, and neuropsychological testing results excluding the scores on the CASI.	LA = 58%/D: 74.2, 7.8; C: 70, 13.3 Osaka 27%/D: 70.7, 8.4; C: 63.6, 9.7 Seattle 63%/D: 78.3.6.0; C: 77.5, 6.4 Tokyo 66%/D: 78.1, 6.7; C: 73.3,4.9 Education: x̄, sd:	CASI	71	.95	.94	76 .93	.93	
		LA = D: 12.1,4.1; C: 12.7, 3.5	CASI-Short	21	.89	.88	21 .89	.92	
		Osaka = D: 11.2, 4.0; C: 11.9, 3.4	HDSS-CE	24	.93	.93	25 .92	.92	
	LA: patients from geriatric neurobehavioral & dementia referral center, control: spouses, community residents Osaka: patients from neuro-psychology clinic of national medical research center; control also patients at clinic. Seattle: patients & control subscribers of a health maintenance program. Tokyo: patients from outpatient clinic of a geriatric hospital; control: students at community college for aged.	Seattle = D: 12.5, 3.0; C: 13.8, 2.9	MMSE-CE	23	.92	.92	21 .94	.94	
		Tokyo = D: 8.4, 2.9; C: 11.1, 4.3	3MS-CE	68	.93	.94	74 .93	.93	

TABLE 8.1 (Continued)

Reference/Instrument	Method of data collection/Clinical criteria	Sampling method/Sample characteristics/Response rate	Method of analysis: Results by group/Validity (Criterion)	Recommendations of investigators
Tsai et al., 1989 HIDS	Can be completed in approximately 10 minutes. Scores of 31–32.5 = nondemented, 22–30.5 = subnormal, 10.5–21.5 = early dementia, 0–10 = demented. Sample: all inhabitants of specific urban and rural communities in Shanghai aged 60 years and older (over 60 according to text). Instrument administered by 2 psychiatrists and 2 nurses, clinical evaluation by the psychiatrists. DSM-III criteria for dementia.	$N = 2573$; 63.3% female; According to score: 35.3% non-demented, 46.3% subnormal, 16.1% early dementia, 2.3% demented; age group/n: 60–64/384, 65–69/792, 70–74/560, 75–79/441, 80–84/307, 85+/89; education level: illiterate: 67.1%. Response rate: 84%.	96.3% diagnostic agreement between clinical and instrument. 80.2% sensitivity, 99.4% specificity (Note: determined from data presented). HDS score ≤ 15: 100% diagnosed as demented, score of 16–21: 94.6% diagnosed as demented, score of 22–27: 8.7% diagnosed as demented, score of 28+: 0% diagnosed as demented. HDS level/% diagnosed with dementia: normal/0%, subnormal/7.1 %, early dementia/97.1 %, demented/100%.	Assessment of dementia by HDS corresponds well with clinical evaluation. It is a useful national and international assessment tool.
Wilder et al., 1995 MSQ; SPMSQ; CARE-Diag; Blessed MIC; MMSE	Subjects were screened and given a dementia/non-dementia diagnosis from a North Manhattan probability sample of 65 and older residents (transcultural pilot study (TIPS) & NMAP Reporting Registry). Criterion diagnosis: DSM-III-R criteria for dementia by clinical core team of neurologists, physicians and neuropsychologists.	$N = 795$; Black: $n = 299$, Latino: $n = 355$, White: $n = 136$. age range (%): 65–74: B: (25.1); L: (41.7); W: (17.6) 75–84: B: (46.2); L: (36.6); W:(30.9) 85+: B: (28.8); L: (21.7); W:(51.5) education: (%): <5: B: (17.6) L: (52.8); W: (11. 4) 5–11: B:(60.0); L: (37.1); W: (40.9) ≥ 12: B: (22.4); L: (10.1); W: (47.7)	Differences in area under the curve (AUC) by race-ethnicity/by education: Blessed MIC: .057/.127; CARE Dementia .040/.094; Kahn Goldfarb MSQ: .044/.112; MMSE: .080/.131; SPMSQ: .068/.176; CARE Homogeneous: .043/.115; "Culture fair": .048/.118. Specificity when sensitivity set at 90% derived from ROC curves with criterion diagnosis: Racial-ethnic groups/Educational groups	Shorter scales perform as well as longer ones, are more consistent across cultural and educational groups and can be more easily modified to improve performance in culturally diverse populations.

TABLE 8.1 (Continued)

Reference/ Instrument	Method of data collection/ Clinical criteria	Sampling method/ Sample characteristics/ Response rate	Method of analysis: Results by group/Validity (Criterion)							Recommendations of investigators
			B	L	W	T	<5	5-11	12	
			Blessed MIC:							
			.72	.47	.74	.60	.33	.55	.80	
			CARE Dementia:							
			.49	.58	.68	.58	.45	.53	.78	
			Kahn Goldfarb							
			MSQ:							
			.57	.55	.62	57	.42	.54	.77	
			MMSE:							
			.54	.38	.59	.44	.24	.51	.74	
			SPMSQ:							
			.46	.42	.62	.48	.27	.46	.74	
			CARE							
			Homogeneous:							
			.60	.59	.71	.62	.43	.62	.77	
			"Culture fair":							
			.60	.53	.69	.58	.40	.57	.83	

simplicity in terms of administration, content and translation as well as for its equivalent validity among different cultural and language groups. Similarly, both the Spanish and the short-Spanish version of the IQCODE were found to have greater diagnostic validity than did the MMSE in terms of classification accuracy for mild dementia among a random sample of community residents in Madrid, Spain (Morales et al., 1995); however, the study included only a small number ($n = 7$) of diagnosed cases.

In another study (Pittman et al., 1992) a quantitative paradigm (based on a battery of neuropsychological tests) showed diagnostic agreement (71.9%) with clinical diagnosis in a sociocultural heterogeneous sample; however, the battery was found more likely (than the physician-derived diagnosis) to classify patients with low educational levels as being demented. When age and education were controlled in a logistic regression model, minority status was found unrelated to diagnosis.

Sensitivity and Specificity Among Asians

Fuh and associates (1995) found the IQCODE to be a better (see Table 8.1) screening tool than the MMSE for detecting dementia, particularly for persons with low educational level, among a sample of Chinese control and demented individuals; however, particularly among the nondemented community resident group the low response rate is of concern when interpreting these results. Similarly, using a logistic regression model Hill and colleagues (1993) found that the Chinese-MMSE (CMMS) (together with a set consisting of history questions, Pfeffer Outpatient Disability Scale [POD], and the Instrumental Activities of Daily Living Scale) was an effective predictor of clinical diagnosis in a community sample in Shanghai. The history instrument and the POD, however, were more closely related to clinical diagnosis than were the CMMS scores, which turned out to load significantly on an education-weighted principal component. Li and colleagues (1989), adjusting the MMSE cut-scores to < 17 (based on a pretest) in order to set sensitivity/specificity at 100% and 89%, respectively, reported the MMSE to be appropriate for surveys of dementia among a Chinese population. Concurring with those who regard the MMSE as education biased, they suggest use of differential cut-scores among populations where low education is prevalent.

Based on consistently high estimates of specificity and sensitivity, the CASI was considered to have cross-cultural applicability (see Teng et al., 1994). This is a relatively new scale derived from a combination of original and/or modified items drawn from established dementia screening scales, such as the MMSE and the Hasegawa. It was tested in two sites in Japan and two sites in the US; the studies relied on convenience samples with no matching for age and/or education across sites or between control/dementia patients. It turned out that performance on the CASI was influenced by educational level, in that nondemented individuals' scores tended to increase with education, and to decrease with age within each education range (see Teng et al., 1994). This is similar to the performance of other cognitive screens, for example the HDS, examined by Tsai and associates (1989) on a sample of community residents in Shanghai.

DISCUSSION

As this chapter suggests, validity results may be confounded and coefficients may be inflated in those instances where cognitive screening scores were also part of the clinical criteria used to establish a dementia diagnosis. Procedures used to standardize item administration and to deal with "nonresponses" (due to handicap, physical problems, etc.) were seldom addressed in the reported studies; error might be introduced in screening if unstandardized procedures were implemented in the handling of nonresponse.

For multisite studies, diagnostic consistency for dementia across sites is of concern when no documentation of a training program, and/or examination of interrater reliability was presented or discussed. Caution should be exercised in interpreting sensitivity/specificity results, particularly in studies where only screened positives or a disproportionate percentage of screened positives comprised the clinically evaluated subsample, because this practice might result in inflated sensitivity estimates.

Few studies used ROC analyses; most either evaluated sensitivity/specificity at standard cut-scores or set cut-scores equal to some value, and then examined false positive rates. As previously discussed, examination of ROC curves allows investigation of performance of the screen across all scale points and provides the strongest evidence of scale performance. Only Fillenbaum and colleagues (1990), Hall and colleagues (1993, 1996), and Wilder and colleagues (1995) performed such analyses.

Caution should be exercised in the generalization of cross-cultural findings derived from studies conducted only in the United States. Screening instruments that performed well for Spanish-speaking Latinos in the United States may perform differently among samples drawn in Latin America or Spain. Similarly, test performance using Chinese American or African American samples might be different from that observed when samples are drawn in China or Africa (see Table 8.1).

The MMSE was the most widely evaluated scale and most investigators reported that it provided high false positive rates (see Anthony et al., 1982; Gurland et al., 1992). When comparisons of several scales have been conducted, the shorter fared as well or better than did longer scales (Fillenbaum et al., 1990; Fuh et al., 1995; Gurland et al., 1992; Wilder et al., 1995). Sometimes unadjusted scores performed better than did statistically adjusted scores (see Kraemer, Moritz, & Yesavage, 1998). Although often recommended, use of raw unadjusted scales scores with adjusted cut-scores for different education or race/ethnicity groups has not always proved optimal, for example Lindeboom, Launer, Schmand, Hooyer, & Jonker

(1996).

Newer scales which may show promise when used in ethnically diverse popula-tions include the CARE-Diagnostic scale (evaluated among representative samples of community resident as well as primary care outpatient Black, Latino and White elders), the Fuld-OME, evaluated among English- and Spanish-speaking commu-nity-residing elders and among memory disorder clinics patients, the CIS'D' evaluated among representative samples of Black community residents in the U.S. and Nigeria, and the informant-based IQCODE evaluated with Chinese and with Spanish representative samples of community residents. Except for the CARE Diagnostic scale none of these newer scales has yet been evaluated for item bias.

The potentially biasing effect of education on the validity of screening scales has been a consistent theme across studies. The question regarding whether rates of dementia are in fact different among individuals reporting different educational levels, or are an artifact resulting from educational or cultural bias remains to be answered. A more in-depth examination is warranted of the relationship between racial/ethnic group, years of education, and literacy in the context of methodological variation across studies in the existing literature. However, the effect of literacy on the specificity and sensitivity of cognitive screens has not been examined fully (see Manly et al., 1999). Some investigators are proponents of cut-score adjustments as a means for dealing with systematic discrepancies in scale performance across racial/ethnic, and/or educational subgroups, while others recommend development of adjusted measures based on algorithms that correct for the effects of education or race/ethnicity (see Magaziner, Bassett, & Hebel, 1987; Mungas, Marshall, Weldon, Haan, & Reed, 1996). Still others advocate reconsideration of the screens' contents, in which educational- and/or culture-weighted domains are less empha-sized (Fillenbaum et al., 1990; Murden et al., 1991), and the individual's functional capacity is more strongly featured (Wilder et al., 1995). Finally, some recommend conducting item bias analysis and removing offending items (see Teresi et al., 1995). However, the role of sociocultural bias in the clinical diagnostic process affecting the case classification and, thus, the validity coefficients, must also be considered. Additionally, as noted in the introduction to this chapter, sensitivities and specificities have limitations when considered as validity coefficients. While cognitive screening scales may never be free of test bias, progress is being made in minimizing the effects of such bias by developing new or modifying old screening scales.

REFERENCES

Albert, S. M., & Teresi, J. A. (1999). Reading ability, education, and cognitive status assessment among older adults in Harlem, New York City. *American Journal of Public Health, 89,* 95-97.

Anthony, J., LeResche, L., Niaz, U., Von Korff, M., & Folstein, M. (1982). Limits of the 'Mini-Mental State' as a screening test for dementia and delirium among hospital patients. *Psychological Medicine, 12*, 397-408.

Berkman, L. F. (1986). The association between educational attainment and mental status examinations: Of etiological significance for senile dementias or not? *Journal of Chronic Disease, 39*,171-174.

Blessed, G., Tomlinson, B. E., & Roth, M. (1968). The association between qualitative measures of dementia and senile change with cerebral matter of elderly subjects. *British Journal of Psychiatry, 114*, 792-811.

Bohnstedt, M., Fox, P., & Kohatsu, N. (1994) Correlates of Mini-Mental Status Examination scores among elderly demented patients: The influence of race-ethnicity. *Journal of Clinical Epidemiology, 47*(12), 1381-1387 .

Callahan, C. M., Hall, K. S., Hui, S. L., Musick, B. S., Unverzagt, F. W., & Hendrie, H. C. (1996). Relationship of age, education and occupation with dementia among a community-based sample of African Americans. *Archives of Neurology, 53*, 134-140.

Eslinger, P. J., Damasio, A. R., Benton, A. L., & Van Allen, M. (1985). Neuropsychologic detection of abnormal mental decline in older persons. *Journal of American Medical Association, 253*, 670-674.

Fillenbaum, G., Heyman, A., Williams, K., Prosnitz, B., & Burchett, B. (1990). Sensitivity and specificity of standardized screens of cognitive impairment and dementia among elderly Black and White community residents. *Journal of Clinical Epidemiology, 43*(7), 651-660.

Folstein, M. F., Folstein, S. E., & McHugh, P. R. (1975). The Mini-Mental State. A practical method of grading the cognitive state of patients for the clinician. *Journal of Psychiatric Research, 12*, 189-198.

Folstein, M.F., & McHugh, P.R. (1976). Phenomenological approach to the treatment of "organic" psychiatric syndromes. In B. Wolman (Ed.), *The therapist's handbook: Treatment methods for mental disorders* (pp. 279-286). New York: Van Nostrand-Reinhold.

Fuh, H., Teng, E., Lin, K., Larson, E., Wang, S., Liu, C., Chou, P., Kou, B., & Liu, H. (1995, January). The Informant Questionnaire on Cognitive Decline in the Elderly (IQCODE) as a screening tool for dementia for a predominantly illiterate Chinese population. *Neurology, 45*, 92-96.

Fuld, P. A. (1981). *Object-memory evaluation.* Woodale, IL: Stoelting Company.

Gurland, B. J., Golden, R. R., & Challop, J. (1982). Unidimensional and bidimensional approaches to the differentiation of depression and dementia in the elderly. In S. Corkin, K. L. Davis, J. H. Crowden, E. Usdin, & R. J. Wurtman, (Eds.), *Alzheimer's disease: A report of progress in research* (pp. 19-125). New York: Raven Press.

Gurland, B. J., Kuransky, J. B., Sharpe, L., Simon, R., Stiller, P., & Birkett, P. (1977). The comprehensive Assessment and Referral Evaluation (CARE): Rationale, development and reliability. *International Journal of Aging and Human Development, 8*, 9-42.

Gurland, B., Wilder, D., Cross, P., Teresi, J., & Barrett, V. (1992). Screening scales for dementia: Toward reconciliation of conflicting cross-cultural findings. *International Journal Geriatric Psychiatry, 7,* 105-113.

Hall, K. S., Hendrie, H. C., Brittain, H. M., Norton, J. A., Rodgers, D. D., Prince, C. S., Pillay, N., Blue, A., W., Kaufert, J.N., Nath, A., Shelton, P., & Postl, B.D. (1993). The development of a dementia screening interview in two distinct languages. *International Journal of Methods in Psychiatric Research, 3,* 1-28.

Hall, K., Ogunniyi, A., Hendrie, H., Osuntokun, B., Hui, S., Musick, B., Rodenberg, C., Unverzagt, F., Guerje, O., & Baiyewu, O. (1996). A cross-cultural community based study of dementias: Methods and performance of the survey instrument Indianapolis, USA, and Ibadan, Nigeria. *International Journal of Methods in Psychiatric Research, 6,* 129-142.

Hanley, J. A., & McNeil, B. J. (1982). The meaning and use of the area under a Receiver Operating Characteristic (ROC) Curve. *Radiology, 143,* 19-36.

Hasegawa, K. (1974). The study on the brief intelligence scale for the demented elderly. *Seishinigaku [Psychiatry], 16,* 965-969.

Hendrie, H., Osuntodkun, B., Hall, K., Ogunniyi, A., Hui, S., Unverzagt, F., Gureje, O., Rodenberg, C., Baiyewu, O., Musick, B., Adeyinka, A., Farlow, M., Oluwole, S., Class, C., Komolafe, O., Brashear, A., & Burdine, V. (1995, October). Prevalence of Alzheimer's disease and dementia in two communities: Nigerian Africans and African Americans. *American Journal of Psychiatry, 152*(10), 1485-1492.

Heyman, A., Fillenbaum, G., Prosnitz, B., Raiford, K., Burchett, B., & Clark, C. (1991, June). Estimated prevalence of dementia among elderly Black and White community residents. *Archives of Neurology, 48,* 594-598.

Hill, L. R., Klauber, M. R., Salmon, D. P., Yu, E. S. H., Liu, W. T., Zhang, M., & Katzman, R. (1993). Functional status, education, and the diagnosis of dementia in Shanghai survey. *Neurology, 43,* 138-145.

Holh, U., Grundman, M., Salmon, D. P., Thomas, R. G., & Thal L. J. (1999). Mini-Mental Status Examination and Mattis Dementia Rating Scale performance differs in Hispanic and non-Hispanic Alzheimer's disease patients. *Journal of Neuropsychological Society, 5,* 301-307.

Jorm, A. F., & Korten, A. E. (1988). Assessment of cognitive decline in the elderly by informant interview. *British Journal of Psychiatry, 152,* 209-213.

Kahn, R. L., Goldfarb, A. I., Polack, M., & Peck, A. (1960). Brief objective measures for the determination of mental status in the aged. *American Journal of Psychiatry, 117,* 326-328.

Katzman, R., Brown, T., Fuld, P., Peck, A., Schechter, R., & Schimmel, H. (1983). Validation of a short orientation-memory-concentration test of cognitive impairment. *American Journal of Psychiatry, 140,* 734-739.

Katzman, R., Zhang, M., Qu, O. Y., Wandg, Z. Y., Liu, W. T., Yu, E., Wong, S. C., Salmon, D. P., & Grant, I. (1988). A Chinese version of the Mini-Mental State Examination: Impact of illiteracy in a Shanghai dementia survey. *Journal of Clinical Epidemiology, 41,* 971-978.

Kendrick, D. C. (1985). *Kendrick Cognitive Test for the elderly.* Windsor, England: NFER-Nelson.

Kittner, S. J., White, L. R., Farmer, M. E., Wolz, M., Kaplan, E., Moes, E., Brody, J., & Feinleib, M. (1986). Methodological issues in screening for dementia: The problem of education adjustment. *Journal of Chronic Disease, 9,* 163-170.

Kraemer, H. C. (1982). Estimating false alarms and missed events from interobserver agreement: Comment on Kaye. *Psychological Bulletin, 92,* 749-754.

Kraemer, H. C., Moritz, D., & Yesavage, J. (1998). Adjusting Mini-Mental State Examination scores for age and educational level to screen for dementia: Correcting bias or reducing validity? *International Psychogeriatrics, 10*(1), 43-51.

Li, G., Shen, Y. C., Chen, C. H., Zhao, Y. W., Li, S. R., & Lu, M. (1989). An epidemiological survey of age-related dementia in an urban area of Beijing. *Acta Psychiatrica Scandinavica, 79,* 557-563.

Lindeboom, J., Launer, L. J., Schmand, B. A., Hooyer, C., & Jonker, C. (1996). Effects of adjustment on the case-finding potential of cognitive tests. *Journal of Clinical Epidemiology, 49,* 691-695.

Loewenstein, D., Duara, R., Arguelles, T., & Arguelles, S. (1995). Use of the Fuld Object-Memory Evaluation in the detection of mild dementia among Spanish- and English-speaking groups. *American Journal of Geriatric Psychiatry, 3*(4), 300-307.

Magaziner, J., Bassett, S. S., & Hebel, R. (1987). Predicting performance on the Mini-Mental Examination: Use of age and education-specific equations. *Journal of American Geriatric Society, 35,* 996-1000.

Manly, J. J., Jacobs, D. M., Sano, M., Bell, K., Merchant, C. A., Small, S. A., & Stern, Y. (1998). Cognitive test performance among nondemented elderly African American and Whites. *Neurology, 50,* 1238-1245.

Manly, J. J., Jacobs, D. M., Sano, M., Bell, K., Merchant, C. A., Small, S. A., & Stern, Y. (1999). Effect of literacy on neurological test performance in nondemented, education-matched elders. *Journal of the International Neuropsychological Society, 5,* 191-202.

Manly, J., Jacobs, D., Touradji, P., Small, S., Merchant, C., Bell, K., Stern, Y. (2000). Are ethnic group differences in neuropsychological test performance explained by reading level? A preliminary analysis. *Journal of the International Neuropsychological Society, 6,* 245.

Morales, J., Fillenbaum, G., Prosnitz, B., Raiford, K., Burchett, B., & Clark, T. (1995). The screening of mild dementia with a shortened Spanish version of the Informant questionnaire on cognitive decline in the elderly." *Alzheimer's Disease and Associated Disorders, 9*(2), 105-111.

Mulgrew, C. L., Morgenstern, N., Shetterly, S. M., Baxter, J., Baron, A. E., & Hamman, R. F. (1999). Cognitive functioning and impairment among rural elderly Hispanics and Non-Hispanic Whites as assessed by the Mini-Mental State Examination. *Journal of Gerontology: Psychological Sciences, 54,* 223-229.

Mungas, D., Marshall, S. C., Weldon, M., Haan, M., & Reed, B. R. (1996). Age and education correction of Mini-Mental State Examination for English and Spanish-speaking elderly. *Neurology, 46,* 700-706.

Murden, R., McRae, T., Kaner, S., & Bucknam, M. (1991). Mini-Mental State exam scores vary with education in Blacks and Whites. *Journal of the American Geriatric Society, 39*(2), 149-155.

Pfeiffer, E. (1975). A short portable mental status questionnaire for the assessment of organic brain deficit in elderly patients. *Journal of the American Geriatric Society, 23,* 433-441.

Pittman, J., Andrews, H., Tatemichi, T., Link, B., Struening, E., Stern, Y., & Mayeux, R. (1992, May). Diagnosis of dementia in a heterogeneous population: A comparison of paradigm-based diagnosis and physician's diagnosis. *Archives of Neurology, 49,* 461-467.

Stern, Y., Andrews, H., Pittman, J., Sano, M., Tatemichi, T., Lantigua, R., & Mayeux, R. (1992). Diagnosis of dementia in a heterogeneous population: Development of a neuropsychological paradigm-based diagnosis of dementia and quantified correction for the effects of education. *Archives of Neurology, 49,* 453-460.

Storandt, M., Botwinick, J., Danziger, W. L., & Hughes, C .P. (1984). Psychometric differentiation of mild senile dementia of the Alzheimer type. *Archives of Neurology, 41,* 497-499.

Teng, E., Hasegawa, K., Homma, A., Imai, Y., Larson, E., Graves, A., Sugimoto, K., Yamaguchi, T., Sasaki, H., Chiu, D., & White, L. (1994). The Cognitive Abilities Screening Instrument (CASI): A practical test for cross-cultural epidemiological studies of dementia. *International Psychogeriatrics, 6*(1), 45-56.

Teresi, J., Golden, R., Cross, P., Gurland, B., Kleinman, M., & Wilder, D. (1995). Item bias in cognitive screening measures: Comparisons of elderly White, Afro-American, Hispanic and high and low education subgroups. *Journal of Clinical Epidemiology, 48*(4), 473-483.

Teresi, J., & Holmes, D. (1997). Methodological issues in cognitive assessment and their impact on outcome measurement. *Alzheimer's Disease and Associated Disorders, 11*(6) 146-155.

Tsai, N., & Gao, Z. (1989). Validity of Hasegawa's Dementia Scale for screening dementia among aged Chinese. *International Psychogeriatrics, 1*(2), 145-152.

Vecchio, T. J. (1966). Predictive value of a single diagnostic test in unselected population. *New England Journal of Medicine, 274,* 1171-1173.

Welsh, K. A., Fillenbaum, G., Wilkinson, W., Heyman, P., Mohs, R. C., Stern, Y., Harrel, L., Edland, M. S., & Beekly, D. (1995). Neuropsychological test performance in African-American and White patients with Alzheimer's disease. *Neurology, 45,* 2207-2211.

Wilder, D., Cross, P., Chen, J., Gurland, B., Lantigua, R. A., Teresi, J., Bolivar, M., & Encarnacion, P. (1995). Operating Characteristics of Brief Screens for

Dementia in a Multicultural Population. *American Association for Geriatric Psychiatry, 3*(2), 96-107.

Wilkin, D., Mashiah, J., & Jolley, D. J. (1976-1977). Changes in behavioral characteristics of elderly population of local authority homes and long-stay hospital wards. *British Medical Journal, 2,* 1274-1276.

Acknowledgments. Analyses were funded in part by the Columbia University Resource Center for Minority Aging Research (RCMAR), the National Institute on Aging (AG15294), by generous support from the Hebrew Home for the Aged at Riverdale, and by the Active Life Expectancy Study funded by the National Institute on Aging (AG10489).

Part IV

Measurement of Health, Mental Health and Quality of Life

9

Self-Assessments of Health and Functional Capacity Among Older Adults

Ronald J. Angel, Michelle L. Frisco

INTRODUCTION

Self-assessments of general health and functional capacity are among the most commonly used measures in gerontology. They tap highly salient aspects of overall well-being and specific functioning that are of immediate practical importance. Health is central to well-being at any age, but given the increasing risk of chronic disease that accompanies the aging process, health considerations are particularly salient among the elderly. The old-old, who represent the fastest growing segment of the population, are at a particularly high risk of poor health and functional impairment. Accurate assessments of their health and functional status, therefore, are crucial in planning their acute and long-term health care, as well as for the estimation of their active life expectancy (Angel, Angel, & Henderson, 1997; Crimmins, Hayward, & Saito, 1994; Katz et al., 1983; Manton, Corder, & Stallard, 1993).

Although concerns over validity are serious in all studies of the general health and functional capacity of the elderly, they are particularly serious when dealing with minority elderly, among whom language, culture, and social class can substantially alter the meaning of responses to standard health probes (Angel & Guarnaccia, 1989; Angel & Williams, 2000). In this chapter we review some of the most commonly used approaches to the assessment of general health and functional capacity, and propose a research agenda to further the understanding of how to improve measurement of health status and functional capacity in culturally diverse populations.

SELF-ASSESSED GENERAL HEALTH

Assessments of general health levels are usually based on answers to questions such as, "in general, how would you rate your health: excellent, very good, good, fair, or poor?" The validity of such probes is reflected in the fact that those individuals who rate their health as fair or poor are more likely to die, to use medical services, and to have other indicators of pathology than those who rate their overall health as good or excellent (Bernard et al., 1997; Hoeymans, Feskens, Kromhout, & Van Den Bos, 1997; Spiers, Jagger, & Clarke, 1996). Because they are easy to administer, such single-item health probes are extremely useful in general health surveys. They are not as time consuming as symptom check lists or more detailed medical histories, nor do they assume that respondents are aware of specific conditions that would be revealed in a physical examination.

Questions concerning one's overall health simply require that the respondent use his or her subjective judgement to arrive at a comparative assessment of his or her health. Of course, one obvious problem with this approach is that the question is not grounded with a specific reference, nor is it specific as to the aspects of health at issue. The probe asks only that the individual rate his or her health along some verbal metric, and it is up to the respondent to determine how that metric is calibrated and how it is anchored. Such assessments are, in fact, cognitively complex and they are potentially affected by culturally based linguistic and cognitive schemata (Angel & Thoits, 1987; Angel & Williams, 2000; Kempen, Steverink, Ormel, & Deeg, 1996). Most individuals appear to make reasonable adjustments when answering questions about health and compare their health to what might be considered an "appropriate" reference group. Some individuals, in fact, are quite optimistic about their health even in the presence of significant decline (Borawski, Kinney, & Kahana, 1996; Taylor, 1989; Taylor & Brown, 1988).

How respondents arrive at assessments of their health, though, is still poorly understood and many studies have found poor convergence between self-reported health information and that provided by physicians and other professionals (Edwards et al., 1994). Several studies reveal numerous potential sources of distortion and altered recall in responses to probes concerning symptoms and health. Previous and current experience with illness and knowledge of disease can affect responses (Kind & Dolan, 1995; Means et al., 1992). The accuracy of recalled information can be influenced by the way a question is worded; unclear or inappropriate questions can lead a respondent to respond with the wrong information (Herrmann, 1995; Jobe & Mingay, 1991; Lesser, 1995).

In order to make self-reports of general health more objective, the central question is often phrased using a variation on the following: "compared to others your age, how would you rate your health?" (Ren & Amick, 1996; Wolinsky, 1998). This phrasing at least identifies an appropriate age group as a reference. Unfortunately, it still leaves the respondent with a fairly unstructured cognitive response task, and it is never certain how s/he interprets the meaning of excellent, very good,

good, fair, or poor or, for that matter, any other health-related term used. There is ample evidence, in fact, to suggest that such categories are social constructions that cannot be assumed equivalent for all individuals or groups, especially when the questions are translated into other languages (Angel & Guarnaccia, 1989; Angel & Thoits, 1987; Angel & Williams, 2000). There is little understanding of the cognitive processes involved in an individual's response to questions concerning general health, let alone of the influence of culture and language on the interpretation of the question or the structure of responses. This makes it difficult for researchers to know how to proceed when comparing racial and ethnic groups.

SELF-ASSESSMENTS OF FUNCTIONAL CAPACITY

Self-assessments of overall health not may be particularly useful for many purposes which require more specific information about consequences of differential health levels. One such area involves assessing functional capacity. In gerontology, functional capacity is highly salient, and its measurement is of major concern (Angel, Angel, & Himes, 1992; Guralnick, Branch, Cummings, & Curb, 1989; Jette & Branch, 1985; Langlois et al., 1996; Wolinsky, Stump, Callahan, & Johnson, 1996). Different diseases, or the same disease at distinct levels of severity, can have very different implications for functioning. From the perspective of social policy and long-term-care planning, one's level of functioning may be of greater salience than the specific associated diseases (Guralnick et al., 1989). Seriously impaired individuals are not only at greater risk of death, but their need for assistance is high, and the quality of their lives is often low (Angel & Angel, 1997; Guralnick et al., 1994).

THE MEASUREMENT OF PHYSICAL CAPACITY

There are two approaches to the measurement of basic functional capacity. The first focuses on self-reports of the ability to carry out basic activities of daily living (ADLs) including bathing, grooming, dressing, eating, getting from bed to a chair, using the toilet, or walking across a room. Respondents are asked if they can perform each activity with or without someone's help or the use of a special device (Jette, 1994; Wolinsky & Johnson, 1992). Those who report no problems are assumed to be fully functional. Those who report difficulties with one or more tasks are assumed to be impaired. The degree of disability is determined by the number of activities that one cannot perform independently and the amount of help needed to complete each activity.

As with single-item general health measures, self-reported functioning appears to have significant predictive and concurrent validity. Individuals who report poor functioning have higher mortality than do those who report better functioning, and they report poorer outcomes on other health-related measures, including global health assessments (Bernard et al., 1997; Guralnick et al., 1994; Hoeymans et al., 1997; Spiers et al., 1996). Like other self-reported measures, questions concerning self-reported functional ability are easy to administer and are therefore useful in general surveys. Given the apparent broad validity of such measures, they are even useful for clinical purposes (Guralnick et al., 1989).

The second approach to the assessment of functional capacity is to directly assess an individual's ability to perform specific tasks. Such direct assessments are referred to as performance-based assessments, or POMAs (Cress et al., 1995; Guralnick et al., 1989). Performance-based measures consist of actual tests of one's ability to perform tasks like standing with one's feet together side by side, or one in front of the other, without losing balance; standing on one leg for a particular period; sitting down and getting up from a chair repeated times; and bending over and picking up some object such as a pencil. Other examples include assessing grip strength using a dynamometer, or timing how long it takes a person to walk across a measured distance. Because they rely on direct observation, these measures do not require the respondent to interpret questions concerning his or her ability to perform the task, and because they are not filtered by the respondent, these measures can serve as a rather narrow validity criterion. However, as we discuss later, even basic physical functioning is a complex concept and POMAs are too narrow in their scope to serve as an unambiguous gold standard. Assessments of waking and standing, for example, measure gait and balance rather than mobility, or even functioning, more generally.

A growing body of research reveals only moderate concordance between self-reported and performance-based assessments of functional capacity. Thus, it is becoming increasingly clear that each measures something different (Cress et al., 1995; Jette & Branch, 1985; Kelley-Hayes, Jette, Wolf, D'Agostino, & Odell, 1992; Kempen et al., 1996; Myers, Holliday, Harvey, & Hutchinsons, 1993; Reuben, Siu, & Kimpau, 1992; Reuben, Valle, Hays, & Siu, 1995; Rozzini, Frisoni, Bianchetti, Zanetti, & Trabucchi, 1993; Sager et al., 1992). Self-reports probably reflect the individual's adaptation to diminished capacity (Myers et al., 1993), and individuals with some impairment may not always need to attend to the impairment. This may lead, in turn, to very positive attitudes about their health status (Borawski et al., 1996; Taylor, 1989). Such individuals may no longer even see themselves as impaired.

Because they are based on external validation, performance-based measures are often regarded as more objective than self-reports. However, neither approach tells the entire story about functional capacity, although each can provide independent and useful information (Guralnick et al., 1994). Practical considerations often limit the use of performance-based measures because, compared to self-reports, they are more difficult to administer, require special equipment and training, are time consuming, and thus are more expensive. As a result, few general surveys employ performance-based measures, although their use is increasing, especially when the assessment of specific aspects of functioning is desired (Rantanen et al., 1998). In occupational therapy, where the assessment of motor skills is vital, their use is common (e.g., O'connor et al., 1999; Stephens, Pratt, & Michlovitz, 1996; Whitney, Poole, & Cass, 1998). The few studies that compare self-assessments to performance-based measures provide useful insight into the validity and utility of each measurement approach; unfortunately, few provide useful information on cultural group differences in the validity of self-reported or performance-based measures of functional capacity.

INSTRUMENTAL ACTIVITIES OF DAILY LIVING

As useful as is information on physical functioning, it does not tell the whole story about one's capacity to live independently. Many older individuals with significant impairments continue to live alone (Angel, Angel, & Himes, 1992). Most persons take for granted the requirements for getting along in the world of mature adulthood. However, in order to survive independently, one must be able to acquire and manage money, buy food, and navigate a number of complex institutions. A logical approach to assessing one's ability to carry out such "instrumental" activities of daily living (IADLs) is to ask about the respondent's ability to, for example, use the telephone, shop for food and other necessities, prepare meals, keep house, do laundry, use public transportation or drive, and manage finances (Barberger-Gateau, Gagnon, Letenneur, Sauvel, & Datrigues, 1992; Langlois et al., 1996; Myers et al., 1993; Reuben et al., 1995). Each of these tasks is more complicated than simply walking across a small room or getting in and out of a chair. Each requires higher-order cognitive and physical capacities and reflects a higher level of functioning. Again, there is little information on how responses to questions concerning higher-order functioning are influenced by cultural, linguistic, or social class factors.

THE VALIDITY OF SELF-ASSESSMENTS OF HEALTH AND FUNCTIONING

As is the case for all subjective phenomena, such as depression and self-esteem, self reported general health and functional capacity are potentially influenced by a large range of individual and social factors that can influence how individuals interpret and respond to questions concerning their health status. From a psychometric perspective, such variability represents distortion which threatens the validity of the information obtained. This shortcoming of self-reports is one of the major motivations for attempting to develop more objective assessment techniques.

Assessing the validity and reliability of either self-reported general health or self-reported functional capacity requires techniques other than those used to assess constructed indexes that are designed to measure a single construct or dimension. Self-assessed health is based on a single item and measures of internal consistency are clearly meaningless. Typical ADL or IADL batteries contain multiple items, and it is clear that individuals who report more problems (those who receive a higher score in psychometric terms) are in poorer health than those who report fewer problems. Yet such lists of activities with which one might have problems are not created or used in the same way as standardized psychological scales. They are not intended to be indexes which reflect a single or specific latent dimension or structure. They are merely lists of problems related to different areas of functioning. Since they do not tap a common domain of content, there is no reason to expect high inter-item correlations. Although different areas of functioning may overlap, they are neither theoretically nor necessarily statistically interdependent. Measures of internal consistency, such as Cronbach's alpha, therefore, may be inappropriate. Although factor analysis has been used to group ADLs into specific functional domains, it represents a categorization technique rather than a scale-building exercise (Wolinsky, 1998). Thus, it is not conceptually or practically useful to view each item as a manifestation of a common latent structure. The fact that we speak of "health" in a global sense can be deceptive when it comes to measurement. For policy purposes, and even for clinical purposes, we are often interested in more specific dimensions of health, and the fact that culture, language, and social class can influence responses to questions concerning health and functional capacity are considerations above and beyond traditional measurement concerns. They go beyond statistical considerations of validity and reliability.

How, then, can the validity and reliability of self-reports of health and functioning be assessed? For the most part, the validity of these measures is based on plausible associations between the measures and behaviors and outcomes that are considered medically relevant. As mentioned earlier, the validity of global health is established concurrently and prospectively, that is, on the basis of its correlation with other health measures and behaviors, as well as with subsequent morbidity and mortality (Benyamini & Idler, 1999; Idler & Benyamini, 1997). The data consistently show that individuals who rate their health in the lowest categories have more debilitating conditions, are more depressed, have poorer functioning, use more medical services, and have higher mortality rates than those who rate their health higher.

The validity of measures of functional status is established in basically the same way. Individuals reporting poorer levels of functioning also report lower general health, have more health conditions, and have higher subsequent mortality than those who report better functioning (Barberger-Gateau et al., 1992; Bernard et al., 1997; Cress et al., 1995; Greiner, Snowdon, & Greiner, 1996; Hoeymans et al., 1997; Reuben et al., 1992). In addition, functioning can be assessed using performance-based measures which make it possible to compare the two approaches. Substantial concordance increases our confidence that both measure the same thing. Table 9.1 summarizes the results of several representative studies that compare self-

TABLE 9.1. Studies Comparing Self-Report and Performance-Based Measures of Physical Function

Study	Self-Report Measures	Performance-Based Measure	Results
Cress, Schechtman, Mulrow, Fiatarone, Gerety, and Buchner, 1995	Summary score ranging from 0–100 on SIP sickness impact profile	Gait speed; chair-stand time; maximal grip strength, and balance score	Self-perceived gait speed is a global indicator of perceived physical function; gait speed is the best predictor of self perceived function
Greiner, Snowdon, and Greiner, 1996	Is your ability to take care of yourself excellent, very good, good, fair or poor?	Performance on 6 Katz ADLs	Self-rated function has a stronger relationship to functional ability and decline than self-rated health; self-rated function may be a better marker of global function than self-rated health.
Guralnick, Simonsick, Ferrucci, Glenn, Berkman, Blazer, Scherr, and Wallace, 1994	Lower body ADL trouble (yes/no)	Summary performance scale based on balance, timed tandem, semi-tandem, and side-by-side stands, walking speed, chair stand	There is a strong association b/w performance measures of lower extremity function and self-reported disability but performance measures contribute more information than self-report; discordance was found for walking assessments.
Hoeymans, Feskens, Kromhout, and Van Den Bos, 1997	Hierarchical disability scales based on IADLs, BADLs and mobility items measure four categories: not disabled, disabled in IADL only, disabled in mobility and IADL and disabled in BADL, mobility and IADLs	Standing balance, walking speed, chair stand and external shoulder rotation	Men w/IADL disabilities had no different health ratings than men w/o disabilities; functional limitations have a small but sig. effect on self-rated health when disabilities are accounted for
Kelly-Hayes, Jette, Wolf, D'Agostino, and Odell, 1992	6 Katz ADL items; uses 4 categories of ability to perform for each measure	Same Katz ADL items measured in previous column	Persons w/restrictions rarely rate disability below their functional

TABLE 9.1. (*Continued*)

Study	Self-Report Measures	Performance-Based Measure	Results
			limitations; self-reports do not underestimate level of disability
Kempen, Gertrudis, Steverink, Ormel and Deeg, 1996	11 Self-Report ADL Items form subscale ranging from 11–44 w/4 response categories: yes, I can do it (1) w/o difficulty, (2) w/some difficulty, (3)w/great difficulty, (4) only with someone's help	Putting on & taking off jacket, walking, and standing up from chair and sitting 5 times without arms	Relationship between self-report and performance-based measures of ADL is not strong; subjects w/low levels of perceived physical competence & mastery and higher levels of depressive symptoms report lower levels of ADL ability compared to their performance-based ADL
Langlois, Maggi, Harris, Simonsick, Ferrucci, Pavan, Sartori, and Enzi, 1996	5 Katz ADLs; Rosow-Breslau index; 5 IADL's are used to generate 4 categories of disability-none, mild, moderate, and strong	Standing from chair, returning to seated position, side-by-side stands; standing with eyes closed; walking; picking up pencil, raising hands above head, external shoulder rotation	Self-reported disability identifies older persons with physical disability not determined by self report of need for help
Myers, Holliday, Harvey, and Hutchinsons, 1993	14 IADLs	14 IADLs 1 in the previous column	Performance measures are not superior or preferred by respondents
Reuben, Valle, Hays, and Siu, 1995	OARS scale measuring IADL function, Katz ADLs; Scores for both are reported as two sums of the number of items performed in-dependently; FSQ containing BADLs and IADLs, scores range from 0–100	Physical Performance Test (PPT) including ability to write, eat, lift a book, put on jacket, pick up penny, turn 360 degrees and walk	Relationship between self-administered, interview-administered and performance-based measures is weak; instruments probably measure different constructs

TABLE 9.1. *(Continued)*

Study	Self-Report Measures	Performance-Based Measure	Results
Reuben, Siu, and Kimpau, 1992	Katz, Spector, and Rosow-Breslau scale	Tinetti Gait scores and PPT	Both performance-based and self-report measures of functional ability are independent predictors of mortality
Rozzini, Frisoni, Bainchetti, Zanetti, and Trabucchi, 1993	BADL (Katz scale and Lawton and Brody scales) and 8 IADL items; disability classification is independent, dependent in 1 function, dependent in 2 or more functions	7-item version of the PPT	Chronic disease affects functional status in a way insensitive to BADL and IADL measures. Performance-based measures capture impairment before functional loss emerges
Sager, Dunham, Schwantes, Mecum, Halverson, and Harlowe, 1992	Modified Katz ADL scale measuring number of reported problems 0–5	Modified Katz ADL items in previous column	There are significant differences in patients' assessment and performance-based measurement of ADL function in hospitalized elderly
Sinoff and Ore, 1997	10-item Barthel Index ADL scale ranging from 0–100	Same 10-item Barthel Index in previous column	Self-report scores are more optimistic than performance-based measures; self-assessed ADLs may have limitations in diagnosing the old-old

TABLE 9.2. Mexican American Elderly Individuals Ability to Complete Timed Walk by Their Self-Reported Mobility[1]

		Self-Reported Mobility (can walk across a small room)			
		Can	Cannot	Missing	Total & Total %
	Completed Walk	2385	45	5	2435
		98.14%	1.85%	.01%	100%
Timed Walk	Could not	183	107	3	293
	Complete Walk	63.10%	36.89%	.01%	100%
	Missing	218	100	4	322
		67.70%	31.06%	1.24%	100%

[1]Data come from the Longitudinal Study of Mexican American Elderly Health, Phase I (the Hispanic HEPESE).

report and performance-based assessments. It reveals that there is general agreement between the two measurement approaches; however, some research indicates that self-reported and performance based measures do not always tap the same dimensions of functioning (Kempen et al., 1996; Langlois et al., 1996; Reuben et al., 1995; Sager et al., 1992; Sinoff & Ore, 1997).

Table 9.2 presents data on the correspondence between self-reported ability to walk across a small room and a performance-based measure of the same task. The data are from the Hispanic Established Populations for Epidemiologic Studies of the Elderly (Hispanic-EPESE) and refer to Mexican Americans over the age of 65 (Markides, 1992). The self-report consists of the answer to a question as to whether an individual can walk across a small room without the help of another person or a device. We distinguish between those who cannot do so or who can do so only with the help of a person or some device, and those who report that they have no trouble completing the task. The performance-based assessment consists of a timed 10-foot walk that the respondent is asked to perform at his or her normal pace. The number of seconds that it took the respondent to complete the walk is recorded. For present purposes we only distinguish between those who could not complete the walk at all and those who were able to do so, regardless of the time it took.

These data reveal general agreement between the two approaches, but also reveal that several respondents who could not complete the POMA report that they can walk across a small room. Even though these individuals are a small fraction of the overall sample, measures of functional ability are supposed to identify those individuals with functional limitations. These data indicate that performance-based measures and self-reports of functional ability may differ significantly among persons with significant impairment. This may be particularly true when examining culturally distinct samples, such as the Mexican-American elderly population, among whom cultural and linguistic factors may affect responses to questions concerning functioning.

CULTURE, SOCIAL CLASS, AND MEASUREMENT ISSUES

There are numerous sources of invalidity or contamination that can affect self-reports of health status and more objective performance assessments. Motivation, adaptation to diminished health and decreased mobility, perceived competence and mastery, and depression are each examples of factors that can influence how individuals respond to probes about health, or even the effort put into completing performance tests (Guralnick et al., 1989; Kempen et al., 1996; Myers et al., 1993). One such package of factors that influences reports of health is culture which, in the case of Black and Hispanic elderly, is associated with social class (Angel & Williams, 2000). Of course, for researchers who focus on race and ethnicity, the influence of culture and social class represents far more than sources of invalidity. Rather, they are intellectually salient dimensions along which world views and social opportunities are structured (Angel & Williams, 2000). For present purposes, though, we focus on the impact of culture on measurement and the problems it poses when making assumptions about cultural invariance of measurement procedures.

Since self-reports are always filtered through an individual's perceptual and linguistic apparatus, they are inevitably influenced by cultural and social class factors that determine how people see the world and assess what is normal or abnormal (Angel & Guarnaccia, 1989; Angel & Thoits, 1987; Angel & Williams, 2000; Guralnick et al., 1989). Culture may also interact with other sources of invalidity found to affect self-reports in ways that are, as yet, unknown. It is becoming increasingly clear that the uncritical application of diagnostic or assessment instruments in different language and cultural groups is fraught with conceptual and methodological dangers (Angel & Williams, 2000). In recent years a growing number of comparative studies of physical and mental health has demonstrated significant variation in how individuals from different cultures categorize and label diseases and symptoms; for example, they think and talk about suffering using different idioms of distress (Kleinman, 1982; Yoder, 1995). This fact has important implications for comparative research (Pelto & Pelto, 1997; Trostle & Sommerfeld, 1996).

The insights derived from both comparative studies and medical anthropology have important implications for both survey research and clinical practice. Among the elderly, many of whom grew up in more culturally homogenous environments than is today's norm, cultural differences remain pronounced. For example, health surveys of older Hispanics find that the majority of respondents speak little English and prefer to be interviewed in Spanish (Markides, Martin, & Gomez, 1983). Given the potentially serious confounding effects of culturally based factors in the measurement of health and functional capacity, it is imperative that we begin to explore how they operate and how culture, language, and social class interact with factors that influence responses to survey probes and performance on tests of functional capacity.

SOMATIZATION AND THE MIND/BODY PROBLEM

One major problem in the assessment of self-reported health and functional capacity is that probes about specific domains of health or functioning are frequently unclear and do not clearly differentiate between the physical and cognitive aspects of health. General health probes simply ask for one's self-evaluation of one's health, and allow the respondent to determine what health means. Questions concerning ADLs often do not clearly refer to specific aspects of activity they refer to. Tasks such as bathing, preparing meals, or taking care of one's finances are complex and include multiple lower-order behaviors (Guralnick et al., 1989). This ambiguity is one of the problems that performance-based assessments seek to avoid, but they do so by focusing on fairly narrow domains of functioning.

Most studies of factors that influence self-assessments of health and functional capacity find that higher levels of depressive affect, measured by scales as the Center For Epidemiologic Studies—Depression (CES-D), are associated with poorer self assessed health and functioning (Angel & Guarnaccia, 1989; Kempen et al., 1996). This could reflect the fact that individuals who are in poor health and whose functioning is impaired are at greater risk of depression. On the other hand, it could be that depression itself can lead one to view one's health and functioning as poor. The fact that people do not differentiate between physical and mental states in their subjective experience has important implications for research on the health of the elderly (Angel & Thoits, 1987; Lock, 1993; Lock & Scheper-Hughes, 1996). A long tradition in medical anthropology and sociology has documented a tendency among members of some cultures to somatize, a clinical term that refers to the expression of affective distress as physical symptomatology (Grau & Padgett, 1988; Katon, Kleinman, & Rosen, 1982a,b.; Kirmayer, 1984a; Kirmayer, 1984b; Kleinman, Good, & Guarnaccia, 1986).

Individuals' tendency to express their affective distress as physical illness is a consistent finding (Grau & Padgett, 1988; Katon, Kleinman & Rosen, 1982a,b.). The potential problems introduced by somatization in the use of self-reports of any sort were demonstrated in a study using the Hispanic Health and Nutrition Examination Survey (H-HANES), a large-scale epidemiological and health survey. In this survey, respondents received a physical examination that served as a comparison for their self-report (Angel & Guarnaccia, 1989). Although the physician's assessment cannot be taken as a gold standard, it is an independent source of information on the respondent's health by a trained observer, and the degree of association between the respondent and the physician is revealing. In this study respondents with high scores on the CES-D rated their health as substantially worse than did physicians. This association was significantly affected by the language in which the survey was conducted. This leads to the conclusion that rates of physical illness and psychological distress found using standard survey instruments are potentially influenced by factors such as the assessment instrument used, translation procedures employed, and samples studied, all of which are salient to studies of comparative health.

Data on Hispanics also reveal large differences between Mexican Americans and Puerto Ricans in levels of affective distress (Angel & Guarnaccia, 1989). Although the association between depressive affect and negative assessments of physical health held for both groups, Puerto Ricans report much higher levels of affective distress and poorer physical health than do Mexican Americans. Numerous other studies also find that Puerto Ricans consistently report more symptoms than do any ethnic group (Dohrenwend & Dohrenwend, 1969; Haberman, 1970, 1976; Srole et al., 1978). Although such differences may reflect true differences in health, some informed observers speculate that these disparities reflect either differences in the social desirability of symptoms used in scales or culturally patterned ways of expressing distress (Angel & Guarnaccia, 1989; Dohrenwend & Dohrenwend, 1969; Haberman, 1976). However, whatever the reason it appears that cultural group membership significantly affects responses to questions about health and subjective states. As our nation becomes more ethnically diverse, and as we increasingly engage in comparative research, it is becoming imperative that we understand the limitations and appropriate uses of general health measures.

FUTURE RESEARCH ON HEALTH ASSESSMENT

It is clear that comparative assessment of health introduces significant measurement problems that we do not yet fully understand. Because the elderly are often more culturally traditional than are the young, research among the old must be informed by a greater appreciation of the impact that language and culturally based health beliefs have on responses to questions concerning health and illness. It is quite possible, and even probable, that aspects of culture and language are confounded with measures of health. In comparisons of culturally distinct groups, health information can be seriously biased, and there is a risk of misinterpretation of response biases as real differences in health occur.

In the long run, more research and different methodologies, including intensive qualitative interviews, will be necessary if health is to be better measured. Today, even predominantly quantitative researchers often recognize the importance of including ethnographic components in epidemiological and health studies. This often facilitates understanding of how individuals interpret questions concerning their health, and how they structure their answers (Pelto & Pelto, 1997; Trostle & Sommerfeld, 1996).

In the short term there is little choice but to use available measures of global health and functional capacity. Such measures are, for the most part, valid and reliable, but it has become increasingly clear that they cannot be used uncritically. Personality, cultural, and social class factors that affect responses to questions concerning health must be accounted for in studies that employ these measures, as independent or dependent variables or as covariates.

There are also practical approaches for dealing with the measures we have in ways that do not ignore the influence of culture and social class. Angel and Gronfein (1988) propose a two staged procedure for dealing with subjective information in statistical models. They propose that responses to questions concerning health not be taken at face value and entered directly into predictive models. Instead factors that influence health should be modeled separately as a first step, and then predicted values should be introduced into outcome models in a second stage. Given the rapid progress in modeling that has occurred in recent years, many such possibilities exist. However, the basic requirement is an appreciation of the fact that self-reported measures cannot be treated as objective entities and that both self-reported and performance-based measures be used in order to understand fully individuals' health status. In order to develop more valid and reliable measures, a better understanding of the impact that culture, language, and social class have on perceptions and the response task must be developed, as well as a more sophisticated methods for using such information.

REFERENCES

Angel, J. L., Angel, R. J., & Henderson, K. J. (1997). Contextualizing social support and health in old age: Reconsidering culture and gender. *The International Journal of Sociology and Social Policy, 17*(9-10), 83-116.

Angel, R., & Gronfein, W. (1988). The use of subjective information in statistical models. *American Sociological Review, 53*(3), 464-472.

Angel, R., & Guarnaccia, P. J. (1989). Mind, body and culture: Somatization among Hispanics. *Social Science & Medicine, 28*(12), 1229-1139.

Angel, R., & Thoits, P. (1987). The impact of culture on the cognitive structure of illness. *Culture, Medicine, and Psychiatry, 11,* 23-52.

Angel, R., & Williams, K. (2000). Cultural models of health and illness. In I. Cuellar & F. A. Paniagua (Eds.), *Handbook of multi-cultural mental health: Assessment and treatment of diverse populations.* New York: Academic Press.

Angel, R. J., & Angel, J. L. (1997). *Who Will Care For Us?: Aging and Long-Term Care in Multicultural America.* New York: New York University Press.

Angel, R. J., Angel, J. L., & Himes., C. L. (1992). Minority group status, health transitions, and community living arrangements among the elderly. *Research on Aging, 14,* 496-421.

Barberger-Gateau, D., Gagnon, M., Letenneur, L., Sauvel, C., & Datrigues, F. (1992). Instrumental activities of daily living as a screening tool for cognitive impairment and dementia in elderly community dwellers. *Journal of the American Gerontological Society, 40,* 1129-1134.

Benyamini, Y., & Idler, E. (1999). Community studies reporting association between self-rated health and mortality: Additional studies, 1995-1998. *Research on Aging, 21*(3), 392-401.

Bernard, S. L., Kincade, J. E., Konrad, T. R., Arcury, T. A., Rabiner, D., Woomert, A., DeFreise, G. H., & Ory, M. (1997). Predicting mortality from community surveys of older adults: The importance of self-rated functional ability. *Journal of Gerontology: Social Sciences, 52B*(3), S155-S163.

Borawski, E. A., Kinney, J. M., & Kahana, E. (1996). The meaning of older adults' health appraisals: Congruence with health status and determinants of mortality. *Journal of Gerontology: Social Sciences, 51B*(3), S157-S170.

Cress, M. E., Schechtman, K. B., Mulrow, C. D., Fiatarone, M. A., Gerety, M. B., & Buchner, D. M. (1995). Relationship between physical performance and self-perceived physical function. *Journal of the American Geriatrics Society, 43*, 93-101.

Crimmins, E. M., Hayward, M. D., & Saito, Y. (1994). Changing mortality and morbidity rates and the health status and life expectancy of the older population. *Demography, 31*, 159-175.

Dohrenwend, B. P., & Dohrenwend, B. S. (1969). *Social Status and Psychological Disorder: A Causal Inquiry.* New York: Wiley-Interscience.

Edwards, W. S., Winn, D. M., Kurlantzick, V., Sheridan S., Retchins S., & Collins, J. G. (1994). Evaluation of national health interview survey diagnostic reporting. National Center for Health Statistics. *Vital and Health Statistics, 2*(120).

Grau, L., & Padgett, D. (1988). Somatic depression among the elderly: A sociocultural perspective. *International Journal of Geriatric Psychiatry, 3,* 201-207.

Greiner, P., Snowdon, D. A., & Greiner, L. H. (1996). The relationship of self-rated function and self-rated health to concurrent functional ability, functional decline and mortality: Findings from the nun study. *Journals of Gerontology:Social Sciences, 48*(5), S234-S241.

Guralnick, J. M., Branch, L. G., Cummings, S. R., & Curb, J. D. (1989). Physical performance measures in aging research. *Journal of Gerontology:Medical Sciences, 44*(5), M141-M146.

Guralnick, J. M., Simonsick, E. M., Ferrucci, L., Glenn, R. J., Berkman, L. F., Blazer, D. G., A., S. P., & Wallace, R. B. (1994). A short physical performance better assessing lower extremity function: Association with self-reported disability and prediction of mortality and nursing home admission. *Journal of Gerontology: Medical Sciences, 49*(2), M85-M94.

Haberman, P. W. (1970). Ethnic differences in psychiatric symptoms reported in community surveys. *Public Health Reports, 85,* 495-502.

Haberman, P. W. (1976). Psychiatric symptoms among Puerto Ricans in Puerto Rico and New York City. *Ethnicity, 3,* 133-144.

Herrmann, D. (1995). Reporting current, past, and changed health status: What we know about distortion. *Medical Care, 33,* (Suppl.) AS89-AS94.

Hoeymans, N., Feskens, E. J. M., Kromhout, D., & Van Den Bos, G. A. M. (1997). Ageing and the relationship between functional status and self-rated health in elderly men. *Social Science & Medicine, 45*(10), 1527-1536.

Idler, E., & Benyamini, Y. (1997). Self-rated health and mortality: A review of twenty-seven community studies. *Journal of Health and Social Behavior, 39*(2), 21-37.

Jette, A. (1994). How measurement techniques influence estimates of disability in older populations. *Social Science and Medicine, 38*(7), 937-942.

Jette, A. M., & Branch, L. G. (1985). Impairment and disability in the aged. *Journal of Chronic Diseases, 38*(1), 59-65.

Jobe, J. & Mingay, D. J. (1991). Cognition and survey measurement: History and overview. *Applied Cognitive Psychology, 5,* 175.

Katon, W., Kleinman, A., & Rosen G. (1982a). Depression and somatization: A review, part 1. *American Journal of Medicine, 72,* 127-135.

Katon, W., Kleinman, A., & Rosen, G. (1982b). Depression and somatization: A review, part 2. *American Journal of Medicine, 72,* 241-247.

Katz, S., Branch, L. G., Branson, M. H., Papsidero, J. A., Beck, J. C., & Greer, D. S. (1983). Active life expectancy. *New England Journal of Medicine, 309,* 1218-1224.

Kelley-Hayes, M., Jette, A. M., Wolf, P. A., D'Agostino, R. B., & Odell, P. M. (1992). Functional limitations and disability among elders in the Framingham Study. *American Journal of Public Health, 82*(6), 841-845.

Kempen, G., Steverink, N., Ormel, J., & Deeg, D. J. H. (1996). The assessment of ADL among frail elderly in an interview survey: Self-report versus performance-based tests and determinants of discrepancies. *Journal of Gerontology:Psychological Sciences, 51B*(5), P254-260.

Kind, P. & Dolan, P. (1995). The effect of past and present illness experience on the valuations of health sates. *Medical Care, 33,* (Suppl.) AS255-AS263, Supplement.

Kirmayer, L. J. (1984a). Culture, affect and somatization, part 2. *Transcultural Psychiatric Research Review, 21,* 237-262.

Kirmayer, L. J. (1984b). Culture, affect and somatization, part 1. *Transcultural Psychiatric Research Review, 21,* 159-188.

Kleinman, A. (1982). Neurasthenia and depression: A study of somatization and culture in China. *Culture, Medicine and Psychiatry, 6,* 117-190.

Kleinman, A., Good, B., & Guarnaccia, P. J. (1986). *Critical review of selected cross cultural literature on depression and anxiety disorders* (PLO No. 85M029642401D). National Institute of Mental Health.

Langlois, J. A., Maggi, S., Harris, T., Simonsick, E. M., Ferrucci, L., Pavan, M., Sartori, L., & Enzi, G. (1996). Clinical investigations: Self-report of difficulty in performing functional activities identifies a broad range of disability in old age. *Journal of the American Geriatrics Society, 44,* 1421-1428.

Lesser, J. T. (1995). Choosing questions that people can understand and answer. *Medical Care, 33,* (Suppl.) AS203-AS208.

Lock, M. M. (1993). *Encounters with aging: Mythologies of menopause in Japan and North America.* Berkeley, CA: University of California Press.

Lock, M. M., & Scheper-Hughes, N. (1996). A critical-interpretive approach in medical anthropology: Rituals and routines of discipline. In C. F. Sargent & T. M. Johnson (Eds.), *Medical Anthropology: Contemporary Theory and Method* (Rev. ed.). Westport CT: Praeger.

Manton, K. G., Corder, L. S., & Stallard, E. (1993). Estimates of change in chronic disability and institutional incidence and prevalence rates in the U.S. elderly population from the 1982, 1984, and the 1989 National Long Term Care Survey. *Journal of Gerontology: Social Sciences, 48*, S153-S166.

Markides, K. S. (1992). *A longitudinal study of Mexican/American elderly health.* Washington, D C: National Institute on Aging.

Markides, K. S., Martin, H. W., & Gomez, E. (1983). *Older Mexican Americans: A study in an urban barrio.* Austin TX: University of Texas Press.

Means, B., Habina, K., Swan, G. E., & Jack, L. (1992). Cognitive research on response error in survey questions on smoking. National Center for Health Statistics. *Vital and Health Statistics, 6*(5).

Myers, A. M., Holliday, P. J., Harvey, K. A., & Hutchinsons, K. (1993). Functional performance measures: Are they superior to self assessments? *Journal of Gerontology: Medical Sciences, 48*(5), M196-M206.

O'Connor, D., Kortman, B., Smith, A., Ahern, M., Smith, M., & Krishnan, J. (1999, December). Correlation between objective and subjective measures of hand function in patients with rheumatoid arthritis. *Journal of Hand Therapy, 12*, 323-329.

Pelto, P. J., & Pelto, G. H. (1997). Studying knowledge, culture, and behavior in applied medical anthropology. *Medical Anthropology Quarterly, 11*, 147-163.

Rantanen, T., Guralnik, J. M., Leveille, S., Izmirlian, G., Hirch, R., Simonsick, E., Ling, S., & Fried, L.P. (1998). Racial difference in muscle strength in disabled older women. *Journal of Gerontology: Biological Sciences, 53A*, B355-B361.

Ren, X. S., & Amick, B. C. (1996). Racial and ethnic disparities in self-assessed health status: Evidence from the National Survey of Families and Households. *Ethnicity and Health, 1*(3), 293-303.

Reuben, D. B., Siu, A. L., & Kimpau, S. (1992). The predictive validity of self-report and performance-based measures of function and health. *Journal of Gerontology: Medical Sciences, 47*(4), M106-M110.

Reuben, D. B., Valle, L. A., Hays, R. D., & Siu, A. L. (1995). Measuring physical function in community-dwelling older persons: A comparison of self-administered, interviewer-administered, and performance-based measures. *Journal of the American Geriatric Society, 43*, 17-23.

Rozzini, R., Frisoni, G. B., Bianchetti, A., Zanetti, O., & Trabucchi, M. (1993). Physical performance test and activities of daily living scales in the assessment of health status in elderly people. *Journal of the American Geriatrics Society, 41*, 1109-1113.

Sager, M. A., Dunham, N. C., Schwantes, A., Mecum, L., Halverson, K., & Harlowe, D. (1992). Measurement of the activities of daily living in hospitalized elderly: A comparison of self-report and performance-based methods. *Journal of the American Geriatric Society, 40*, 457-462.

Sinoff, G., & Ore, L. (1997). The Barthel Activities of Daily Living Index: Self-reporting versus actual performance in the Old-Old. *Journal of the American Geriatric Society, 45*, 832-836.

Spiers, N., Jagger, C., & Clarke, M. (1996). Physical function and perceived health: Cohort differences and interrelationships in older people. *Journal of Gerontology, 51B,* S226-S233.

Srole, L., Langner, T. S., Michael, S. T., Kirkpatrick, P. O., Marvin, K., & Rennie, T. A. C. (1978). *Mental health in the metropolis: The midtown Manhattan study.* New York: McGraw-Hill.

Stephens, J. L., Pratt N., & Michlovitz, S. (1996). The reliability and validity of the Tekdyne hand dynamometer: Part II. *Journal of Hand Therapy, 9,* 18-26.

Taylor, S. E. (1989). *Positive illusions: Creative self-deception and the healthy mind.* New York: Basic Book.

Taylor, S. E., & Brown, J. D. (1988). Illusions and well being: A social psychological perspective on mental health. *Psychological Bulletin, 103*(2), 193-210.

Trostle, J. A., & Sommerfeld, J. (1996). Medical anthropology and epidemiology. *Annual Review of Anthropology, 25,* 253-274.

Whitney, S. L., Poole, J. L., & Cass, S. P. (1998). A review of balance instruments for older adults. *American Journal of Occupational Therapy, 52,* 666-71.

Wolinsky, F. D. (1998). Self-rated health and adverse health outcomes: An exploration and refinement of the trajectory hypothesis. *Journals of Gerontology: Social Sciences, Series B, 53*(6), S336-S351.

Wolinsky, F. D., & Johnson, R. J. (1992). Widowhood, health status, and the use of health services by older adults: A cross sectional and prospective approach. *Journals of Gerontology: Social Sciences, 47,* S8-S16.

Wolinsky, F. D., Stump, T. E., Callahan, C. M., & Johnson, R. J. (1996). Consistency and change in functional status among older adults over time. *Journal of Aging and Health, 8*(2), 155-182.

Yoder, P. S. (1995). Ethnomedical knowledge of diarrheal disorders in Lubumbashi Swahili. *Medical Anthropology, 16,* 211-247.

10

Cross-Cultural Assessment of Geriatric Depression: A Review of the CES-D and GDS

Ada C. Mui, Denise Burnette, Li Mei Chen

T he United States is on the threshold of two dramatic demographic changes: the aging and increased racial and ethnic diversity of its population. The number of persons aged 65 and over is projected to double, from 34 million, or 13% of the population in 2000, to nearly 70 million, or one in five Americans by 2030. By 2030, minority populations are projected to represent one in four older adults, up from 16% in 1998. Between 1998 and 2030, the elderly non-Hispanic White population is projected to increase by 79%, compared with 226% for older minorities, including Hispanics (341%), African Americans (130%), American Indians, Eskimos, and Aleuts (150%), and Asians and Pacific Islanders (323%) (U.S. Bureau of the Census, 1998).

These demographic trends have contributed to increased interest in the prevalence and presentation of psychological distress among ethnic minority populations. However, research on cross-cultural differences in the experience and expression of depressive illnesses has received far less attention, particularly in geriatrics, despite epidemiological and clinical emphases on the importance of effective assessment and treatment of late-life depression.

Estimates of the prevalence of major depression vary widely depending on the definition and procedures used to count persons with depression (Gallo & Lebowitz,1999). Using DSM-based criteria for major depression, Gurland, Cross, and Katz (1996) estimate a 1-year prevalence rate of about 5% or less among community dwelling persons aged 65 and older. Depressive symptoms and syndromes are far more common, having been identified in 8% to 20% of older community residents (Gallo & Lebowitz, 1999). Both prevalence and incidence studies that rely on DSM-based diagnosis of major depression suggest age-related declines, whereas symptom-based assessment studies show increased rates of depression among elders, especially women (U. S. Department of Health and Human Services, 1999). Cultural influences on symptom reporting, which remain underexamined (Gallo, Cooper-Patrick, & Lesikar, 1998), are the central concern of this article.

Data from the Epidemiological Catchment Area study suggest there are few racial/ethnic group differences in either one-year or lifetime prevalence rates for diagnosable mental disorders among older adults (Robins & Regier, 1991; see Aneshensel, Clark, & Frerichs, 1983; Blazer et al., 1998). But estimated prevalence rates for ethnic minority elders may be biased as a result of low acceptability of standardized measures of symptom reporting. Sociocultural factors, such as differences in perception, interpretation, valuation, expression, and tolerance of symptoms may contribute to this bias (Mui, 1996a, b), as does physical, cognitive, and functional impairment.

The appropriateness of total standardized scales and specific items, which are typically normed on general populations of Western countries, thus need to be properly evaluated for their applicability to cultural subgroups within the United States and cross-nationally. Instruments commonly used to screen for depressive symptomatology include the Beck Depression Inventory (Beck, Ward, & Mendelson, 1961), Hamilton Depression Rating Scale (Hamilton, 1960), Zung Self-Rating Depression Scale (Zung, 1965), Center for Epidemiological Studies-Depression Scale (CES-D; Radloff, 1977) and Geriatric Depression Scale (GDS; Brink et al., 1982).

This chapter reviews published studies on the utility and psychometric properties of the CES-D and the GDS, the two most widely used screening instruments for depressive symptoms among elderly persons. The articles included in this chapter were identified through a systematic search of Ageline, Health and Psychosocial Instruments (HaPI), Medline, PsycINFO, ProQuest Direct, Social Work Abstracts, Social Science Abstracts, and Sociological Abstracts for English language studies published from 1975 to present on cross-cultural use of these two instruments. Most articles appeared in the 1990s, suggesting a recent growth of interest in this topic. Abstracts were initially reviewed online to select articles with primary data on use of the instruments with U.S. ethnic minority and non-U.S. elderly populations. Several additional articles were identified through literature cited in primary sources.

The CES-D has been used in numerous local, national, and international studies across age groups, while the GDS was developed specifically for geriatric populations. Both measures have a dual purpose and have thus undergone different types of testing, with the CES-D more widely and rigorously evaluated cross-culturally than the GDS. Studies that treat the scales as a continuous measure of depressive symptoms typically examine factor structure, validity, and reliability. Others use an established cut-point score to classify respondents at risk for depressive disorder; these assess sensitivity and specificity. The two instruments are described next, then studies involving their use with elderly samples across cultural groups are discussed.

DESCRIPTION OF INSTRUMENTS

The CES-D is a 20-item inventory for screening for depressive symptomatology (Radloff, 1977). Factor analytic studies in North America show four distinct domains: depressive affect (7 items), positive affect (4 items) somatic symptoms (7 items) and interpersonal relationships (2 items) (Berkman et al., 1986; Clark, Aneshensel, Frerichs, & Morgan, 1981; Radloff, 1977; Ross & Mirowski, 1984). Respondents are asked how often they experienced each symptom during the past week (rarely, some of the time, occasionally, or most of the time). Each item is scored 0-3, yielding a range of possible summary scores of 0-60, with higher levels indicating more frequent symptomatology. When used as a screening instrument, summary scores typically indicate probable cases of depressive disorder. Some argue this cutoff point is too low (Husaini et al., 1980); and, as studies reviewed herein will show, it may need to be altered for use in other cultures to approximate the diagnostic performance of the original scale (Bahar, Henderson, & Mackinnon, 1992).

The psychometric properties of the CES-D have been established in numerous community-based studies across age, socioeconomic, and racial/ethnic groups, and it has become a standard indicator of depressive symptomatology among older adults (Berkman et al., 1986; Blazer, Burchett, Service, & George, 1991; Davidson, Feldman, & Crawford, 1994; Husaini et al., 1980). The scale correlates well with clinical ratings of depression (Roberts & Vernon, 1983; Weissman et al., 1977), and it has good internal consistency, acceptable test-retest reliability, good concurrent validity on clinical and self-report criteria, and good construct validity.

As with other screening tools, the CES-D aims to obtain information on a range of depressive symptoms, but it does not assess severity relevant to diagnosis or clinical assessment. Callahan and Wolinksy (1994) cite studies supporting the scale's sensitivity and specificity as a screening tool for case finding in clinical populations, measuring change in depressive symptoms over time, and identifying patients with functional morbidity. Data on criterion validity in elderly community-based samples are sparse, but Beekman and colleagues (1997) report satisfactory sensitivity and specificity in a general population of older adults in the Netherlands.

The Geriatric Depression Scale (GDS) is a 30-item screening inventory for depressive symptomatology in older populations (Brink et al., 1982). To alleviate respondent fatigue, Sheikh and Yesavage (1986) developed a 15-item short form of the GDS, a subset of the original 30-item scale. Long-form scores range from 0 to 30; those who report 10 or fewer symptoms are considered normal, 11-20 symptoms is mildly depressed, and 21 or more symptoms, moderately to severely depressed (Brink et al., 1982). Short-form scores range from 0 to 15; those who report 4 or fewer symptoms are considered normal, 5-9 symptoms is mildly depressed, and 10 or more symptoms, moderately to severely depressed (Sheikh & Yesavage, 1986).

Both GDS forms have undergone extensive validation. As with the CES-D, GDS study populations have been primarily Anglo and include psychiatric and medical patients and normal older adults. Reliability estimates for the normative sample have been good (internal consistency = .94; test-retest = .85), and the scale has been validated against Research Diagnostic Criteria (RDC; Dunn & Sacco, 1989; Yesavage et al., 1983). It can discriminate among normal and mildly and severely depressed elders, and performs as well as the DSM-III-R symptom checklist in predicting clinical diagnoses (Parmelee, Lawton, & Katz, 1989).

There is concern that comorbid physical disease, functional impairment, and medication use, all of which are known to affect diagnosis of depression in older adults, may inflate scores on depression inventories (Gallo, Anthony, & Muthén, 1994; Gatz & Hurwicz, 1990; Reifler, 1994). Therefore, a strength of the GDS is that it contains no somatic items (Kessler, Foster, Webster & House, 1992). The scale also uses a simple Yes/No response format for symptom endorsement, which is easier for older adults and for persons whose formal education is limited (Olin et al., 1992).

ESTABLISHING MEASUREMENT EQUIVALENCE

In order to evaluate racial/ethnic group differences in the epidemiology and etiology of depression, symptom scales must assess the same underlying disorder of depression across all groups. Cross-cultural measurement equivalency requires at least three interrelated conditions: conceptual equivalence, metric equivalence, and structural equivalence (Hui & Triandis, 1985; see also Burnette, 1998 and Liang, in this book).

Conceptual equivalence refers to similarity in meaning of research concepts across cultural groups. Fidelity of translation is a major requisite for conceptual equivalence. Translation typically involves translation from a source language to a target language by a bilingual translator who has specialized knowledge of the research topic, independent back translation, and reconciliation of discrepancies and refinement through piloting (Bracken & Barona, 1991). Language readability and comprehension are central to this process (Weidmer, Brown, & Garcia, 1999). Conceptual equivalence involves judgment, and similarity is typically deemed sufficient when the variance in respondents' replies that are attributable to the language of the instrument is inconsequential (Rogler, 1999).

As Mackinnon, McCallum, Andrews, and Anderson (1998) point out, however, when a scale is used to screen for clinical disorders fidelity of translation may be of secondary importance if acceptable accuracy against a gold standard can be demonstrated (realizing that cut-points may need to be altered). Moreover, as Rogler (1999) observes, while arriving at negotiated meanings through an iterative translation process addresses linguistic equivalence, it does not ensure comparable conceptual meaning or significance to mental health across cultural groups. Qualitative methods such as ethnography and semiotics are best suited to understanding these aspects of conceptual equivalence and to uncovering indigenous idioms of distress and culture-bound syndromes.

Metric equivalence assumes conceptual equivalence and means that observed indicators have the same relationships with their respective latent concepts or factors across groups. In confirmatory factor analysis, similar factor structures and a similar configuration of zero and salient factor loadings of a scale's items across groups represents metric equivalence. Finally, structural equivalence assumes conceptual and metric equivalence and refers to similarities in causal linkages between a construct of interest and its consequences. Path analysis and structural equation modeling are usually used to evaluate structural equivalence (Tran, 1997; see Liang, in this volume). In all likelihood, the studies reviewed herein that were conducted in non-U.S. countries used translated versions of the instruments. However, few mentioned translation, so this aspect of conceptual equivalence could not be evaluated. The tables thus present information on study site rather than the language of administration. The articles also lacked information on other relevant aspects of conceptual equivalence, so the next section reviews studies on metric and structural equivalence of the CES-D with samples of older adults across various cultural groups. Research on the GDS, which focuses heavily on criterion-related validity of the 15-item short-form and internal consistency and test-retest reliability of the 30-item version, is then summarized. To highlight the two different uses of the scales, the tables are subdivided into studies that treat the measure as a continuous variable (Tables 10.1a and 10.2a) and those that focus on criterion-related validity (Tables 10.1b and 10.2b). Finally, conclusions and implications for future research and practice are discussed.

CROSS-CULTURAL RESEARCH WITH THE CES-D (TABLE 10.1)

As noted above, community-based studies in the United States report few racial/ethnic group differences in prevalence rates for mental disorders among older adults. Cross-national epidemiological studies show lower rates of depressive symptomatology among Asian samples (Weissman et al., 1996). Comparing group means on the CES-D in four national samples, Krause and Liang (1992) found that Japanese elders had the lowest rates of depressive symptomatology, followed by Taiwanese, American Whites, and American Blacks, in that order. However, while noting that no studies of non-immigrant Asian samples have reported depression levels higher than those found in Western countries, Mackinnon and colleagues (1998) found higher means in three of the Southeast Asian countries (Myanmar, Thailand, and Sri Lanka) than in Australia.

TABLE 10.1A. Studies Assessing Cross-Cultural Use of CES-D as Continuous Variable With Older Adults

Author	Study Site	Sample Characteristics	Study Methodology	Response Rate	Results
Baker et al., 1996	U.S.	$N = 96$ African Americans age 60+ drawn from home health agency in Tennessee. Stratified evenly by urban/ rural, age group (60–69, 70–79, 80+), and gender. 34% married; 47% grade school educ, 42% lived alone.	Assess presence of depressive symptoms, using the 20-item CESD, in African American community-dwelling elders. Multiple regression analysis examined the association of medical illness, medication use, social network, and functional impairment on depressive symptoms.		19.8% scored ≥16 on CES-D. Persons with 6 + chronic illnesses and those using 4 + prescription medications had higher scores, as did urban dwellers. Strongest predictors of depressive symptoms were medical illness and social networks.
Barón et al., 1989	U.S.	$N = 314$ American Indians 45+ from 4 Pacific Northwest reservation groups. Median age = 59; 70.0% female; 48.4% married; 58% H.S. education.	Principal Components Factor Analysis with varimax rotation		Cronbach's alpha = .86. Four-factor model explained 49% of total variance. Factor loadings did not correspond to previous research. No specific somatic factor was identified and the positive affect factor separated into two factors.
Blazer et al., 1998	U.S.	Data are from Duke site of the Established Populations for Epidemiologic Studies of the Elderly (EPESE). $N = 3041$ community-dwelling North Carolinians age 65+. African American oversample (54% of unweighted sample and 35% of weighted sample) and Whites.	Confirmatory factor analysis and LISREL used to confirm four-factor structure; bivariate analysis used to determine prevalence of individual symptoms by race; LISREL performed to control for potential confounding demographic and social risk factors.		Four-factor structure replicated. In bivariate analysis, Blacks more likely to report less hope about future, poor appetite, trouble concentrating, more effort for usual activities, less talking, and feeling people are unfriendly. In multivariate analysis, only the racial difference in interpersonal relations persisted.

TABLE 10.1A. *(Continued)*

Author	Study Site	Sample Characteristics	Study Methodology	Response Rate	Results
Boey, 1999	Hong Kong	$N = 554$ Community-dwelling Chinese elders in Hong Kong. $N = 31$ patients from a psychogeriatric assessment clinic of a voluntary agency participated in small-scale validation study.	Tested the reliability of the 10-item short form of the CES-D cross-sectionally and longitudinally. Examined associations between CES-D-10 and ADLs, Life Satisfaction Scale (LLS), Lubben Social Network Scale and self-rated health.		Cronbach's alpha of CES-D-10 = .79. consistency over 3 years (r = .44, p < .01); accuracy of classification of cases with depressive symptoms comparable to 20-item form (Kappa = .84); significant correlations with ADLs, life satisfaction, social support, and self-rated health.
Callahan & Wolinsky, 1994	U.S.	$N = 3047$ Urban primary care setting. Overall mean age 69, range 60–102; 30% male; 65% Black, 34.5% White. Black women (mean age 69.8; ≤ 8 yrs educ, 40%; ≤ $800/mo income, 85%); White women (mean age 67.2, ≤ 8 yrs educ, 43%; ≤ $800/mo income, 84%) Black men (mean age 69.5; ≤ 8 yrs educ, 54%; ≤ $800/mo income, 72%); White men (mean age 67.4; ≤ 8 yrs educ, 51%; ≤ $800/mo income, 66%).	Separate principal components factor analysis performed for each of the four race/gender groups and for respondents with imputed values for missing data (37%) and those who answered all items. Imputed values were most common for the positive affect construct. Cognitive impairment, alcoholism, and chronic illnesses also assessed.		Cronbach's alpha = .85 (both male groups, .80, Black women, .84, White women, .87). Factor structures for race/ gender groups differed markedly, as did groups with and without imputed data. Disparities were not resolved by removing persons with low education, cognitive impairment, alcoholism, or varying assumptions for imputation. But they were resolved by eliminating 5 items, suggesting a need to modify the CES-D in these populations.

TABLE 10.1A. *(Continued)*

Author	Study Site	Sample Characteristics	Study Methodology	Response Rate	Results
Chapleski et al., 1997	U.S.	$N = 277$ American Indian elders age 55+ in eastern Great Lakes region. Stratified by area of residence, with oversample rural and reservation elders (125 urban, 83 off-reservation rural, 101 on reservation). Age 55–64, 37%; 65–74, 43%, 75+, 19%; 36% male; (12 yrs educ, 55%, 12 yrs educ, 23%, 12 yrs educ, 22%; 51 % married).	Confirmatory factor analysis (LISREL-8) used to examine factor structure of CES-D and test alternate models for the full sample and for the three residential sub-groups. The 20-item and 12-item versions were evaluated.	73%	12-item version of Liang et al. (1989) for Mexican Americans provided superior fit over 20-item version for overall sample. Factor structure and factor loadings were similar across residential strata. Cronbach's alpha for the 12-item scale = .83.
Chi & Boey, 1993	Hong Kong	$N = 91$ Chinese elders in Hong Kong. 1. Normals ($N = 3$ 1; age 60–69, 45 %, 70–79, 39%, 80+, 16%; 42% male; 48% married; 53% no formal educ) 2. Normals matched to clinical group ($N = 30$; age 60–69,17 %, 70–79, 53%, 80+, 30%; 53% male, 53% married; 43% no formal educ) 3. Clinical ($N = 3$ 1; age 60–69, 16%, 70–79, 45%, 80+, 26%; 26% male, 29% married; 81% no formal educ).	Evaluated validity and reliability of four geropsychiatric screening instruments: CES-D, Life Satisfaction Index-A form, General Health Questionnaire, and Short Portable Mental Status Questionnaire.		CES-D: Cronbach's alpha = .80, split-half = .74. Test-retest not performed. Discriminated well between matched normal (mean = 28. 1) and clinical (mean = 38.0) group (p <.005). High correlation with clinical assessments of psychiatrists.
Davidson, Feldman, & Crawford, 1994	U.S. (NYC)	$N = 303$ frail elders in New York City area senior housing (mean age 79.8; 15% male; 15% married; 47% White and 53% non-White–26% identified as Hispanic).	Confirmatory factor analysis used to test 4-factor structure of the CES-D and the existence of a single underlying second-order factor. Also examined contribution of somatic factor to total symptom score and associations of age, race, functional status and health with the four factors.		Overall mean score 18.6 (Whites, 21.6; non-Whites, 15.9). Four-factor model replicated and one underlying second-order factor found. Somatic items did not unduly impact total scores. Age and health did not affect somatic subscale more than other subscales. Functional limitation was associated with

TABLE 10.1A. (Continued)

Author	Study Site	Sample Characteristics	Study Methodology	Response Rate	Results
Krause & Liang, 1992	U.S., Japan, Taiwan	Data are from three nationwide surveys. 1) $N = 1094$ American Whites (mean age = 70 ± 7.4; $3\ 3\ \%$ male; yrs educ 11.2 ± 3.3) $N = 464$ American Blacks (mean age = 69.8 ± 7.4; 32% male; yrs educ 8.4 ± 3.9). 2) $N = 2041$ Japanese (mean age 69.0 ± 6.7; 45% male; yrs educ 8.7 ± 2.8), 3) $N = 3865$ Taiwanese (mean age = 68.6 ± 6.4; 43% male; yrs educ 4.0 ± 4.6).	Using an 11-item CES-D, ANOVA and ANCOVA (adjusting for age, sex, and education) to estimate the prevalence of depressive symptoms in four culturally diverse groups (overall scale) and to evaluate cultural variations in the ways symptoms are manifest (subscales).	U.S. 67% Japan 69% Taiwan 91.8%	Japanese elders had lowest overall levels of depressive symptoms, then Taiwanese, American Whites, and American Blacks. Hypotheses that Japanese elders express depressive symptoms as interpersonal complaints and Taiwanese as somatic symptoms were not supported. Americans had higher scores than Asians on all three symptom clusters (depression, somatic, interpersonal). No major cross-cultural variations in symptom manifestation.
Krause & Liang, 1993	China	$N = 2721$ Chinese in China. Three-stage probability sample of persons age 60+ in Wuhan City (mean age 68.7 ± 6.1; 46% male; yrs educ 2.6 ± 4.0).	LISREL-7 was used to estimate a model of relationships among stress, social support, and depressive symptoms. The latter was assessed by 3 latent constructs: depressed affect, somatic symptoms, and positive affect. Exploratory factor analysis of the CES-D.	83%	Original four-factor solution replicated. Financial strain was associated with economic support but also related to high levels of somatic symptoms, low levels of positive self-evaluation, and high levels of depressive affect.

TABLE 10.1A. *(Continued)*

Author	Study Site	Sample Characteristics	Study Methdology	Response Rate	Results
Mackinnon et al., 1998	Indonesia Korea Myanmar Sri Lanka Thailand	Data are from the WHO South East Asian Regional Office (SEARO). Indonesia (N = 1191), Korea (N = 1161), Myanmar (N = 1215), Sri Lanka (N = 1186), Thailand (N = 1172). Sample aged 60+ ; stratified by age, sex, and rural/urban status.	Confirmatory factor analysis (LISREL-8.2) was used to test fit of four-factor model, relative importance of four sub-scales and adequacy of a single second-order factor. Used 17 of the 20 CES-D items (3 were deemed culturally inappropriate) and a 3-point response scale.		Original four-factor solution replicated for all countries. A single-factor model adequately fit the data at all sites and sub-scales added little additional information. Comparable performance of CES-D in these countries and North American and European cultures. There was no evidence that somatization predominated in these countries, but items with high loadings on well-being loaded low on general factor.
Mahard, 1988	U.S. (NYC)	N = 60. Puerto Ricans aged 55–82 in New York City; half diagnosed as clinically depressed. (Mean age 64.7 ± 6.2; 80% female; median yrs educ = 4). All born in P.R.; 75% had lived in the U.S. 30+ yrs).	Assessed internal consistency; ability to discriminate clinical and non-clinical populations; construct validity (in relation to stress, coping, and social desirability).		Cronbach's alpha = .87 in patient and nonpatient groups. CES-D discriminates well between patients (mean 29.5 ± 12.8) and nonpatients (mean 16.2 ± 10.6) at p<.001. Higher rates of depressive symptoms were related to increased levels of stress and fewer coping resources. Scores may be affected by social desirability.
McCallum et al., 1995	Australia	N = 2805. Prospective community study of Australians. Age 60 +; Study population generally representative of Australian-born elders in the Australian population (44% male).	Confirmatory factor analysis (LISREL 7.20) used to test the four-factor model; assess the adequacy of a single second-order depression factor; and examine associations of factors	73%	Original four-factor solution replicated. Aligns with research on North American populations and confirms the exceptional functioning of well-being scale in Japan. A single dominant factor

TABLE 10.1A. (*Continued*)

Author	Study Site	Sample Characteristics	Study Methodology	Response Rate	Results
			with age, gender, and education. 16-item CES-D and 3 response categories used.		accounted for 75% of shared variance. With the exception of the interpersonal factor, scores were higher for women; with exception of well-being, all scales correlated positively with age and negatively with age of leaving school.
Miller, Markides, & Black, 1997	U.S.	Data are from the Hispanic EPESE[a] N = 2536 Hispanic Americans (mean age = 73; 42.5% male; 44% born in Mexico. N = 330 Three Generation Study of Mexican Americans in San Antonio, Texas (age range 65–80; 30% male).	Exploratory factor analysis to explore viable factor structures for the CES-D. Confirmatory factor analysis (MIMIC) to test predictive strength of background vars. (age, gender, education, language of interview) and dimensionality of CES-D.	86% in H-EPESE	Two factors identified: Depression (cc .90) and Well-being (a =.88). Affect, somatic, and interpersonal scales highly correlated; well-being not as highly correlated with others. Goodness-of-fit lower for Three Generation Study data.
Somervell et al., 1992	U.S.	N = 120 Northwest Coast American Indian elders.	Exploratory factor analysis.		Factor structure differed from that in the literature. No clear distinction between depressed and somatic factors.
Tran, 1997	U.S.	Data are from 1986 National Survey of Americans' Changing Lives. Black females (N = 438 aged 24–59, yrs educ 11.8 ± 2.7, 34.5% married; N =3 40 aged 60+, yrs educ 8.6 (3.7, 27.6% married; White females (N = 652 aged 24–59, yrs educ 12.7± 2.6, 64.7% married; N = 764 age 60+, yrs educ 11.2 ± 3.1, 51.2% married).	Exploratory factor analysis with oblique rotation used to evaluate equivalence of factor structure of 11-item CED-D across groups. A four-factor restriction for each group was used to compare the factor structure of this short version with the original 20-item version.		Factor structures for the 11-item CES-D differed among the four age by race categories. Factor structure for the 11-item version also differed from that of the 20-item scale.

TABLE 10.1B. Studies Assessing Cross-Cultural Use of CES-D as Screening Instrument With Elderly Persons

Author	Study Site	Sample Characteristics	Study Methdology	Response Rate	Results
Baker et al., 1995	U.S.	$N = 39$ Psychiatric patients age 50+ (49% African American; 61 % White; 51% 70–92 years old, 77% female; 51% widowed.	All patients had diagnosis of affective disorder confirmed by SCID interview.		Sensitivity = 71% for Blacks and 85% for Whites. Specificity not reported.
Barón et al., 1989	U.S.	$N = 314$ American Indians age 45+ from 4 Pacific Northwest reservation groups. Median age=59; 70.0% female; 48.4% married; 58% H.S. education.	Criteria: DSM-III and RDC diagnoses. Receiver Operating Characteristics (ROC) procedures used to determine optimal cut-point.	38%	Sensitivity = 100% for both criteria; specificity 73% and 71% relative to DSM-III and RDC, respectively. ROC analysis suggests cut-point of 24 to maintain high sensitivity and reduce false positive rate.
Beekman et al., 1997	U.S.	$N = 487$ Longitudinal Aging Study, Amsterdam. Selection based on 1-month prevalence of major depression based on Diagnostic Interview Schedule (DIS). Stratified on age (55–64, 32%; 65–74, 28%; 75–85, 40%); gender (42% male); and urbanization. Educ. level: 45% low, 42% mid, 13% high; 55% married.	Baseline interview included CES-D; those scoring ≥16 received adapted version of DIS including DSM-III affective and anxiety disorders sections to establish criterion validity. Other background, cognitive, and physical health data included.	81.7%	Weighted sensitivity 100%; specificity 88%; positive predictive value 13.2%. False positives not more likely among elders with physical illness, cognitive decline, or anxiety.
Madianos Gournas, & Stefanis, 1992	Greece	$N = 251$ Residents of two boroughs of Athens, Greece. Age 65+. Mean age 74 ± 6.6; 37% male; 39.8% married; illiterate/ some elementary educ, 43%; SES: 3% upper; 19.2% middle; 53.2% lower middle; 25.3% lower.	Affective disorders estimated by a clinical examination with semistructured psychiatric interview (PEF) supplemented by DSM-III criteria.	82%	27.1% dysphoric or depressive symptoms. Cut-off ≥16, sensitivity and specificity = 83.4% and 85.9%. Construct validity: lower SES, widowed, high stress and live

TABLE 10.1B. *(Continued)*

Author	Study Site	Sample Characteristics	Study Methdology	Response Rate	Results
Papassoti- ropoulos & Heun, 1999	Germany	$N = 287$ Stratified random sample drawn of community-dwelling persons age 60+ in Rheinland-Pfalz, Germany. (25% in each age group 60–69; 70–79; 80–89; 90–99; 60. 1% female; 49.8% married).	Compares the performance of the CES-D and the General Health Questionnaire-12 using DSM-III-R criteria.		depressive symptoms. Test- retest reliability = .76. Prevalence of depression was 3.5%. Both discrimi- nated well between de- pressed and nondepressed subjects, but also high rates of false positives (CES-D, 90. 1 %). ROC analysis showed optimal cut-off for case identification = 9 /10, with corresponding sensitiv- ity and specificity 75% and 72%.
Somervell et al., 1993	U.S.	$N = 120$ Northwest coast American Indian elders.	Criterion was DSM-III-R diagnosis derived from the Lifetime version of the Schedule for Affective Disorders and Schizophrenia.		Sensitivity for major depres- sion 100%; specificity, 8 2. 1 %. For broad category of depressive disorders, sensi- tivity = 77.8%; specificity, 84.7%. ROC derived cut- points did not improve per- formance of CES-D.

A major issue is the extent to which such group comparisons reflect true differences in the prevalence of depressive symptomatology or conversely, how much is due to measurement variance in the construct of interest. Studies reviewed on the CES-D confirm earlier findings that the scale is unidimensional and robust to minor changes. Testing two shorter forms of the CES-D with persons age 65 and over, Kohout, Berkman, Evans, and Cornoni-Huntley (1993) reported that little precision was sacrificed. These studies used test versions consisting of 10, 12, 16, or 17 items, and many adopted a three- rather than four-option response format. Reasons given for abbreviating the scale were to reduce respondent burden and eliminate culturally inappropriate items. The studies also found high reliability (internal consistency, split-half, and test-retest), good validity, and good ability to discriminate between normal and clinical subjects, with acceptable levels of sensitivity and specificity in all.

For example, three items: "I felt I was just as good as other people," "I felt hopeful about the future," and "I had crying spells" were deemed inappropriate in several studies with elderly Asian groups. Chapleski and associates (1997) found that a 12-item version of the CES-D developed by Liang, Tran, Krause, and Markides (1989) for Hispanics was a more superior fit to data with American Indians than the original 20-item scale. In a four-group (race/gender) study of Black and White Americans, Callahan and Wolinsky (1994) recommended dropping five items to maximize comparability across groups. The CES-D appeared robust in the face of these changes; but, as McCallum, Markinnon, Simons, and Simons (1995) point out, potential costs include reduced reliability and lack of comparability in norms for screening.

In studying whether the four factors of the CES-D stem from one superordinate factor, Hertzog and colleagues (1990) concluded that there appears to be a general underlying factor measuring depressed mood across older populations. Several studies reviewed herein offer confirmation. Models for samples as diverse as five Southeast Asian cultures (Mackinnon et al., 1998), White and non-White elders in New York City (Davidson, Feldman, & Crawford, 1994), and a semirural community in Australia (McCallum et al., 1995) were dominated by a single factor, suggesting that very diverse groups experience the same phenomenon, regardless of its label. This finding affirms Radloff's (1977) original assertion that the high internal consistency of the CES-D (a=.87) argues for treating it as a single scale rather than emphasizing its factor structure.

But some of these studies support Liang et al.'s (1989) observation of lack of consensus on the factor structure of the CES-D. Factor solutions differ in terms of item content and number and hierarchy of factors; and factor loading thresholds also vary. As a result, some studies delete items and others force a four-factor subgroup solution. Most factor analytic work with depressive symptom scales in the U.S. suggests three symptom clusters: cognitive aspects of depression, somatic symptoms, and interpersonal problems. Others argue that positive affect is a fourth distinct domain. Radloff (1977) included the latter dimension in order to weaken response set tendencies and to obtain a more comprehensive view of mental health. Still others contend that the scale has only two general dimensions—depressive affect and positive affect or well-being.

As in earlier studies (Angel & Thoits, 1987; Liang et al., 1989), factor structure was found to vary across cultural groups. This finding raises concern about how uniformly the scale is measuring depressive symptomatology. Most studies replicated the original four-factor solution, but solutions were forced and the amount of variance explained ranged from .49 for an American Indian sample to .75 for Australians. An exception is the study by Miller, Markides, and Black (1997), who found that a two-factor model of depression and well-being provided a better fit for the Hispanic EPESE data.

Variations were also observed in the performance of somatic, interpersonal, and positive affect dimensions of the CES-D. Many studies on cross-cultural manifestations of depressive symptomatology suggest a need to differentiate between cognitive and somatic aspects of depression (Kleinman, 1977; Marsella, 1987). Kleinman and Kleinman (1985) argue that a main cultural difference in the expression of psychological distress is that members of non-Western societies tend to somatize psychological distress, expressing it in bodily complaints and service use, while those in Western cultures express it as psychological affect. Somatic symptoms were associated with high levels of depression in several of the studies reviewed, but the data did not confirm this generalization. Using exploratory factor analysis, Somervell and associates (1992) found no clear distinction between depressed affect and somatic factors in an American Indian sample. Confirmatory factor analytic studies offer further evidence of cultural variation in factors. Krause and Liang's (1992) hypothesis that Taiwanese would express depressive symptoms as somatic symptoms was not supported. MacKinnon and coworkers (1998) found no evidence that somatization predominated in any Asian samples they studied. And Davidson, Feldman, and Crawford (1994) found that functional impairment was associated with higher somatic scores in a sample of urban African American, White, and Hispanic elders, but somatic items did not unduly impact total scores.

These studies also raised concerns about the positive affect dimension of the CES-D. Krause and Liang (1992) found that Japanese elders were less depressed but also less happy than were Americans. They cite a study by Yatomi, Liang, Krause, and Akiyama, (1993) that confirmed a four-factor structure of the CES-D with Japanese elders but also found that the well-being factor correlated poorly with other factors. In several Southeast Asian samples, high loadings on well-being were coupled with low loadings of these items on the general factor (Mackinnon et al., 1998). This factor was also not as highly correlated with other factors in the Hispanic EPESE (Miller, Markides, & Black, 1997). And, in a Korean version of the CES-D developed for an adult Korean population of all ages, Cho and Kim (1998) found the positive affect dimension to be problematic. A significant issue in cross-cultural use of the CES-D thus appears to be atypical responses to the well-being items in non-Western as compared to Western cultures.

Several studies reported cultural group-related findings on the interpersonal dimension of the CES-D. Krause and Liang's (1992) national data on Japanese elders living in Japan failed to support their hypothesis that this group would express depressive symptomatology primarily as interpersonal complaints. Blazer and associates (1998) found minimal differences in symptom frequency between African American and White elders in the North Carolina EPESE, but they did observe differences on the interpersonal relations factor. The salience of this factor persisted for African Americans even with the effects of education, income, cognitive impairment, chronic health problems and disability controlled.

Finally, several studies noted the need to consider the impact of culture in conjunction with other sociodemographic and health factors known to impact depressive symptoms in older adults. For example, Callahan and Wolinsky (1994) found different patterns of item endorsement and factor structure among four race/ gender groups in a low-income, chronically ill population (see also Tran, 1997). Overall response rates for these studies were high, but authors also reported high rates of item-specific and overall nonresponse on the CES-D, which they attributed to sociocultural and contextual factors rather than presence or absence of depression.

CROSS-CULTURAL RESEARCH WITH THE GDS (TABLE 10.2)

In general, research shows that the psychometric properties and utility of the English version of GDS with elderly Anglos is satisfactory, with both sensitivity and specificity scores typically exceeding 80% (see Stiles & McGarrahan, 1998 for a review). Studies to date that evaluate the utility of this instrument with elderly persons in different cultural groups are inconclusive. Most focus on criterion validity and reliability rather than item analysis or factor structure of the scale, and most use the short form of the scale. In developing the short form, Sheikh and Yesavage (1986) used a small sample (18 normal and 17 depressed elders) to establish its correlation with the long form ($r=.84, p<.001$) and its sensitivity to depression among elders with mild to moderate dementia. A later study of 47 community dwelling and 34 nursing home elders found a modest correlation between the short and long forms ($r=.66, p<.01$), leading them to question the adequacy of the former study (Alden, Austin, & Sturgeon, 1989). The extent to which the GDS short form is representative of or as reliable as the long form remains questionable.

The GDS long form has respectable internal consistency, test-retest reliability, inter-rater reliability, and split-half reliability (coefficients .80 - .99) with Anglo elders (Stiles & McGarrahan, 1998). Studies reviewed suggest that the reliability of the GDS long form with diverse elderly populations is also satisfactory. The highest Cronbach's alpha coefficient reported is .90 for a community sample of Chinese immigrant elders in New York City (Mui, 1996a). Studies with elderly Chinese mental patients in Hong Kong and a community sample of elders in Spain also

TABLE 10.2A. Studies Assessing Cross-Cultural Use of GDS as Continuous Variable With Older Adults

Author	Study Site	Sample Characteristics	Study Methodology	Response Rate	Results
Al-Shammari & Al-Subaie, 1999	Saudi Arabia	N = 7,970 elders, age 60+ in Saudi Arabia sampled from primary health care centers (PHCs) for the first-stage sampling and family health records in a PHC catchment area for the second-stage sampling (overall mean age 68.8 ± 7.7, male 69.1 ± 7.7, female 67.7 ± 7.7; urban 65.9%, rural 31.7%, remote 2.5%; single 9.4%, married 70.1%, divorced/widowed 20.5%; illiterate 79.3%; not working 55.1%).	GDS long form Bivariate analyses by socio-demographic characteristics, housing, financial status, diagnoses and medication, living arrangements, loss of close relative, recreational activities, health perceptions, ADL and other health problems. ICD-9 used to classify clinical diagnoses via history, physical examinations, and appropriate lab tests.	Male 98.8% Female 79.8%	Prevalence rate for severe depressive symptoms was 8.4%. Correlates of depression were poor education, unemployed, old age, being female, divorced or widowed, and living in remote rural area (social association). Also, more common among those who had poor housing arrangements and limited privacy.
Black et al., 1995	Denmark	N = 47 Danish geriatric patients.	GDS long form Using Danish GDS, each patient was tested by two physicians and one nurse. Samples stratified by Merck Manual Geriatrics diagnoses groups.	62%	Interrater correlations ranged from .89 to .92. Data suggested that Danish translation of the GDS has a high level of inter-rater precision, independent of whether the rater was a physician or nurse.
Ferraro et al., 1997	U.S.	N = 22 Native American elders from reservation in North Central Dakota who were fluent in English (overall mean age 66.3 ± 10.2, average educational level 8.9 ± 3.8).	GDS short form Other demographic and psychometric information collected (sex, self-rated health, types/numbers of medications currently taken, and performance on the vocabulary sub-test of the WAISR). Correlation coefficient calculated.	100%	Prevalence rate 23% (elders scored between 6–15). The result was higher than in previous studies that have obtained GDS long form from non-Native American elders.

TABLE 10.2A. (Continued)

Author	Study Site	Sample Characteristics	Study Methodology	Response Rate	Results
Haller et al., 1996		$N = 880$ European elders living in different towns born between 1913 to 1918, ages 74 to 79 years old (male $N = 433$, female $N = 452$).	GDS short form Sample stratified by age and sex. Mental health, food intake and anthrometric data, blood samples and other data were also collected. Bivariate analyses and correlation coefficients examined.	100%	Prevalence rate 11.6% for men and 27.5% for women. Data suggested that the prevalence of depression was high in this sample (one-fifth of the sample). Significant differences in GDS scores according to the different types of education and in women.
Liu et al., 1997	China	$N = 1,313$ Chinese elders in rural area of Kinmen, an islet located west of Taiwan and off the coast of mainland China, > 65 years of age in two of the four towns on this islet (male $N = 880$, female $N = 1175$: no education, 67%, less than 6 years of education, 93%: farmers, 47%).	GDS short form Retained those who scored ≥ 5 on the GDS short form, then stratified by depressive symptoms. Bivariate analyses tested.	64%	Sensitivity or specificity was not computed. Based on DSM III-R criteria, 13% were diagnosed as having depression, using cutoff of ≥ 5, 26%-screened positive on GDS.
Mui, 1996a	U.S. (NYC)	$N = 50$ immigrant Chinese elders in New York City who live in the community, ages 62–91 (male $N = 25$, female $N = 25$; overall mean age, 75.1 ± 6.5; most subjects finished 8 years of education; average length of stay in U.S. 19 years, all born abroad; over 80% received less than $500/month from SSI or Social Security).	GDS long form Principal components analysis with varimax rotation to examine factor structure of the new GDS short form.	100%	GDS long form was reliable (alpha = .90; split half = .82), GDS short form was not as reliable as long form (alpha =.72), GDS new short form (alpha = .89), New short form may be culturally more sensitive. Two-factor solution was identified.
Zalsman et al., 1998	Israel	$N = 27$ clinically depressed inpatient elders ages 62–91 and $N = 21$ normal healthy elders ages 62–85 in Israel (overall mean age of inpatient elders 73.3, overall mean age of control group, 70.3).	GDS short form.	100%	Interrater reliability was maximal (kappa = 1.0), test-retest reliability (kappa = .88). Neither sensitivity nor specificity was determined.

TABLE 10.2B. Studies Assessing Cross-Cultural Use of GDS as Depression Screening With Older Adults

Author	Study Site	Sample Characteristics	Study Methodology	Response Rate	Results
Abas et al., 1998	U.K.	$N = 164$ African Caribbean primary care migrant elders, age 60+ in south London (54% women, 46% men; overall mean age 68.3 ± 5.9; 84% born in Jamaica; Mean and median years living in UK, $36 + 3.8$).	GDS short form. Standardized psychiatric diagnosis of depression and specific diagnosis of cultural specific "depressed/lost spirit" were used as criteria for validation of GDS.	71%	Cut-off ≥ 5, sensitivity 82%; specificity 62%. Modest agreement between the medical and the culture-specific approaches to diagnosing depression. Performance was best at the lower cut-off of 4; African-Caribbean adults may be significantly depressed when they admit to a small number of symptoms regarding low mood.
Baker et al., 1993	U.S.	$N = 58$ African American elders living in senior citizen complex. $N = 41$ Mexican Americans age 55+ with affective disorder in-patients in Texas area.	GDS short form. Depressive symptoms were stratified by DSM-IIIR diagnoses using bivariate analyses.	African Americans, 94% Mexican Americans 72%	African Americans: Cut-off score ≥ 6 yields sensitivity of 35% and specificity of 100%. Cut-off score ≥ 4, sensitivity improved to 64% and specificity 95%. Mexican Americans: Cut-off ≥ 6, sensitivity 64% and cut-off ≥ 4 improved sensitivity to 75%. Specificity not calculated as total Mexican sample had affective disorder.
Chan, 1996	Hong Kong	$N = 461$ Chinese psychiatric out-patients in Hong Kong 60+ (males $N = 167$, females $N = 290$; overall mean age $70.2 + 7.27$; married 54.3%, widowed 37.4%, other 8.2%; income < city median HK\$5,170/ mo. 91.4%, at or below public assistance levels 59.7%; no education, 42.1 %).	GDS long form. Discriminant analysis using canonical discriminant functions (linear regression) tested to compare original results using the Research Diagnostic Criteria.	99%	Sensitivity 70.6%, specificity 70.1%, false negative 29.4%, false positive 29.9% was not satisfactory. Internal consistency reliability .89 (alpha); test-retest reliability .85. Criterion-related (psychiatrist di-

TABLE 10.2B. *(Continued)*

Author	Study Site	Sample Characteristics	Study Methdology	Response Rate	Results
Cwkel & Ritchie, 1988	Jerusalem	$N = 20$ clinically depressed elders in outpatient psychiatric clinics matched with $N = 20$ normal elders from Jerusalem, Israel (age of samples ranged from 60–84; men $N = 30$, female $N = 7$; nationalities consisted of Russian $N = 9$, Romanian $N = 3$, North African $n = 3$, Western European $n = 4$, and Israeli $n = 2$; no education $n = 1$, 1–8 years of education $n = 7$, 8+ years of education $n = 12$).	GDS short form. Stratified by dementia and clinical status, which were checked by neurologist and clinical psychologist.	100%	.95 and concurrent validity (with CES-D) was .96. Cut-off ≥ 7, sensitivity 70%, specificity 75%. Thus, use of short GDS with heterogeneous population of elders, as many as 30% who experienced depression may be missed and that among those who were not clinically depressed, 25% may be wrongly diagnosed as depressed. Low levels of sensitivity and specificity may be due to cultural reasons. Jewish elders may be reluctant to report feelings that might reflect a lack of faith.
Espino et al., 1996	U.S.	$N = 48$ community-based, monolingual and bilingual Mexican American elders 65+, recruited from a county-financed community-based psychiatric care clinic, and the VA community-based outpatient psychiatric unit (overall mean age 75.24 ± 9.07, female 48%, hypertension 27%, diabetes mellitus 22.9%, arthritis 18.7%).	GDS long form. Screened elders with depression that were treated for 3+ weeks, severe dementia by Mini Mental Status Exam, and unstable bipolar illness. Principal components factor analysis with varimax rotation was conducted and 5-factor solution was identified.	73%	Cut-off ≥ 11, sensitivity 80%, specificity 61%. Based on the clinical diagnosis, sensitivity 80% and specificity 50%. The factor structure obtained is different from other studies on non-Mexican elders. This suggests that these signs and symptoms of depression in older Mexican Americans may be different from other elderly Americans.

TABLE 10.2B. *(Continued)*

Author	Study Site	Sample Characteristics	Study Methdology	Response Rate	Results
Izal & Montorio, 1993	Spain	$N = 60$ elderly living in public residence attached to the National Institute of Social Services in Spain (Overall mean age, 84; female, 61%, male, 39%; widowed, 61% married, 23%, single, 16%; average period of stay in residence, 7 years).	GDS long form.	100%	Cut-off ≥ 11 showed prevalence of 50%, cut-off ≥ 14 showed prevalence of 35%. Alpha coefficient .89, test-retest reliability .89.
Lee et al., 1993	Hong Kong	$N = 113$ normal Chinese elders and $N = 80$ clinically depressed elders in Hong Kong ages 60–87 (male $N = 49$, female $N = 144$; overall mean age $72.8 + 6.4$; residing in community $N = 113$).	GDS short form. Interviewed and retained those without any significant medical and psychiatric problems. Diagnoses set by DSM III-R criteria. Discriminant analysis was used.	100%	Cut-off ≥ 8, Sensitivity 96.3%, specificity 87.5%.
Woo et al., 1994	Hong Kong	$N = 1,611$ Chinese elders living in community in Hong Kong age 70+ (male $N = 877$; female $N = 734$).	GDS short form. Univariate analyses and stepwise logistic regression used.	60%	Cut-off ≥ 8, sensitivity 96.3%, specificity 87.5%. Prevalence rate 29.2% for males and 41.1% for females.

168   *Measurement of Health & Quality of Life*

obtained acceptable alpha, split-half, and test-retest reliability coefficients, ranging from .82 to .92 (Chan, 1996; Izal & Montorio, 1993). Inter-rater and test-retest reliability coefficients in a study using the short form with normal and depressed Israeli elders were also good (.88 - 1.00) (Zalsman et al., 1998). Overall, studies in other countries have thus established that the reliability of the GDS as a continuous scale is more than adequate.

Most studies of the validity of the GDS assess the scale's criterion validity in terms of sensitivity and specificity. In their original study, Yesavage and Brink (1983) established a cut-off point of 11 with a sensitivity/specificity ratio of 84% / 95%, which appeared to afford an optimal balance of false negatives and false positives. With a cut-off point of 14, sensitivity was 80% and specificity was 100%. A higher cut-off point may be used if false positives are a concern. In their review, Stiles and McGarrahan (1998) conclude that the GDS long form has shown respectable sensitivity and specificity scores, with most above 80% with Anglo elders. Studies on the validity of the GDS with other racial/ ethnic groups are less conclusive.

Most studies that assessed criterion validity in this article used the GDS short form. Since they used different cut-off points, it is difficult to compare sensitivity and specificity scores. The highest sensitivity with the short form was 96% (cut-off at 8) in a Hong Kong sample (Lee et al., 1993). Sensitivity/specificity ratios were 70%/75% (cut-off at 7) in a sample of diverse national origins in Israel (Cwikel & Ritchie, 1989), and 82%/62% in an African Caribbean sample in South London (cut-off at 5) (Abas et al., 1998). Using the GDS long form with a cut-off point at 14, the sensitivity/specificity ratio was 70.6%/70.1% with a psychiatric sample in Hong Kong (Chan, 1996), with false negative (29.4%) and false positive (29.9%) rates unacceptably high.

For Mexican American elders, the GDS long form yielded a sensitivity/specificity ratio of 80%/61% (cut-off at 11) (Espino et al., 1996). Another study using the short form found poor sensitivity with Mexican American and African American elders (64%/35% and 75%/64%; using 6 and 4 as cut-off points, respectively) (Baker, Espino, Robinson, & Stewart, 1993). Taken together, these studies suggest that neither the long nor short form of the GDS is adequate for cross-cultural use. More rigorous validation studies are particularly needed to improve the scale's validity in diverse populations of older adults.

There are very few factorial studies on the GDS. Four studies used principal component analysis to analyze the long form with samples of Anglo elders (Abraham, Wofford, Lichtenberg, & Holroyd, 1994; Parmelee, Lawton, & Katz, 1989; Salamero & Marcs, 1992; Sheikh et al., 1991), and another factor analyzed the short form with a sample of older Chinese Americans and Chinese immigrants (Mui, 1996a). Sheikh and colleagues (1991) found five distinct factors: 1. sad mood (nine items); 2. lack of mental and physical energy (six items); 3. positive mood (six items); 4. agitation (three items); and 5. social withdrawal (two items). Four items did not load on any factors. Abraham et al. (1994) found a six-factor solution: 1. life dissatisfaction; 2. dysphoria; 3. hopelessness; 4. anxiety; 5. social withdrawal; and 6. decreased cognition. Two other studies concluded that the GDS was basically unidimensional and strongly recommended its use as a single composite score (Parmelee et al., 1989; Salamero & Marcos, 1992).

Mui (1996a) used principal components analysis to create a new 15-item GDS short form (retaining 10 items from the original short form) for Chinese immigrant elders. This scale had two factors (happy mood and sad mood) and an alpha coefficient comparable to that of the GDS long form. Overall, existing factor analytic work on the GDS has used only exploratory factor analyses and the results were inconsistent. There is thus clearly a need for confirmatory factor analyses of the GDS with both Anglo and other racial/ ethnic elderly populations.

CONCLUSION

Future growth and increased pluralism of the U.S. elderly population, much of which is expected to result from immigration, underscore the need to better understand cultural influences on the assessment of depressive symptoms, the ways in which symptoms are configured into disorders, and the interplay of personal and sociocultural factors in depressive illness (Tran, 1997). Very few depression screening or diagnostic instruments are normed on or adequately validated across cultural groups (Lebowitz et al., 1997).

This chapter has reviewed published English-language studies on two of the most widely used screening instruments for depressive symptomatology among older adults, the CES-D and the GDS. It is important to note that variation in objectives, samples, and analytic techniques in these studies makes it impossible to compare specific findings. For example, some used newer, more sophisticated analytic techniques, such as multiple indicators, multiple causes (MICIC) confirmatory factor analysis models, which permit simultaneous testing of factor structure and effects of background variables (Muthén, 1989). As Miller and colleagues (1997) caution, findings from these studies may be cause to reevaluate those from earlier, less rigorous analyses.

Nevertheless, several conclusions, however tentative, can be drawn. Studies on the CES-D confirm its general usefulness for assessing depression in diverse groups of older adults, while highlighting important areas of caution. These studies affirmed the unidimensional nature of the scale and its robustness with minor alterations. While various versions of the scale demonstrated excellent reliability, it needs to be further calibrated against clinical assessments of depression in various cultural groups. Stronger evidence of convergent validity is also needed, by relating the scale to other indicators and correlates of depression in these groups.

Sociocultural and health-related factors appeared to influence differential patterns of item endorsement and factor structures of the CES-D. The composition and hierarchy of factors varied by group: the well-being factor was consistently problematic in non-Western cultures, two rather than four factors were a better fit for Hispanic elders, the interpersonal problems factor was most salient for African Americans, and the depressed affect and somatic factors were conflated for a group of American Indians. These findings suggest that cultural factors may impact the reporting of depressive symptoms and that changes in various items and factors may improve the metric and structural equivalence of the CES-D with cultural groups other than Western Anglos.

High internal consistency and criterion validity of the GDS long form with Anglo elders has generated widespread use of this instrument. However, research on psychometric properties of the GDS suggests that without alterations it may not be as valid for use in many non-Western cultures. The long form is more reliable than the short form, and further study is needed to determine whether and under what conditions the short form can be substituted. Factorial studies on the GDS are limited and have produced mixed results. Studies using confirmatory factor analytic techniques are particularly lacking. In the absence of consistent findings, the scale should be used as a single factor instrument (Stiles & McGarrahan, 1998).

Additional research on the comparative performance of various screening instruments with different populations could also prove fruitful. At least one study found that the CES-D was more reliable than the 15-item GDS in detecting depressive symptoms in both African American and White elders (Baker, Okwumabua, Philipose, & Wong, 1996). More in-depth qualitative studies of perceptions, expressions, and reporting of depressive symptoms could also lead to improvements in the conceptual and measurement equivalence of these and other screening instruments.

Reliable and culturally valid screening instruments are also an essential component of competent clinical practice. George (1992) suggests that perhaps the best population-based indicator of need for mental health treatment is prevalence of psychiatric disorder. If screening instruments are unable to identify depressive disorder for specific cultural groups, rates of depressive symptoms for these groups will likely be misestimated. Adequate measures will thus help improve detection of and, in turn, interventions for depressive illnesses and could facilitate targeting of high-risk subgroups of older adults in the U.S. and in other nations.

Pending further research, practitioners should exercise caution in using these instruments when screening for depressive symptoms with diverse groups of older adults, and they should be aware of the limitations. At minimum, they should recognize that racial/ethnic groups within the U.S. and those from abroad vary considerably in how they experience and express depressive symptoms and in how society, health, and culture influence differential patterns of distress. They should also be aware that biases that stem from poor equivalence may produce erroneous estimates of symptoms, and that adjustments such as deletion of culturally inappropriate items and changes in cut-off scores, particularly if false positives are a concern, may be warranted. Bilingual, bicultural practitioners are particularly well suited to attend to such issues. Finally, findings confirming the unidimensionality of both scales suggest that full scales should be used, again while remaining cognizant of group-related differences in the salience of specific factors. The systematic collection and dissemination of sound clinical data on the experience of using the CES-D and the GDS, and other screening instruments, would contribute significantly to the task of improving their performance across diverse groups of older adults.

REFERENCES

Abas, M. A., Phillips, C., Carter, J., Walter, J., Banerjee, S., & Levy, R. (1998). Culturally sensitive validation of screening questionnaires for depression in older African Caribbean people living in south London. *British Journal of Psychiatry, 173*, 249-254.

Abraham, I. L, Wofford, A. B., Lichtenberg, P. A., & Holroyd, S. (1994). Factor structure of the Geriatric Depression Scale in a cohort of depressed nursing-home residents. *International Journal of Geriatric Psychiatry, 9*, 611-617.

Alden, D., Austin, C., & Sturgeon, R. (1989). A correlation between the Geriatric Depression Scale long and short forms. *Journal of Gerontology, 44*, P124-P125.

Al-Shammari, S. A., & Al-Subaie, A. (1999). Prevalence and correlates of depression among Saudi elderly. *International Journal of Geriatric Psychiatry, 14*(9), 739-747.

Aneshensel, C. S., Clark, V. A., & Frerichs, R. R. (1983). Race, ethnicity, and depression: A confirmatory analysis. *Journal of Personality and Social Psychology, 44*, 385-398.

Angel, R. J., & Thoits, P. (1987). The impact of culture on the cognitive structure of illness. *Culture, Medicine, and Psychiatry, 11*, 465-494.

Baker, F. M., Espino, D. V., Robinson, B. H., & Stewart, B. (1993). Depression among elderly African Americans and Mexican Americans. *American Journal of Psychiatry, 150*, 987-988.

Baker, F. M., Velli, S .A., Freidman, J., & Wiley, C. (1995). Screening tests for depression in older Black versus White patients. *American Journal of Geriatric Psychiatry, 3*, 43-51.

Baker, F. M., Okwumabua, J., Philipose, V. & Wong, S. (1996). Screening African American elderly for the presence of depressive symptoms: A preliminary investigation. *Journal of Geriatric Psychiatry and Neurology, 9* (3), 127-132.

Barón, A. E., Manson, S. M., Ackerson L. M., & Brenneman, D. L. (1989). Depressive symptomatology in older American Indians with chronic disease: Some psychometric considerations. In C. Attkisson & J. Zich (Eds), *Screening for depression in primary care* (pp. 217-231). New York: Routledge.

Beck, A. T., Ward, C. H., & Mendelson, M. (1961). An inventory for measuring depression. *Archives of General Psychiatry, 4*, 561-571.

Beekman, A. T. F., Deeg, D.J. H., Van Limbeek, J., Braam, A. W., De Vries, M. Z., & Van Tilburg, W. (1997). Criterion validity of the Center for Epidemiologic Studies Depression Scale (CES-D): Results from a community-based sample of older subjects in the Netherlands. *Psychological Medicine, 27*, 231-235.

Behar, E., Henderson, A. S., & Mackinnon, A. J. (1992). An epidemiological study of mental health and socio-economic conditions in Sumatra, Indonesia. *Acta Psychiatrica Scandinavica, 85*, 257-263.

Berkman, L. F., Berkman, C. S., Kasl, S., Freenan, D. H. Jr., Loe, L., & Ostfeld, A. M. (1986). Depressive symptoms in relation to physical health and functioning in the elderly. *American Journal of Epidemiology, 124*, 372-388.

Black, C. H., & Auerbach, H. (1995). A Danish version of the geriatric depression scale. *Clinical Gerontologist, 16* (2), 67-70.

Blazer, D., Burchett, B., Service, C., & George, L. K. (1991). The association of age and depression among the elderly: An epidemiologic exploration. *Journal of Gerontology: Medical Sciences, 46*, M210-M215.

Blazer, D. G., Landerman, L. R., Hays, J. C., Simonsick, E .M., & Saunders, W. B. (1998). Symptoms of depression among community-dwelling elderly African American and White older adults. *Psychological Medicine, 28*, 1311-1320.

Boey, K. W. (1999). Cross-validation of a short form of the CES-D in Chinese elderly. *International Journal of Geriatric Psychiatry, 14* (8), 608-617.

Bracken, B. A., & Barona, A. (1991). State of the art procedures for translating, validating, and using psychoeducational tests in cross-cultural assessment. *School Psychology International, 12*, 119-132.

Brink, T. L., Yesavage, J. A., Lum, B., Heersma, P., Adey, M., & Rose, T. A. (1982). Screening tests for geriatric depression. *Clinical Gerontologist, 1*, 37-44.

Burnette, D. (1998). Conceptual and methodological considerations in research with non-white ethnic elders. *Journal of Social Service Research, 23* (3/4), 71-91.

Callahan, C. M., & Wolinsky, F. D. (1994). The effect of gender and race on the measurement properties of the CES-D in older adults. *Medical Care, 32*(4), 341-356.

Chan, A. C. (1996). Clinical validation of the geriatric depression scale (GDS): Chinese version. *Journal of Aging and Health, 8*(2), 238-253.

Chapleski, E. E., Lamphere, J. K., Kaczynski, R., Lichtenberg, P. A., & Dwyer, J. W. (1997). Structure of a depression measure among American Indian elders: Confirmatory factor analysis of the CES-D scale. *Research on Aging, 19*(4), 462-485.

Chi, I., & Boey, K. W. (1993). Hong Kong validation of measuring instruments of mental health status of the elderly. *Clinical Gerontologist, 13*(4), 35-51.

Cho, M. J., & Kim, K. H. (1998). Use of the Center for Epidemiologic Studies Depression (CES-D) Scale in Korea. *The Journal of Nervous and Mental Disease, 186*(3), 304-310.

Clark, V. A., Aneshensel, C. S., Frerichs, R. R., & Morgan, T. M. (1981). Analysis of effects of sex and age in response to items of the CES-D scale. *Psychiatry Research, 5*, 171-181.

Cwikel, J., & Ritchie, K.(1988). The short GDS evaluation in a heterogeneous multilingual population. *Clinical Gerontologist, 8*(2), 63-83.

Davidson, H., Feldman, P. H., & Crawford, S. (1994). Measuring depressive symptoms in the frail elderly. *Journal of Gerontology: Psychological Sciences, 49*(4), P159-P164.

Dunn, V. K., & Sacco, W. P. (1989). Psychometric evaluation of the Geriatric Depression Scale using an elderly community sample. *Psychology and Aging, 4*, 125-126.

Espino, D. V., Bedolla, M. A., Perez, M., & Baker, F.M. (1996) Validation of the geriatric depression scale in an elder Mexican American ambulatory population: A pilot study. *Clinical Gerontologist, 16* (4), 55-67.

Ferraro, F. R., Bercier, B., & Chelminski, I. (1997). Geriatric depression scale-short form (GDS-SF) performance in Native American elderly adults. *Clinical Gerontologist, 18* (1), 52-55.

Gallo, J. J., Anthony, J. C., & Muthén, B. O. (1994). Age differences in the symptoms of depression: A latent trait analysis. *Journal of Gerontology: Psychological Sciences, 49*, P251-P264.

Gallo, J. J., Cooper-Patrick, L., & Lesikar, S. (1998). Depressive symptoms of Whites and African Americans aged 60 years and older. *Journal of Gerontology: Psychological Sciences, 53B* (5), P277-P286.

Gallo, J. J., & Lebowitz, B. D. (1999). The epidemiology of common late-life mental disorders in the community: Themes for the new century. *Psychiatric Services, 50*, 1158-1166.

Gatz, M., & Hurwicz, M. (1990). Are older people more depressed? Cross-sectional data on CES-D factors. *Psychology and Aging, 5*, 284-290.

George, L. K. (1992). Social factors and the onset and outcome of depression. In K. W. Schaie, J. S. House, & D. G. Blazer (Eds). *Aging, health behaviors, and health outcomes* (pp. 137-159). Hillsdale, NJ: Erlbaum Associates.

Gurland, B. J., Cross, P., & Katz, S. (1996). Epidemiological perspectives on opportunities of treatment of depression. *American Journal of Geriatric Psychiatry, 4* (Suppl 1), S7-S13.

Haller, J., Weggemans, R. M., Ferry, M., & Guigoz, Y. (1996). Mental health: Mini-mental state examination and geriatric depression score of elderly Europeans in the SENECA study of 1993. *European Journal of Clinical Nutrition, 50*, Suppl. 2, S112-S116.

Hamilton, M. (1960). A rating scale for depression. *Journal of Neurology, Neurosurgery, Psychiatry, 23*, 56-62.

Hertzog, C., Alstine, J. V., Usala, P. D., Hultsch, D. F & Dixon, R. (1990). Measurement properties of the Center for Epidemiological Studies depression scale in older populations. *Psychological Assessment, 2,* 64 -72.

Hui, H. C., & Triandis, H. C. (1985). Measurement in cross-cultural psychology: A review and comparison of strategies. *Journal of Cross-Cultural Psychology, 16,* 131-152.

Husaini, B. A., Neff, R. H., Harrington, J. B., Hughes, M. D., & Stone, R. H. (1980). Depression in rural communities: Validating the CES-D scale. *Journal of Community Psychology, 8,* 20-27.

Izal, M., & Montorio, I. (1993). Adaptation of the geriatric depression scale in Spain: A preliminary study. *Clinical Gerontologist, 13*(2), 83-91.

Kessler, R. C., Foster, C., Webster, P. S., & House, J. S. (1992). The relationship between age and depressive symptoms in two national surveys. *Psychology and Aging, 7*(1), 119-126.

Kleinman, A. (1977). Depression, somatization and the new cross-cultural psychiatry. *Social Science and Medicine, 11,* 3-10.

Kleinman, A., & Kleinman, J. (1985). Somatization: The interconnection in Chinese society among culture, depressive experiences, and the meaning of pain. In A. Kleinman & B. Good (Eds.) *Culture and Depression.* Los Angeles: University of California Press.

Kohout, F. J., Berkman, L. F., Evans, D. A., & Cornoni-Huntley. (1993). Two shorter forms of the CES-D depression symptoms index. *Journal of Aging and Health, 5,* 179-193.

Krause, N., & Liang, J. (1992) Cross-cultural variations in depressive symptoms in later life. *International Psychogeriatrics, 4,* Supplement 2, 185-202.

Krause, N., & Liang, J. (1993). Stress, social support, and psychological distress among the Chinese elderly. *Journal of Gerontology: Psychological Sciences, 48*(6), P282-P291.

Lebowitz, B. D., Pearson, J. L., Schneider, L. S., Reynolds, C .F., III, Alexopoulos, G. S., & Linvingston, M. (1997). Diagnosis and treatment of depression in late life. Consensus statement update. *Journal of the American Medical Association, 278,* 1186-1190.

Lee, H. C. B., Chiu, H. F. K., Kwok, W. Y., Kuong, K. P., Leung, C. M., & Chung D. W. S. (1993). Chinese elderly and the GDS short form: A preliminary study. *Clinical Gerontologist 14*(2), 37-42.

Liang J., Tran, T., Krause, N., & Markides, K. (1989). Generational differences in the structure of the CES-D scale in three generations of Mexican Americans. *Journal of Gerontology: Social Sciences, 44,* S110-S120.

Liu, C. Y., Teng, E. L., Fuh, J. L., Lin, C. C., Lin, K. N., Chen, H. M., Lin, C. H., Wang, P. N., Yang, Y. Y., Larson, E. B., Chou, P., & Liu, H. C. (1997). Depressive disorders among older residents in a Chinese rural community. *Psychological Medicine, 27,* 943-949.

Mackinnon, A., McCallum, J., Andrews, G., & Anderson, I. (1998). The Center for Epidemiological Studies Depression Scale in older community samples in Indonesia, North Korea, Myanmar, Sri Lanka, and Thailand. *Journal of Gerontology: Psychological Sciences, 53B*(6), P343-P352.

Madianos, M. G., Gournas, G., & Stefanis, C. N. (1992). Depressive symptoms and depression among elderly people in Athens. *Acta Psychiatrica Scandinavia, 86*, 320-326.

Mahard, R. E. (1988). The CES-D as a measure of depressive mood in the elderly Puerto Rican population. *Journal of Gerontology, 43* (1), P24-P25.

Marsella, A. (1987). The measurement of depressive experience and disorder across cultures. In A. Marsella, R. Hirschfeld, & M. Katz (Eds.) *The measurement of depression* (pp. 389-394). New York: Guilford Press.

McCallum, J., Mackinnon, A., Simons, L., & Simons, J. (1995). Measurement properties of the Center for Epidemiological Studies Depression Scale: An Australian community study of aged persons. *Journal of Gerontology: Social Sciences, 50B* (3), S182-S189.

Miller, T. Q., Markides, K. S., & Black, S. A. (1997). *Journal of Gerontology: Social Sciences, 52B* (5), S259-S269.

Mui, A. C. (1996a). Depression among elderly Chinese immigrants: An exploratory study. *Social Work, 41* (6), 633-645.

Mui, A. C. (1996b). Geriatric depression scale as a community screening instruments for elderly Chinese immigrants. *International Psychogeriatrics, 8* (3), 445-458.

Muthén, B. O. (1989). Latent variable modeling in heterogeneous populations. *Psychometrika, 54*, 557-585.

Olin, J. T., Schneider, L. S., Eaton, E. M., Zemansky, M. F., & Pollock, V. E. (1992). The Geriatric Depression Scale and the Beck Depression Inventory as screening instruments as an older adult outpatient population. *Psychological Assessment, 4*, 190-102.

Papassotriropoulos, A., & Heun, R. (1999). Screening for depression in the elderly: A study on misclassification by screening instruments and improvement of scale performance. *Progress in Neuro-Psychopharmacology and Biological Psychiatry, 23* (3), 431-446.

Parmalee, P. A., Lawton, M. P., & Katz, I. R.(1989). Psychometric properties of the Geriatric Depression Scale among the institutionalized aged. *Psychological Assessment, 1*, 331-338.

Radloff, L. S. (1977). The CES-D scale: A self-report scale for research in the general population. *Applied Psychological Measurement, 1*, 385-401.

Reifler, B. V. (1994). Depression: Diagnosis and co-morbidity. In *Diagnosis and treatment of depression late life: Results of the NIH Consensus Conference* (pp. 55-61). Washington, DC: American Psychiatric Press.

Roberts, R. E., & Vernon, S. W. (1983). The Center for Epidemiological Studies Depression Scale: Its use in a community sample. *American Journal of Psychiatry, 140*, 41-46.

Robins, L. N., & Reiger, D. A. (Eds.). (1991). *Psychiatric disorders in America.* New York: Free Press.

Rogler, L. H. (1999). Implementing cultural sensitivity in mental health research: Convergence and new directions. *Psychline Inter-Transdisciplinary Journal of Mental Health, 3,*(1, 2,3), 1-12.

Ross, C. E., & Mirowski, J. (1984). Components of depressed mood in married men and women. *American Journal of Epidemiology, 119,* 997-1004.

Salamero, M., & Marcus, T. (1992). Factor study of the Geriatric Depression Scale. *Acta Psychiatrica Scandinavica, 86,* 282-286.

Shiekh, J.J., & Yesavage, J. A. (1986). Geriatric Depression Scale (GDS): Recent evidence and development of a shorter version. *Clinical Gerontologist, 5,* 165-173.

Shiekh, J. J., Yesavage, J. A., & Brooke, J. O. (1991). Proposed factor structure of the Geriatric Depression Scale. *International Psychogeriatrics, 3,* 23-28.

Somervell, P. D., Beals, J., Kinzie, J. D., Boehnlein, J., Leung, P., & Manson, S. M. (1992). Use of the CES-D in an American-Indian Village. *Culture, Medicine, and Psychiatry, 16,* 503-517.

Somervell, P. D., Beals, J., Kinzie J. D., Boehnlein, J., Leung, P., & Manson, S. M. (1993). Criterion validity of the Center for Epidemiological Studies Depression Scale in a population sample from an American Indian village. *Psychiatry Research, 47,* 255-266.

Stiles, P. G., & McGarrahan, J. F. (1998). The geriatric depression scale: A comprehensive review. *Journal of Clinical Geropsychology, 4* (2), 89-110.

Tran, T. V. (1997). Exploring the equivalence of factor structure in a measure of depression between Black and White women: Measurement issues in comparative research. *Research on Social Work Practice, 7* (4), 500-517.

U.S. Bureau of the Census. (1998). Population Projections of the United States by Age, Sex, Race and Hispanic Origin: 1995-2050, Current Population Reports, P25-P130.

U.S. Department of Health and Human Services, (1999). *Mental Health: A Report of the Surgeon General.* Rockville, MD: U.S. Department of Health and Human Services, Substance Abuse and Mental Health Services Administration, Center for Mental Health Services, National Institutes of Health, National Institute of Mental Health.

Weidmer, B., Brown, J., & Garcia, L. (1999). Translating the CAHPS 1.0 survey instruments into Spanish. *Medical Care, 37* (3), MS89-MS96.

Weissman, M. M., Sholomskas, D., Pottenger, M., Prusoff, B.A., & Locke, B. Z. (1977). Assessing depressive symptoms in five psychiatric populations: A validation study. *Journal of Epidemiology, 106,* 203-214.

Weissman, M. M., Bland, R. C., Canino, G. J., Faravelli, D., Greenwald, S., & Hwu, H. G. (1996). Cross-national epidemiology of major depression and bipolar disorder. *Journal of the American Medical Association, 276,* 293-296.

Woo, J., Ho, S. C., Lau, J., Yuen, Y. K., Chiu, H., Lee, H. C., & Chi, I. (1994). The prevalence of depressive symptoms and predisposing factors in an elderly Chinese population. *Acta Psychiatrica Scandinavia, 89,* 8-13.

Yatomi, N., Liang, J., Krause, N., & Akiyama, H. (1993). Cross-cultural differences in depressive symptoms among the aged: Comparisons of the factor structure of the CES-D. *Shakai Roonengaku, [Social Gerontology] 37,* 37-47.

Yesavage, J. A., & Brink, T. L. (1983). Development and validation of a screening scale: A preliminary report. *Journal of Psychiatric Research, 17,* 37-49.

Zalsman, G., Aizenberg, D., Sigler, M., Nahshoni, E., & Weizman, A. (1998). Geriatric depression scale-short form: Validity and reliability of the Hebrew version. *Clinical Gerontologist, 18* (3), 3-9.

Zung, W. (1965). A self-rating depression scale. *Arch Gen Psychiatry, 12,* 63-70.

11

Applying Health Locus of Control and John Henryism Active Coping Theories to Older African American Adults

Marvella E. Ford, Deanna Hill, Ameera Butler, Suzanne Havstad

E fforts to improve health promotion among older adults may benefit by addressing mental health constructs. Two such constructs are health locus of control and the John Henryism theory of active coping. While they grew from disparate theoretical frameworks, the two constructs are similar in that individuals with a strong sense of internal control over their health or a strong sense of John Henryism are more likely than others to be involved in health promoting activities (Bild et al., 1993; Weaver & Gary, 1996; Wrightson & Wardle, 1997).

In order to develop targeted health position programs, the constructs of health locus of control and active coping need to be measured in a culturally appropriate manner. In recent years, increasing attention has been paid to accessing the cross-cultural validity and reliability of measurement instrument. Measures found reliable in one population group may not be so in another group. Each racial and ethnic group has its own set of cultural values, norms, attitudes, and expectancies (Ferketich, Phillips, & Verran, 1993; Marin & Perez-Stable, 1995a; Marin et al., 1995b). Given these differences, it may be unrealistic to assume that constructs can be measured in the same way for all groups of people.

The purpose of this chapter is to provide an overview of the development and application of health locus of control and John Henryism theories to older African American adults. Limitations of previous studies assessing these constructs among older African American adults will be discussed, along with recommendations for future studies.

HEALTH LOCUS OF CONTROL THEORY

The construct of health locus of control is derived from social learning theory and refers to the extent to which individuals feel that they control their own health or, conversely, that their health is controlled by factors or events outside of their control (Bailey & Lherisson-Cedeno, 1997; Sugarek, Deyo, & Holmes, 1988). According to social learning theory, an individual's belief that behaviors will result in certain outcomes is reinforced by the value of the outcomes to the individual (Tabb, 1990). Control is defined as the ability to cause an effect in an intended direction, and sense of control is an individual's view that s/he has control over her/his health, as well as the belief that s/he can gain control if desired (Fontaine, McKenna, & Cheskin, 1997; Graveley, & Oseasohn, 1991; Konen, Summerson, & Dignan, 1993; Monga, Tan, Ostermann, & Monga, 1997; Nemcek, 1989; Rotter, 1972; Shapiro et al., 1993; Younger, Marsh, & Grap, 1995). Mirowsky (1997) suggests that adjusting for education and impairment explains approximately 30% to 40% of the association between age and sense of control. The "Horizon Hypothesis" postulates that the longer the subjective life expectancy, the higher a person's sense of internal control (Mirowsky, 1997).

A number of researchers have highlighted associations between a sense of control and health. For example, an inverse relationship has been reported between sense of control and levels of mortality and activity limitations (Seeman & Lewis, 1995). Eizenman, Nesselroade, Featherman, and Rowe (1998) point out that a sense of control is linked with positive health outcomes (cognitive, psychological, and physical) in older adults. Additionally, Erwin, Spatz, Stotts, Hollenberg, & Deloney (1996) found that internal control beliefs are related to positive decisions concerning preventive and screening behaviors. Similarly, in a study including data from 311 older (aged 55-91 years) African American adults, Weaver and Gary (1996) found that people reporting low levels of internal control and high levels of depression did not exercise regularly. Conversely, in a study of 95 African American women aged 25 to 60 years, it was discovered that individuals with higher levels of belief in the control of powerful others (in this case, health professionals), compared to those with higher levels of health-related internal control beliefs, had lower rates of breast self-examination (Erwin et al., 1996).

Based on social learning theory, Wallston, Kaplan, and Maides (1976) developed the Multidimensional Health Locus of Control Scale (MHLC scale). This scale consists of three separate health locus of control subscales measuring expectancies regarding locus of control developed for predicting health-related behavior (Theisen et al., 1995; Toedter et al., 1995; Wallston et al., 1976). The Internal subscale of the MHLC measures an individual's belief that her/his health is a consequence of her/his own actions and is under her/his personal control (Galanos, Strauss, & Pieper, 1994). In contrast, individuals with a sense of external control believe that their health is affected by chance or by powerful others (Galanos,

Strauss, & Pieper, 1994). The Chance subscale assesses the degree to which an individual attributes health status to chance factors, while the Powerful Others subscale addresses the perceived influence of health professionals or family on health (Galanos, Strauss, & Pieper, 1994). Individuals who perceive themselves as exerting control over their own health may be more likely than other individuals to engage in health-related activities (Greimel, Padilla, & Grant, 1997).

The MHLC scale was developed in a study that included 98 Caucasian college students at a small southern university. The construct validity of the MHLC scale and its reliability are discussed by Wallston, Kaplan, and Maides (1976), who found this instrument to have relatively modest internal consistency estimates, that is, Cronbach's alphas of 0.71 (Internal), 0.69 (Chance) and 0.72 (Powerful Others).

A variant of the MHLC scale, the Diabetes Locus of Control Scale (Ferraro, Price, & Desmond, 1987) was used in California to assess locus of control related to diabetes self-management (Bailey & Lherisson-Cedeno, 1997). This cross-sectional study included 24 African Americans and 80 Caucasians with diabetes. The mean ages of the sample were 53.5 years SD = 11.18 (African Americans) and 57.9 years SD = 11.58 (Caucasians). The Cronbach's alphas were 0.66 for the Internal subscale, 0.72 for the Powerful Others subscale, and 0.72 for the Chance subscale (Bailey & Lherisson-Cedeno, 1997). This study was limited by the small sample size and the inclusion of only 24 African Americans, which precluded testing the MHLC scale in this racial subgroup.

Bazargan, Baker, and Bazargan (1998a) examined the extent to which the Powerful Others subscale of the MHLC scale was associated with recency of eye examinations in a cross-sectional study of 998 older (aged 62+ years) African Americans sampled from 23 senior citizen centers in New Orleans. For the six-item subscale, the authors report a Cronbach's alpha estimate of 0.77 (Bazargan, Baker, & Bazargan, 1998a). A limitation of this study is the fact that only one subscale (Powerful Others) of the MHLC scale, rather than the entire scale, was included in the study. However, these investigators went on to use the entire scale in a cross-sectional study of emergency department use, hospital admissions, and physician visits among a sample of 1,114 low-income older (aged 62+ years) African American adults; interviews were completed with 998 of the potential participants (90% response rate) (Bazargan et al., 1998b). Cronbach's alphas for the subscales were 0.69 for Internal Health Locus of Control, 0.69 for Chance and 0.78 for Powerful Others (Bazargan et al., 1998b). A limitation of the study is the fact that the reliability of the MHLC scale was not examined separately by gender.

In a study assessing the MHLC scale in a population-based sample of 342 community dwelling older adults aged 65+ years (185 African Americans and 157 Caucasians), Galanos, Strauss, and Pieper (1994) reported Cronbachs alphas of 0.73 for Internal, 0.58 for Chance and 0.68 for Powerful Others. A limitation of this study is that the reliability of each subscale was not assessed separately for each racial group.

Graveley and Oseasohn (1991) studied male veterans aged 65 years and older in order to identify individuals at risk for medication noncompliance. Seventeen (7%)

of the 249 participants were African Americans, 134 (54%) were Caucasian, 89 (36%) were Hispanic, and 9 (3%) were Asian. The internal consistency of the three MHLC subscales, as measured by Cronbach's alpha, were 0.75 for the Internal subscale, 0.60 for the Powerful Others subscale, and 0.55 for the Chance subscale. A limitation of this study is the fact that few African Americans were included.

THE JOHN HENRYISM ACTIVE COPING THEORY

John Henry Martin was an illiterate sharecropper (named after the steel driver John Henry, legend of the 19th century) who taught himself to read and write (James, Hartnett, & Kalsbeek, 1983). By the age of 40 years, he had purchased 75 acres of land in North Carolina despite the odds against him. James, Hartnett, and Kalsbeek (1983) describe John Henry Martin as having a "single-minded relentless pursuit of economic self-sufficiency." According to James, Strogatz, Wing, and Ramsey (1987), "John Henryism" connotes a strong personality predisposition toward active coping and is based upon Syme's (1979) theory of active coping.

Active coping is similar to internal health locus of control in terms of mastery expectations (James et al., 1983). While internal health locus of control refers to an individual's expectancies regarding the extent of control he or she has over their own health, active coping refers to expectancies on the part of the individuals that they can master difficult situations in life that cause distress (Scribner, Hohn, & Dwyer, 1995). Mui & Burnette (1996) suggest that having a higher sense of internal control may actually lead to active coping, which may in turn result in more positive health outcomes.

The John Henryism Active Coping theory refers to an individual's self-perception that environmental demands or challenges can be met through hard work and determination (James et al., 1983). This theory was originally developed as a predictor of mean blood pressure among African Americans of low socioeconomic status (James et al., 1987). According to this theory, high blood pressure levels are likely to occur when:

1. an environmental stressor is faced;
2. the individual lacks the resources with which to address the environmental stressor;
3. the individual believes the stressor can be controlled and therefore repeatedly attempts to control it (James et al., 1983).

The theory also postulates that the inverse relationship between socioeconomic status and blood pressure is modified by an individual's level of John Henryism (James et al., 1987). That is, among individuals with high levels of John Henryism, this inverse relationship is likely to be stronger than among individuals of low levels of John Henryism. This postulate has been confirmed among African Americans with low socioeconomic status but not among African Americans or Caucasians of high socioeconomic status (James et al., 1987).

The John Henryism Active Coping (JHAC12) scale measures a behavioral predisposition to cope actively with psychosocial environmental stressors (Broman, 1996; Duijkers, Drijver, Kromhout, & James, 1988; James et al., 1987; Scribner et al., 1995). This 12-item scale has three mutually reinforcing subthemes: efficacious mental and physical vigor; a commitment to hard work; and a single-minded determination to achieve goals (James, 1994; James, Keenan, Strogratz, Browning, & Garrett, 1992; James et al., 1987). The JHAC12 scale was developed among a community probability sample of 132 southern, working-class African American men between the ages of 17 and 60 years; the response rate was 91% (James et al., 1983; Weinrich, Weinrich, Keil, Gazes, & Potter, 1988). The sample represented approximately one-third of the occupied Black households in a small, poor, predominantly African American town in North Carolina (James et al., 1983).

In a community sample of 820 adults aged 21-50 years, Cronbach's alphas were 0.71 for African American women, 0.74 for Caucasian women, 0.67 for African American men and 0.66 for Caucasian men (James et al., 1987). In another study of 1,784 25-50 year-old African Americans in Pitt County, North Carolina, the reliability of the JHAC12 scale, as measured by Cronbach's alpha, was 0.77 for the women in the sample and 0.80 for the men in the sample (James et al., 1992). This study was limited in that the scale was tested only among younger African Americans, and Cronbach's alphas were not presented for each of the three socioeconomic status groups (low, medium and high) included in the study sample.

Three published studies have been identified in which the JHAC12 scale was used to assess active coping in samples that included older African American adults and in which reliability estimates were reported. In the first study, an eight-item version of the scale was used to predict blood pressure in a sample of 132 southern, working-class African American men between the ages of 17 and 60 years, although the median age of the study participants was only 30 years (James et al., 1983). The scale had a Cronbach's alpha of only 0.45. This study is limited by the fact that the reliability coefficients of the scale were not reported by age or socioeconomic status group and by the relatively young median age of the sample.

In the second study, Dressler, Bindon, & Neggers (1998) examined the interaction between gender and John Henryism in relation to arterial blood pressure, using the JHAC12. The study sample consisted of 600 individuals aged 25-65 years who were randomly selected from an African American community in the rural southern United States. The mean age of the sample (234 men and 366 women) was 44.7 years. The JHAC12 had a Cronbach's alpha of 0.71 for the entire sample. Reliability coefficients were not reported by gender, age group or socioeconomic status.

In the third study, the reliability of the JHAC12 scale was examined by Weinrich, Weinrich, Keil, Gazes, & Potter (1988). In their study of 1,017 participants in the Charleston Heart Study, these investigators reported Cronbach's alphas of 0.75 for African Americans aged 65+ years, 0.72 for African Americans aged 50-65 years, 0.70 for Caucasians aged 65+ years, and 0.61 for Caucasians aged 50-65 years (Weinrich et al., 1988). Thus, the JHAC12 scale was found to have modest reliability in this sample of African Americans ($n = 401$) and Caucasians ($n = 616$) aged 50+ years. A limitation of this study is the fact that reliability coefficients were not presented separately within racial group by socioeconomic status or by gender.

RECOMMENDATIONS FOR FUTURE RESEARCH

This chapter provided an overview of the constructs of health locus of control and John Henryism. Several limitations of previously conducted studies using these two constructs are clear. For example, measures of these constructs need to be examined in large samples of older African American adults, and within racial groups rather than across racial groups. Future studies can assess whether these constructs are equally (conceptually) relevant across different age, gender, socioeconomic status and ethnic groups, and among individuals from different geographic locations, including urban versus rural and northern versus southern locations.

This chapter focused on issues related to the internal consistency or reliability of the Multidimensional Health Locus of Control scale and the John Henryism Active Coping scale. Issues related to the validity of these scales remain to be addressed in future studies. For example, it is not clear whether these constructs are conceptually equivalent across different ethnic groups. It is possible for a measurement instrument to have high reliability and still represent an invalid measure of a particular construct.

In summary, while progress has been made in the research literature in assessing the psychometric properties of the Multidimensional Health Locus of Control scale and the John Henryism Active Coping scale, much work remains. The face of America is changing in terms of sociocultural representation. Measurement instruments need to be tested for their applicability and relevance for use with the diverse population groups that comprise the American public. This is particularly important since public policy decisions and health promotion programs are often based upon the results of published research incorporating measurement instruments based on mental health constructs. These decisions need to reflect research conducted using culturally appropriate measurement instruments.

REFERENCES

Bailey, B. J., & Lherisson-Cedeno, D. (1997). Diabetes outcomes and practices: Comparison of African Americans and Caucasians. *Journal of the National Black Nurses Association, 9,* 66-75.

Bazargan, M., Baker, R. S., & Bazargan, S. (1998a). Correlates of recency of eye examination among elderly African Americans. *Ophthalmic Epidemiology, 5,* 91-100.

Bazargan, M., Baker, R .S., & Bazargan, S. (1998b). Emergency department utilization, hospital admissions, and physician visits among elderly African Americans. *The Gerontologist, 38,* 25-36.

Bild, D. E., Jacob, D. R., Sidney, S., Haskell, W. L., Anderssen, N., & Obeiman, A. (1993). Physical activity in young Black and White women: The CARDIA study. *Annals of Epidemiology*, 3, 636-644.

Broman, C. L. (1996). The health consequences of racial discrimination: A study of African Americans. *Ethnicity & Disease, 6*, 148-153.

Dressler, W. W., Bindon, J. R., & Neggers, Y. H. (1998). John Henryism, gender and arterial blood pressure in an African American community. *Psychosomatic Medicine, 6*, 62-624.

Duijkers, T. J., Drijver, M., Kromhout, D., & James, S. A. (1988). "John Henryism" and blood pressure in a Dutch population. *Psychosomatic Medicine, 50*, 353-359.

Eizenman, D. R., Nesselroade, J. R., Featherman, D. L., & Rowe, J. W. (1998). Intraindividual variability in perceived control in an older sample. The MacArthur Successful Aging Studies. *Psychology and Aging, 12*, 489-502.

Erwin, D. O., Spatz, T. S., Stotts, R. C., Hollenberg, J. A., & Deloney, L. A. (1996). Increasing mammography and breast self-examination in African American women using the Witness Project TM Model. *Journal of Cancer Education, 11*, 210-215.

Ferketich, S., Phillips, L., & Verran, J. (1993). Focus on psychometrics: Development and administration of a survey instrument for cross-cultural research. *Research in Nursing & Health, 16*, 227-230.

Ferraro, L. A., Price, J. H., & Desmond, S. M. (1987). Development of a diabetes locus of control scale. *Psychological Reports, 61*, 763-770.

Fontaine, K. R., McKenna, L., & Cheskin L. J. (1997). Support group membership and perceptions of control over health in HIV+ men. *Journal of Clinical Psychology, 53*, 249-252.

Galanos, A. N., Strauss, R. P., & Pieper, C. F. (1994). Sociodemographic correlates of health beliefs among Black and White community dwelling elderly individuals. *International Journal of Aging and Human Development, 38*, 339-350.

Graveley, E. A., & Oseasohn, C. S. (1991). Multiple drug regimens: Medication compliance among veterans 65 years and older. *Research in Nursing and Health, 14*, 51-58.

Greimel, E. R., Padilla, G. V., & Grant, M. M. (1997). Self-care responses to illness of patients with various cancer diagnoses. *Acta Oncologica, 36*, 141-150.

James, S. A. (1994). John Henryism and the health of African Americans. *Culture, Medicine, and Psychiatry, 18*, 163-182.

James, S. A., Strogatz, D. S., Wing, S. B., & Ramsey, D. L. (1987). Socioeconomic status, John Henryism, and hypertension in Blacks and Whites. *American Journal of Epidemiology, 126*, 664-673.

James, S. A., Hartnett, S. A., & Kalsbeek, W .D. (1983). John Henryism and blood pressure differences among Black men. *Journal of Behavioral Medicine, 6*, 259-278.

James, S. A., Keenan, N. L., Strogatz, D. S., Browning, S. R., & Garrett, J. M. (1992). Socioeconomic status, John Henryism, and blood pressure in Black adults. *American Journal of Epidemiology, 135*, 59-67.

Konen, J. C., Summerson, J. H., & Dignan, M .B. (1993). Family function, stress, and locus of control: Relationships to glycemia in adults with diabetes mellitus. *Archives of Family Medicine, 2,* 393-402.

Marin, G., Burhansstipanov, L., Connell, C. M., Gielen, A. C., Helitzer-Allen, D., Lorig, K., Morisky, D. E., Tenney, M., & Thomas, S. (1995). A research agenda for health education among underserved populations. *Health Education Quarterly, 22,* 346-363.

Marin, G., & Perez-Stable, E. J. (1995). Effectiveness of disseminating culturally appropriate smoking-cessation information: Programa Latino para Dejar de Fumar. *Journal of the National Cancer Institute Monographs, 18,* 155-163.

Mirowsky J. (1997). Age, subjective life expectancy, and the sense of control: The horizon hypothesis. *Journal of Gerontology, 52B,* S125-S134

Monga, U., Tan, G., Ostermann, H. J., & Monga, T. N. (1997). Sexuality in head and neck cancer patients. *Archives of Physical Medicine and Rehabilitation, 78,* 298-304.

Mui, A., & Burnette, D. (1996). Coping resources and self-reported depressive symptoms among frail older ethnic women. *Journal of Social Service Research, 21,* 19-37.

Nemcek, M. A. (1989). Factors influencing Black women's breast self-examination practice. *Cancer Nursing, 12,* 339-343.

Rotter, J .B. (1966). Generalized expectancies for internal versus external control of reinforcement. *Psychological Monographs, 80,* 1-28.

Scribner, R., Hohn, A., & Dwyer, J. (1995). Blood pressure and self-concept among African American adolescents. *Journal of the National Medical Association, 87,* 417-422.

Seeman, M., & Lewis, S. (1995). Powerlessness, health and mortality: A longitudinal study of older men and mature women. *Social Science and Medicine, 41,* 517-486.

Shapiro, D. H., Potkin, S. G., Jin, Y., Brown, B., Carreon, D., & Wu, J. (1993). Measuring the psychological construct of control: Discriminant, divergent, and incremental validity of the Shapiro Control Inventory and Rotter's and Wallston's locus of control scales. *International Journal of Psychosomatics, 40,* 35-46.

Sugarek, N. J., Deyo, R. A., & Holmes, B. C. (1988). Locus of control and beliefs about cancer in a multi-ethnic clinic population. *Oncology Nursing Forum, 15,* 481-486.

Syme, S.L. (1979). Psychosocial determinants of hypertension. In E. Onesti & C. Klimt (Eds.), *Hypertension: Determinants, complications and intervention.* (pp. 95-98). New York: Grune and Stratton.

Tabb, S.L. (1990). Locus of control in the Black elderly. *Journal of Human Hypertension, 4,* 108-109.

Theisen, M. E., MacNeill, S. E., Lumley, M. A., Ketterer, M. W., Goldberg, A. D., & Borzak, S. (1995). Psychosocial factors related to unrecognized acute myocardial infarction. *American Journal of Cardiology, 75,* 1211-1213.

Toedter, L. J., Schall, R. R., Reese, C. A., Hyland, D. T., Berk, S. N., & Dunn D. S. (1995). Psychological measures: Reliability in the assessment of stroke patients. *Archives of Physical Medicine and Rehabilitation, 76,* 719-725.

Wallston, K. A., Kaplan, G. D., & Maides, S. A. (1976). Development and validation of the Health Locus of Control (HLC) Scale. *Journal of Consulting and Clinical Psychology, 44,* 580-585.

Weaver, G. D., & Gary, L. E. (1996). Correlates of health-related behaviors in older African American adults: implications for health promotion. *Family and Community Health, 19,* 43-57.

Weinrich, S .P., Weinrich, M. C., Keil, J. E., Gazes, P. C., & Potter, E. (1988). The John Henryism and Framingham Type A scales: Measurement properties in elderly Blacks and Whites. *American Journal of Epidemiology, 128,* 165-178.

Wrightson, K. J., & Wardle, J. (1997). Cultural variation in health locus of control. *Ethnicity and Health, 2,* 13-20.

Younger, J., Marsh, K. J., & Grap, M.J. (1995). The relationship of health locus of control and cardiac rehabilitation to mastery of illness-related stress. *Journal of Advanced Nursing, 22,* 294-299.

Acknowledgments. Manuscript preparation was supported by the National Institute on Aging, the National Institute of Nursing Research, and the Office of Research on Minority Health, National Institutes of Health, Resource Center for Minority Aging grant number P30 AG15286.

12

Use of Health-Related Quality of Life Measures in Older and Ethnically Diverse U.S. Populations

Anna M. Nápoles-Springer, Anita L. Stewart

Health-related quality of life (HrQoL) refers to aspects of health, functioning and well-being that are affected by treatments and diseases. Applications of HrQoL measures have grown in the past two decades, including exploration of the HrQoL consequences of various chronic diseases, determining the cost-effectiveness of quality improvement strategies in health care systems, and evaluating treatment effectiveness through clinical trials.

By the year 2050, non-Whites will comprise approximately 50% and those aged 65 and older will make up 20% of the U.S. population (U.S. Census Bureau, 1999). Representation of these ethnically diverse and rapidly growing segments of the population in health research is increasing in the U.S. Thus, it will be important to assure the use of HrQoL instruments that are culturally sensitive in terms of being reliable, valid and relevant across cultural and racial groups. Evidence is needed of the adequacy of HrQoL measures for use in diverse groups to facilitate large-scale epidemiologic, health services, and other cross-cultural research in the U.S. where groups need to be compared on the same measures. This chapter will describe the need for measurement studies in ethnically diverse and older populations, and will illustrate this point by referring to a larger literature review of HrQoL measures used in diverse populations (Stewart & Nápoles-Springer, 2000).

METHODS FOR ASSESSING CONCEPTUAL AND MEASUREMENT EQUIVALENCE

Assessing the validity of a study's results involves considering the plausibility of alternative explanations. When HrQoL measures are used in older, culturally diverse samples where evidence of the measures' validity has not been established, a plausible alternative explanation for observed group differences is that the HrQoL measures may be biased in terms of cultural, sociodemographic, or educational characteristics of respondents (Warnecke et al., 1997). HrQoL instruments may be differentially interpreted, or biased, for a subgroup due to cultural differences in attitudes, norms, and behaviors related to health (Cella, Lloyd, & Wright, 1996; Geisinger, 1994; McHorney, 1996; Warnecke et al., 1997). Cultural factors may also influence response styles or response sets to health-related questions (Byrne & Campbell, 1999; McHorney, 1996; Warnecke et al., 1997). Translation errors and varying administration conditions may also result in bias (Little, 1997).

Comparisons between age or ethnic groups on mean levels of HrQoL are based on the assumption that the measures of HrQoL are understood and answered in a similar fashion across groups (McHorney, 1996). The more explicitly the assumptions of the universality (conceptual and measurement equivalence) of HrQoL measures are tested and met in a study, the better supported are the claims of the study's internal validity. Tests of the universality of HrQoL measures can be grouped into two broad categories: conceptual equivalence, also referred to as content validity, and measurement or empirical equivalence. These approaches generally require different scientific methods.

The first approach uses qualitative methods of focus groups and open ended probe interviews of respondents to examine the conceptual adequacy of measures. The aim of this approach is to assess whether specified constructs are relevant across subgroups, if all relevant constructs are included, and if the constructs are represented adequately by items in a particular measure (Cella et al., 1996; Gandek, 1998; Patrick, Wild, Johnson, Wagner, & Martin, 1994). Cognitive interviews can also be used to examine individual respondents in terms of the cognitive tasks required to answer various survey questions. Cognitive interviews allow the examination of cultural differences in the cognitive processes used to respond to survey items. These methods can identify problems with unclear wording of items, response formats, or response styles (Harris-Kojetin, Fowler, Brown, Schnaier, & Sweeny, 1999; Oksenberg, Cannell, & Kalton, 1991; Sudman, Bradburn, & Schwarz, 1996; Sudman, Warnecke, Johnson, O'Rourke, & Davis, 1994; Warnecke et al., 1997).

The second approach uses quantitative analytic methods to evaluate the measurement properties of an instrument administered to large samples. These methods include:

1. Use of item response theory to assess differential item functioning (measurement bias);
2. Structural equation modeling to simultaneously test across groups the invariance of a measurement model that specifies the relationships between the observed items (actual measures) and the latent variables representing the constructs; and
3. More traditional methods such as multitrait scaling analysis to examine the extent which hypothesized scales meet the assumptions of Likert scaling (with a focus on item convergent and discriminant validity).

An informed interpretation of scores rests on the successful integration of both quantitative and qualitative methods to identify possible sociocultural differences that may influence the meaning of responses. There are a number of ways to combine these methods. Prior to psychometric analyses, qualitative methods can be used to assess whether a concept is defined similarly across groups and if any additional items are required to fully represent a concept for a particular subgroup. In international studies, where translation and adaptation are integral to the use of self-report measures, qualitative methods are often used to explore their content validity prior to translation and administration of standard HrQoL measures to populations. As suggested by the International Quality of Life Assessment (IQOLA) Project Group, if content validity is not investigated to determine the extent to which a concept is adequately represented in a measure, the measure may be less likely to meet standards of empirical validity (Gandek, 1998).

In U.S. studies, popular HrQoL measures are often administered to diverse ethnic and age groups without attention to their content validity. When widely used HrQoL measures are applied in diverse U.S. groups and psychometric differences are found, investigators can also employ cognitive interview techniques to explore retrospectively if differences in the interpretation of items or in response styles may explain observed measurement differences. Additionally, efforts have begun to identify biased items of HrQoL measures across language subgroups using differential item functioning techniques (Bjorner, Kreiner, Ware, Damsgaard, & Bech, 1998). Still, no clear guidelines exist on the appropriate methodology to use when measurement differences are found between comparison groups. Much more measurement research is needed to build an evidence base to identify recommended procedures for using HrQoL measures in diverse U.S. subpopulations.

THE NEED FOR MORE STUDIES OF CONCEPTUAL AND MEASUREMENT INVARIANCE

To determine how much is known about the conceptual and measurement equivalence of HrQoL measures in diverse groups, a literature search was performed for measurement studies of HrQoL instruments, conducted in the U.S., that reported findings by ethnic subgroups (Stewart & Napoles-Springer, 2000). The portion of that review pertaining to older and ethnically diverse U.S. subgroups will be discussed here to illustrate the need for more studies. Essentially, we reviewed studies to determine what was known about the conceptual equivalence (whether the measures included all relevant concepts and adequately represented the concepts for each of the groups studied) and the psychometric or measurement equivalence (the extent to which basic psychometric criteria were met within diverse groups and were equivalent across groups) of HrQoL instruments. Extensive methods for adaptation of measures to new cultures and language groups have been developed in international studies, such as the IQOLA Project (Bjorner et al., 1998; Gandek, 1998; Keller et al., 1998). These studies provide useful methods for the translation, adaptation, and evaluation of the equivalence of HrQoL measures. The review noted above examined U.S. studies only, for two reasons:

1. Processes of acculturation may influence the interpretation of and responses to HrQoL measures among immigrant groups in the U.S.; and
2. There are English-speaking subgroups of the U.S. population whose culture or life experiences may influence the meaning and responses associated with HrQoL measures and may make the use of standard measures problematic. There we highlight key results for older and ethnically diverse adults in the U.S.

The review found very few measurement studies of any HrQoL instruments in older and ethnically diverse groups (16 studies total). Studies have been conducted on only a few measures. Most studies focused on the Medical Outcomes Study (MOS) long- and short-form health surveys (8 studies) (Andresen, Patrick, Carter, & Malmgren, 1995; Azen et al., 1999; Gonzalez, Stewart, Ritter, & Lorig, 1995; Harada, Chiu, Tsuneishi, Fukuhara, & Makinodan, 1998; McHorney, Ware, Lu, & Sherbourne, 1994; Ren, Amick, Zhou, & Gandek, 1998; Sherbourne & Meredith, 1992; Wolinsky & Stump, 1996) and the Center for Epidemiological Studies Depression Scale (CES-D; 4 studies) (Callahan & Wolinsky, 1994; Hertzog, Van Alstine, Usala, Hultsch, & Dixon, 1990; Liang, Van Tran, Krause, & Markides, 1989; Miller, Markides, & Black, 1997). A few studies of measures of activities of daily living (ADLs; 2 studies) (Colsher & Wallace, 1989; Reuben, Valle, Hays, & Siu, 1995) and other depression measures (2 studies) (Arnold, Cuellar, & Guzman, 1998; Teresi, 1994) were also found. Even for the most commonly tested measures, the CES-D and the MOS measures, the paucity of studies in older and ethnic subgroups does not allow for conclusive generalizations. For example, the four studies that reported psychometric findings on the CES-D in older adults by ethnic subgroup, focused on different groups and findings were inconsistent. One of these compared older African Americans and non-Latino Whites (Callahan & Wolinsky, 1994), two included only older Mexican Americans (Liang et al., 1989; Miller et al., 1997), and one included mostly older non-Latino Whites (Hertzog et al., 1990). These four studies used confirmatory factor analysis and found factor structures that varied considerably across ethnic groups; several did not conform to the originally hypothesized structure (Radloff, 1977).

As a further example, of the three studies that report on the item convergent and discriminant validity of the SF-36 in older ethnic groups, one does so in older Japanese Americans (Harada et al., 1998), one in an older Chinese sample (Azen et al., 1999), and one in older African Americans (McHorney et al., 1994). The two SF-36 studies conducted in Asian groups involved translated versions of the measure, so studies of English versions in these ethnic groups are lacking. No measurement studies of Latinos were found. Consequently, for item convergence/ discrimination, as was the case for most of the criteria, the evidence is scant by ethnic, language, and age subgroup.

Of all the studies reviewed, most examined one or more aspects of traditional psychometric criteria (e.g., variability, reliability, construct validity); only one study examined the conceptual equivalence of the instrument using qualitative methods (Cella et al., 1998).

FUTURE DIRECTIONS

With recent policy initiatives striving for reductions in ethnic and socioeconomic disparities in health, measures of HrQoL that are valid, reliable, and conceptually equivalent across groups will be necessary. Since ethnically and socioeconomically diverse groups have been underrepresented in the development of standard HrQoL measures, systematic evidence of the conceptual and measurement invariance of instruments across these groups is needed.

As noted above, we now have available an arsenal of quantitative and qualitative analytic methods that have been underutilized in the clinical, epidemiologic, and health services literature, with the exception of cross-cultural psychology and psychiatry. The availability of these techniques should make the evaluation of conceptual and measurement equivalence across diverse groups a more standard practice.

The time has come for a critical assessment of the adequacy of commonly used HrQoL instruments for use in diverse populations. The widespread use of HrQoL instruments without attention to their measurement properties across ethnic groups implies reification of their validity in spite of a dearth of "culturally grounded validity studies" (Vega & Rumbaut, 1991). Issues of conceptual and measurement equivalence in older, ethnically diverse samples cannot be overlooked if we expect our research findings to be scientifically defensible.

REFERENCES

Andresen, E. M., Patrick, D. L., Carter, W. B., & Malmgren, J. A. (1995). Comparing the performance of health status measures for healthy older adults. *Journal of the American Geriatrics Society, 43*(9), 1030-1034.

Arnold, B. R., Cuellar, I., & Guzman, N. (1998). Statistical and clinical evaluation of the Mattis Dementia Rating Scale-Spanish adaptation: An initial investigation. *Journals of Gerontology. Series B, Psychological Sciences and Social Sciences, 53*(6), 364-9.

Azen, S. P., Palmer, J. M., Carlson, M., Mandel, D., Cherry, B. J., Fanchiang, S.-P., Jackson, J., & Clark, F. (1999). Psychometric properties of a Chinese translation of the SF-36 Health Survey Questionnaire in the Well Elderly Study. *Journal of Aging & Health, 11*(2), 240-251.

Bjorner, J. B., Kreiner, S., Ware, J. E., Damsgaard, M. T., & Bech, P. (1998). Differential item functioning in the Danish translation of the SF-36. *Journal of Clinical Epidemiology, 51*(11), 1189-1202.

Byrne, B. M., & Campbell, T. L. (1999). Cross-cultural comparisons and the presumption of equivalent measurement and theoretical structure. *Journal of Cross-Cultural Psychology, 30*(5), 555-574.

Callahan, C. M., & Wolinsky, F. D. (1994). The effect of gender and race on the measurement properties of the CES-D in older adults. *Medical Care, 32*(4), 341-356.

Cella, D., Hernandez, L., Bonomi, A. E., Corona, M., Vaquero, M., Shiomoto, G., & Baez, L. (1998). Spanish language translation and initial validation of the functional assessment of cancer therapy quality-of-life instrument. *Medical Care, 36*(9), 1407-1418.

Cella, D. F., Lloyd, S. R., & Wright, B. D. (1996). Cross-cultural instrument equating: Current research and future directions. In B. Spilker (Ed.), *Quality of Life and Pharmacoeconomics in Clinical Trials* (pp. 707-715). Philadelphia, PA: Lippincott-Raven Publishers.

Colsher, P. L., & Wallace, R. B. (1989). Data quality and age: Health and psychobehavioral correlates of item nonresponse and inconsistent responses. *Journals of Gerontology, 44*(2), 45-P52.

Gandek, B. (1998). Methods for validating and norming translations of health status questionnaires: The IQOLA Project approach. *Journal of Clinical Epidemiology, 51*(11), 953-959.

Geisinger, K. F. (1994). Cross-cultural normative assessment: Translation and adaptation issues influencing the normative interpretation of assessment instruments. *Psychological Assessment, 6*(4), 304-312.

Gonzalez, V. M., Stewart, A., Ritter, P. L., & Lorig, K. (1995). Translation and validation of arthritis outcome measures into Spanish. *Arthritis and Rheumatism, 38*(10), 1429-46.

Harada, N., Chiu, V., Tsuneishi, C., Fukuhara, S., & Makinodan, T. (1998). Cross-cultural adaptation of the SF-36 health survey for Japanese-American elderly. *Journal of Aging and Ethnicity, 1*(2), 59-80.

Harris-Kojetin, L. D., Fowler, F. J. J., Brown, J. A., Schnaier, J. A., & Sweeny, S. F. (1999). The use of cognitive testing to develop and evaluate CAHPS 1.0 Core Survey Items. *Medical Care, 37* (Suppl. 3), MS10-MS21.

Hertzog, C., Van Alstine, J., Usala, P. D., Hultsch, D. F., & Dixon, R. (1990). Measurement properties of the Center for Epidemiological Studies Depression Scale (CES-D) in older populations. *Psychological Assessment: A Journal of Consulting and Clinical Psychology, 2*(1), 64-72.

Keller, S. D., Ware, J. E., Jr., Gandek, B., Aaronson, N. K., Alonso, J., Apolone, G., Bjorner, J. B., Brazier, J., Bullinger, M., Fukuhara, S., Kaasa, S., Leplege, A.,

Sanson-Fisher, R. W., Sullivan, M., & Wood-Dauphinee, S. (1998). Testing the equivalence of translations of widely used response choice labels: Results from the IQOLA Project. *Journal of Clinical Epidemiology, 51*(11), 933-944.

Liang, J., Van Tran, T., Krause, N., & Markides, K. S. (1989). Generational differences in the structure of the CES-D scale in Mexican Americans. *Journal of Gerontology, 44*(3), S110-S120.

Little, T. D. (1997). Mean and covariance structures (MACS) analyses of cross-cultural data: Practical and theoretical issues. *Multivariate Behavioral Research, 32*(1), 53-76.

McHorney, C. A. (1996). Measuring and monitoring general health status in elderly persons: Practical and methodological issues in using the SF-36 health survey. *The Gerontological Society of America, 36*(5), 571-583.

McHorney, C. A., Ware, J. E., Jr., Lu, J. F., & Sherbourne, C. D. (1994). The MOS 36-item Short-Form Health Survey (SF-36): III. Tests of data quality, scaling assumptions, and reliability across diverse patient groups. *Medical Care, 32*(1), 40-66.

Miller, T. Q., Markides, K. S., & Black, S. A. (1997). The factor structure of the CES-D in two surveys of elderly Mexican Americans. *Journals of Gerontology. Series B, Psychological Sciences and Social Sciences, 52*(5), S259-S269.

Oksenberg, L., Cannell, C., & Kalton, G. (1991). New strategies for pretesting survey questions. *Journal of Official Statistics, 7*(3), 349-365.

Patrick, D. L., Wild, D. J., Johnson, E. S., Wagner, T. H., & Martin, M. A. (1994). Cross-Cultural Validation of Quality of Life Measures. In J. Orley & W. Kuyken (Eds.), *Quality of life assessment : International perspectives* (pp. 19-32). Proceedings of the joint-meeting organized by the World Health Organization and the Foundation IPSEN in Paris, July 2-3, 1993. Berlin; New York: Springer-Verlag.

Radloff, L. S. (1977). The CES-D scale: A self-report depression scale for research in the general population. *Applied Psychological Measurement, 1*(3), 385-401.

Ren, X. S., Amick, B. I., Zhou, L., & Gandek, B. (1998). Translation and psychometric evaluation of a Chinese version of the SF-36 health survey in the United States. *Clinical Epidemiology, 51*(11), 1129-1138.

Reuben, D. B., Valle, L. A., Hays, R. D., & Siu, A. L. (1995). Measuring physical function in community-dwelling older persons: A comparison of self-administered, interviewer-administered, and performance-based measures. *Journal of the American Geriatrics Society, 43*(1), 17-23.

Sherbourne, C. D., & Meredith, L. S. (1992). Quality of self-report data: A comparison of older and younger chronically ill patients. *Journal of Gerontology, 47*(4), S204-S211.

Stewart, A. L., & Nápoles-Springer, A. M. (2000). Health-related quality of life assessments in diverse population groups in the United States. *Medical Care, 38*(9), Supplement II, II-102 - II-124.

Sudman, S., Bradburn, N. M., & Schwarz, N. (1996). *Thinking about answers: The application of cognitive processes to survey methodology.* San Francisco, CA: Jossey-Bass, Inc.

Sudman, S., Warnecke, R., Johnson, T., O'Rourke, D., & Davis, A. M. (1994). *Cognitive aspects of reporting cancer prevention examinations and tests* (Series 6, No. 7). Hyattsville, MD: National Center for Health Statistics, Public Health Service.

Teresi, J. A. (1994). Overview of methodological issues in gerontological and geriatric Measurement. In M. P. Lawton & J. A. Teresi (Eds.), *Annual Review of Gerontology and Geriatrics* (Vol. 14, pp. 1-22). New York: Springer Publishing Company.

U.S. Census Bureau. (1999). *Population Projections of the United States by Age, Sex, Race, and Hispanic Origin: 1995 to 2050; [Online]. Available: www.census.gov/ prod/www/titles.html#popest>.*

Vega, W. A., & Rumbaut, R. G. (1991). Ethnic minorities and mental health. *Annual Review of Sociology, 17*, 351-383.

Warnecke, R. B., Johnson, T. P., Chavez, N., Sudman, S., O'Rourke, D. P., Lacey, L., & Horm, J. (1997). Improving question wording in surveys of culturally diverse populations. *Annals of Epidemiology, 7*(5), 334-342.

Wolinsky, F. D., & Stump, T. E. (1996). A measurement model of the Medical Outcomes Study 36-Item Short-Form Health Survey in a clinical sample of disadvantaged, older, Black, and White men and women. *Medical Care, 34*(6), 537-548.

Acknowledgments. Work on this project was supported by the Resource Center on Minority Aging Research program, funded by the National Institute on Aging (P30 AG15272), the National Institute of Nursing Research, and the Office of Research on Minority Health. We are grateful for the valuable comments of anonymous reviewers and the editors.

Part V
Religiosity & Ethnicity

13

Advances in the Measurement of Religiosity Among Older African Americans: Implications for Health and Mental Health Researchers

Linda M. Chatters, Robert Joseph Taylor,
Karen D. Lincoln

T he past decade has witnessed major growth in research on the significance and functional roles of religion in the lives of the elderly (Levin & Chatters, 1998a). Although still evolving, a systematic body of research findings (Chatters, 2000; Ellison & Levin, 1998; Levin & Chatters, 1998a) suggests that religion is positively associated with a variety of psychosocial factors and physical and mental health outcomes, including various indicators of morbidity, disability, mortality (Bryant & Rakowski, 1992; Colantonio, Kasl, & Ostfeld, 1992; Craigie, Larson, & Lieu, 1990; Dwyer, Clarke, & Miller, 1990; Ferraro & Albrecht-Jensen, 1991; Hummer, Rogers, Nam, & Ellison, 1999; Idler & Kasl, 1997; Kark, Shemi, Friendlander, Martin, & Blondheim, 1996; Kennedy, Kelman, Thomas, & Chen, 1996; Koenig, George, & Peterson, 1998; Koenig et al., 1997; Krause, 1998a,b; Larson et al., 1989; Larson et al., 1992; Levin & Schiller, 1987; Levin & Markides, 1985, 1986, 1988; Levin, Markidos, & Ray, 1996; Meador et al., 1992; Musick, 1996; Strawbridge et al., 1997; Wright, Frost, & Wisecarver, 1993) and perceptions of well-being (Levin & Chatters, 1998a,b; Levin & Tobin, 1996). Taken as a whole, the research literature suggests that religious factors bear an important and largely beneficial connection with a variety of mental and physical health measures. Better physical and mental health status is moderately associated with higher levels of religious involvement, even when defined by numerous indicators and examined within diverse groups (i.e., as defined by clinical disorder, gender, age cohort, denomination, race/ethnicity, social class) within the population (Ellison & Levin, 1998; Levin et al., 1996; Matthews et al., 1998). In addition, several studies indicate that religious involvement is associated with better outcomes for persons who are recovering from physical and mental illnesses (Koenig et al., 1997; Oxman et al., 1995; Pressman et al., 1990; Propst et al., 1992).

The health and medical sciences have begun to address religious and spiritual concerns in clinical care and as a way to understand a range of health-related behaviors, attitudes, and beliefs. Further, health education and health promotion efforts are increasingly attentive to spirituality and spiritual well-being as important components of an individual's overall health (Bensley, 1991; Diaz, 1993; Waite, Hawks, & Gast, 1999). Finally, in various areas of clinical practice, there is growing recognition that religion and spirituality may hold distinct therapeutic benefits for persons whose health is compromised (Bearon & Koenig, 1990; Koenig, 1998).

Persistent questions remain, however, concerning key conceptual, methodological and analytic issues that complicate attempts to gain a clear understanding of the exact nature of the functional mechanisms underlying these relationships (Chatters, 2000; Ellison & Levin, 1998; Levin & Chatters, 1998a) and efforts to appreciate the varied meanings and purposes of religion in relation to issues of health. Currently, no single index or scale of religion/spirituality is recognized as the gold standard that adequately represents the construct of religiosity. Given the variety of religious/spiritual phenomena and the recognized complexity of their diverse relationships to physical and mental health outcomes, a meaningful scale of this sort is not feasible (Fetzer Institute NIA Report, 1999). However, significant progress has been made with respect to the conceptual meanings, methods, and analytic approaches that are best suited to study these relationships. Current programmatic efforts in this area demonstrate greater clarity in defining the nature and boundaries of relevant content areas (e.g., conceptual definitions, multidimensionality) and careful consideration to the research methodologies and procedures (e.g., measurement, sampling, study design) that are appropriate to these questions. These programs of research are involved in developing conceptually based and empirically validated measures of religious involvement for use in health research, in conjunction with developing and testing explicit theoretical linkages connecting religious phenomena and diverse health outcomes (Chatters, 2000; Ellison & Levin, 1998; Fetzer Institute NIA Report, 1999; Idler & George, 1998).

This chapter has several purposes. First, it provides a brief overview of research on religious involvement among older African Americans. Second, a description of conceptualization and measurement issues is provided, with a particular focus on the multidimensionality of religious phenomena. Third, ongoing programs of research are described that focus on the development of conceptually based, empirically validated measures of religious involvement for use in health research. Several dimensions of religious involvement are discussed as they pertain to the measurement of religious involvement, among specifically older African Americans. Finally, the chapter closes with a discussion of the implications of these developments for health and mental health research among older African Americans and future research directions. With respect to terminology, religion and religious involvement are used interchangeably in this chapter to indicate these phenomena in a general sense, while specific designations refer to discrete forms of religious expression (e.g., prayer, service attendance). Given the range of topics addressed in this literature, this chapter is merely representative in its coverage; a number of reviews of this literature provide a more comprehensive survey of research in this area (Chatters, 2000; Levin, 1994; Levin, Chatters, Ellison, & Taylor, 1996; Levin & Vanderpool, 1992; Pargament, 1997).

RELIGIOUS INVOLVEMENT AMONG
OLDER AFRICAN AMERICANS

Research on religious involvement documents that Black Americans generally, and older Black adults in particular, are invested in and committed to religious pursuits (Chatters & Taylor, 1989; Chatters, Taylor & Lincoln, 1999; Ellison & Sherkat, 1995; Levin & Taylor, 1993; Taylor, 1988a, 1988b; Taylor & Chatters, 1991a) as indicated across a variety of religious indicators, including church membership rates, frequency of public behaviors (e.g., church attendance), private devotional practices (e.g., prayer and reading religious materials), and subjective appraisals of religiosity and spirituality. In addition, race comparative analyses among older adults (Levin, Taylor, & Chatters, 1994) and adults (Taylor, Chatters, Jayakody, & Levin, 1996) indicate that African Americans are more religious than Whites from comparable social backgrounds, for both public and private involvement (e.g., church attendance, frequency of prayer). Within the Black population, there is evidence of significant variation in religious involvement, suggesting that religious concerns may be differentially important for particular segments of this population (e.g., older persons).

Investigations of religion, health, and well-being have typically focused on the general population. A small body of research, however, documents the specific health benefits of religious involvement for African Americans. Work in this area finds a beneficial effect of religious involvement on distress and depression (Brown, Ndubuisi, & Gary, 1990; Brown, Gary, Greene, & Milburn, 1992; Ellison, 1995; Ellison, Levin & Taylor, 1997; Musick, Koenig, Hays, & Cohen, 1998), subjective health (Musick, 1996), mortality risk (Bryant & Rakowski, 1992) and life satisfaction and other measures of psychological well-being (Ellison & Gay, 1990; Levin, & Chatters, 1998b; Levin, Chatters, & Taylor, 1995; Levin & Taylor, 1998;

Oretega, Crutchfield, & Rushing, 1983; St. George & McNamara, 1984; Thomas & Holmes, 1992). In addition, religious involvement among African Americans is inversely related to negative health behaviors, such as alcohol use/abuse and smoking (Ahmed, Brown, Gary, & Saadatmand, 1994; Brown & Gary, 1994; Krause, 1991; Wallace & Forman, 1998).

CONCEPTUALIZATION AND MEASUREMENT ISSUES

One of the most fundamental and difficult issues in this field concerns the conceptualization and measurement of religion and religious involvement. Pargament (1997), in defining religion as ". . a process, the search for significance in ways related to the sacred" (p. 32), incorporates both the substantive content (e.g., beliefs, practices, feelings directed toward God) and the functional aspects (e.g., a process focused on questions of ultimate meaning and concern) of religious phenomena. For well over 20 years, researchers in the social and behavioral sciences have defined religious involvement as comprising multiple dimensions that reflect behavioral (i.e., public and private) and subjective (i.e., attitude, belief and experience) dimensions (Chatters, Levin, & Taylor, 1992; Ellison, 1994; Idler & George, 1998; Krause, 1993; Levin, Chatters, & Taylor, 1995; Pargament, 1997; Schiller & Levin, 1988; Williams, 1994). The behavioral component refers to activities that involve organizational or public religious expression (e.g., denominational affiliation, religious service attendance), as well as private activities or nonorganizational practices that are performed independently of formal religious institutions (e.g., private prayer, devotional reading). On the other hand, attitudes, experiences, self-perceptions and attributions that involve religious or spiritual content (e.g., religious identity, feelings of closeness to God) are designated as subjective dimensions of religious involvement (Levin, Taylor, & Chatters, 1995; Williams, 1994).

Despite advances in the conceptualization and measurement of religious involvement (Ainlay & Smith, 1984; Chatters et al., 1992; Chatters & Taylor, 1989; Matthews et al., 1998; Mindel & Vaughan, 1978), some studies continue to use church attendance as the only indicator of religious involvement (see Kennedy et al., 1996 and editorial response by Packer, 1997). Research in the health and medical professions (e.g., psychiatry, social epidemiology, clinical medicine), in particular, often defines religious involvement with respect to behavioral measures of a single dimension (e.g., church attendance or denominational affiliation) and is based on samples from community and national probability surveys. This is particularly the case in studies investigating the independent effects of church attendance on mental health outcomes such as depression, anxiety, suicide, drug and alcohol abuse, and psychiatric care utilization (Gartner, Larson, & Allen, 1991). This practice disregards efforts to define and measure religious involvement comprehensively (i.e., as a multidimensional construct) and precludes the investigation of the distinct mechanisms through which religious effects influence diverse health outcomes

(Ellison, & Levin, 1998; Levin, Taylor, & Chatters, 1995; Levin & Vanderpool, 1987; Schiller & Levin, 1988; Williams, 1994).

Research in the psychology and sociology of religion, which is typically based on samples of college students or members of a single religious denomination (e.g., Presbyterians: King & Hunt, 1972; Mormons: Cornwall, 1989), examines religious involvement as a dependent variable. In this line of research, religiosity is defined in a very broad manner and may embody 10 or more dimensions and include up to 70 individual items (e.g., King & Hunt, 1969; 1972). Many of these scales have never been utilized beyond their initial introduction and most are self-administered (see Hill & Hood, 1999 for a detailed discussion of the reliability and validity of these scales). Further, many of these scales (King & Hunt, 1972) include items that are not measures of religiosity (e.g., "my life is full of joy and satisfaction," "my life is often empty and filled with despair," and are more appropriately classified as indicators of subjective well-being. Given the specialized samples on which the majority of this research is based and the arduous task demands of these scales, there are valid concerns as to the representativeness and validity of findings. For example, there may be selection factors operating whereby only extremely religious persons or those required to participate (e.g., psychology undergraduate students) would complete a battery of 50 to 70 items. The self-administration may be particularly problematic for elderly adults generally, and Black elderly in particular, who may suffer from vision and other serious health problems and reading difficulties. Finally, in terms of understanding religion-health relationships, the use of restrictive nonprobability samples obscures how social factors pattern religious involvement and, in turn, how discrete aspects of religiosity (e.g., attitudes, public versus private behaviors) operate with respect to health and well-being outcomes.

Excellent discussions of the theoretical and conceptual frameworks for under-standing religion's potential effects on health are available (Chatters, 2000; Ellison, 1994; Ellison & Levin, 1998; Idler & George, 1998). This work acknowl-edges that religion and health are multidimensional constructs and related to one another by means of several possible explanations and functional mechanisms (e.g., direct effects, mediated effects through other factors). Several broad categories of factors constitute potential links between religion and health, including: (a) specific lifestyle and health behaviors, including help-seeking (b) social re-sources, (c) coping resources and behaviors, (d) attitudes, beliefs, and emotional states and feelings, and (e) generalized beliefs about the world. Further, the meaning and relationships between religion and health factors potentially differ across defined population groups (e.g., race/ethnicity, age, social class), as well as within groups, regional variations among African Americans (Ellison & Levin, 1998).

MEASURE DEVELOPMENT EFFORTS

A number of recent investigations have examined various dimensions of religious involvement and their association with discrete health outcomes. Research in social gerontology has focused on the development of multidimensional, yet parsi-monious measures of religious involvement. A three-dimensional model of religious involvement, consisting of organizational, nonorganizational, and subjective religiosity, has been verified in several LISREL-based analyses on Black adults (Levin, Taylor, & Chatters, 1995) and older Blacks (Chatters, Levin, & Taylor, 1992) and in analyses of older Whites (Ainlay & Smith, 1984). Several programs of research on the conceptualization and measurement of religious involvement are currently under way that will hopefully yield conceptually based, empirically validated measures of religious involvement that are consequential for health and permit the investigation of the proximate causes and mechanisms that link religion and health (Ellison & Levin, 1998; Fetzer Institute/NIA, 1999; Idler & George, 1998).

Measurement development efforts by the Fetzer Institute/National Institute on Aging Working Group resulted in the development of a brief, multidimensional measure of religion/spirituality for use in health research (Fetzer Institute/NIA Report,1999). Initially, this work identified 12 domains of religious involvement that were thought to be significant for health outcomes; these domains were later used to develop the Brief Multidimensional Measure of Religiousness/Spirituality: 1999 (BMMRS). Several of these domains are well represented in existing research (e.g., religious preference, organizational religiousness, private religious practices, daily spiritual experiences, religious/spiritual coping, religious support). However, other domains have been identified as potentially important, but have not been extensively examined in research on religion and health (e.g., meaning, values, beliefs, forgiveness, religious/spiritual history, commitment). The BMMRS was included in the 1997-1998 General Social Survey; initial information on the psychometric properties of the measure verify the value of the multidimensional approach; further, the items formed reliable indices that were only moderately correlated with one another (Fetzer Institute/NIA,1999). With continued use and wider application in diverse samples, the BMMRS holds real promise for generating useful information on religion-health relationships.

This discussion, however, is not intended to be an assessment of the adequacy of the BMMRS for use among African American elderly. Instead, the following section briefly discusses several commonly employed domains and measures of religious involvement (which are represented in the BMMRS) and the conceptual and methodological challenges inherent in their use. In addition, a number of social context factors are discussed that may affect the general suitability of these religious involvement measures for use in samples of older African Americans.

DIMENSIONS OF RELIGIOUS INVOLVEMENT

Denomination

Of all the religious factors, denominational affiliation is seemingly one of the most reliable, valid, and straight-forward measures of religiosity. However, denominational designations introduce challenging conceptual and analytic issues. One approach that is commonly used in research employs broad denominational labels without consideration for acknowledged subgroups within major denominations that may differ with respect to belief, practice, and governance. For instance, traditional Black Baptists are organized in three main bodies—the National Baptist Convention of the U.S.A., Inc., the National Baptist Convention of America, and the Progressive National Baptist Convention, Inc. Further, anecdotal evidence indicates that there is major variation across Black Baptist congregations within the same convention, with some churches exhibiting more conservative, "Pentecostal-style" services and theology, while others display more liberal and progressive orientations. Given that over half of Black Americans report Baptist affiliation, it is likely that there are within-denomination differences along these and other relevant dimensions (e.g., region, socioeconomic status). In sum, broad denominational classifications that are taken at face value may conceal important within-group variability in beliefs, practices, and institutional structures (Ellison, 1999; Woodberry & Smith, 1998). Of particular significance for religion-health research, there may be important differences across denominations in the centrality and meaning of various types of religious phenomena (e.g., ritual, scripture, direct spiritual experience) and their relationships to physical and mental health outcomes (Levin & Vanderpool, 1987).

Open-ended items or an expanded checklist can be used to maximize the amount of information about denominational affiliation (Ellison, 1999). However, the large number of recognized religious denominations that is generated is often unmanageable and poses difficulties in multivariate analyses. This problem can be addressed in situations where denominational information is fairly well specified, in which constellations of religious factors (e.g., belief systems, congregational climate, worship styles, organizational structures) are created that differentiate broad religious cultures (e.g., mainline Protestant, conservative Protestant). These classifications effectively cluster different denominations into distinctive and meaningful categories which then serve as proxies for the relevant underlying traits or beliefs (see, for example, Ellison, Gay, & Glass, 1989; Ellison & George, 1994; and Ellison & Sherkat, 1993). This approach, however, is not without problems (see Woodberry & Smith, 1998, for a discussion) in that religious groups that appear similar (e.g., beliefs, values and behaviors) could differ with respect to specific attitudes and behaviors (e.g., attitudes about use of professionals for mental health problems, abstinence from alcohol) and even theological beliefs and ritual practices (e.g., divine grace) that are critical for mental health and well-being. Finally, Ellison (1999) suggests that denominational affiliation (however measured) typically assesses identification with or closeness to a religious tradition. As such, it may not necessarily be an accurate measure of present membership or affiliation with a given group, which would require a more direct assessment.

Organizational Religious Participation

Organizational religious participation or public religious behavior (often measured as frequency of service attendance) is one of the most extensively studied dimensions of religious involvement. Organizational religiosity is generally a strong predictor of perceptions of well-being among African Americans (Levin, Chatters, & Taylor, 1995) and its effects appear to be greater among those residing in the South and for older persons (Ellison & Gay, 1990). Despite the seemingly straightforward nature of this construct, there are important conceptual and measurement issues. First, the meaning and place of formalized religious activities (e.g, church attendance) varies substantially across denominations. For example, on average, Catholics attend religious services more frequently than Protestants (Greeley, 1989) and religious services are held more frequently in Catholic churches (up to 12-15 times per week) than among Protestant churches. Further, weekly attendance may be normative for most Protestant groups, whereas more frequent attendance is often expected of Catholics (as well as some Conservative Protestant groups).

Recent research has questioned the accuracy of the standard measure of self-reported religious service attendance used in personal interviews. Hadaway, Marler and Chaves (1993) found that actual church attendance counts for 18 Protestant and Catholic churches in a county in Ohio were only half the level of attendance reported in surveys. The propensity to overreport frequency of service attendance in personal interviews is consistent with overreporting of other socially desirable activities such as voting and charitable contributions. A recent examination of social desirability bias in assessments of religious attendance (Presser & Stinson, 1998) found that time use questions (i.e., having respondents report everything that they did yesterday in chronological order) or self-administered questions tend to provide more accurate estimates of attendance than do standard frequency of religious service attendance items (i.e., personal interviews).

Nevertheless, for a number of empirical and practical reasons, the standard measure of service attendance is acceptable for use in most health and mental health surveys. Presser and Stinson (1998) report that the relationship between major demographic variables and service attendance is equivalent, regardless of whether frequency of attendance is assessed using the standard measure or a time-use item. We recommend that researchers interested in providing reliable national estimates of service attendance over time should incorporate time use items in their survey. However, researchers who are interested in service attendance solely as an independent variable and have time and budgetary constraints on the number of religious items that can be included in a survey, can utilize the standard measure.

A diverse set of measures of organizational religious participation (e.g., involvement in choirs, auxiliary groups, and various leadership positions) may provide a more accurate measure of degree of involvement in a religious organization. Alternative measures of organizational involvement could use assessments of the amount of time (hours per week) that individuals devote to organized religious activities. Measures of time usage, while common in sociology and economics, have rarely, if ever, been used in the measurement of religious participation. Assessments of the amount of time spent in organized activities provide a means of grounding these behavioral reports and are critical for understanding the meaning (i.e., time commitment) of organizational involvement. For instance, "weekly" attendance could involve a 5-8-hour commitment including Sunday school, the regular church service, dinner at the church, and an afternoon/evening program as opposed to a 1-hour service.

Finally, there are persistent difficulties in determining what exactly is being assessed by measures of organizational religious participation. Religious service attendance (and other forms of organizational religious participation) is potentially confounded by selection factors (e.g., functional health status, personality factors) that distort its relationship to mental health outcomes (e.g., depression). In research among older groups, in particular, religious service attendance (and other indicators of organizational participation), may partially function as a proxy for functional health status (i.e., persons who are generally in better health are more likely to attend services), suggesting the importance of controlling for the independent effects of functional health status. Similarly, a significant effect for service attendance (particularly involving comparisons across denominations) tells us little about the operational linkages to mental health outcomes. Organizational religious participation effects are more appropriately understood by examining constructs that are proximal to health outcomes (e.g., congregational climate, worship styles).

Nonorganizational Religious Involvement

This construct includes private religious behaviors that can be conducted outside of the context of an organization, such as reading religious materials (e.g., Bible, Koran), broadcast religious programming (e.g., radio and television), and private prayer. Nonorganizational religious participation is a critical dimension of religious involvement because it indicates the degree to which religiosity is an integral component of daily activities. Unlike organizational religious participation, persons with functional limitations can still engage in these activities. However, it is precisely due to this potential dynamic that observed relationships between nonorganizational religious involvement and health are complex and require careful interpretation. In cross-sectional analyses of older adults, higher levels of nonorganizational religious involvement may be associated with poorer physical and mental health status; suggesting that increased levels of nonorganizational religious practices are characteristic of persons who have reduced their organizational participation for reasons of poor health or disability; longitudinal designs are needed to accurately chart the relationships between nonorganizational religious participation and health outcomes (Levin, 1999).

Careful attention should also be paid to issues regarding literacy levels within a given group, the degree to which older African Americans use specifically written religious resources, and the overall patterns of use of various forms of nonorganizational practices and outlets. Analyses among older African Americans suggest that the likelihood of reading religious materials is positively related to income and educational levels (Taylor & Chatters, 1991b). Other sorts of sociodemographic factors (e.g., gender, region) may also be important in the patterns of nonorganizational religious involvement. Finally, the meaning and significance attached to these types of private religious behaviors is critically important. Different faith traditions and denominations may place greater or lesser emphasis on participation in various types of nonorganizational pursuits (e.g., prayer versus scripture reading). As with organizational religious practices, assessments of the amount of time devoted to these practices (i.e., time use data) and how this varies over time and in relation to specific personal circumstances and events (e.g., periods of sickness), may provide important insights as to the centrality of nonorganizational behaviors for particular health outcomes.

Prayer and Religious Coping

Prayer is a dimension of religious participation that is often designated as a type of nonorganizational religious activity. However, given the complexities of prayer and the significance of prayer experiences for many faiths and traditions, it is discussed here separately. Prayer is typically measured by simply assessing how frequently an individual reports praying during a given time period. While this approach is straightforward and easily administered, it fails to capture the context of prayer and its different elements and the reasons why individuals engage in prayer. Poloma and Gallup (1991) operationalized four dimensions of prayer: (a) ritual prayer includes reciting memorized prayers, (b) conversational prayer can be characterized as informal talks with God, (c) petitionary prayer involves specific material or spiritual requests, and (d) meditative prayer includes quietly thinking about or worshiping God (see Levin & Taylor, 1997 for a recent analysis of the correlates of prayer).

Although writings about African American religious experiences and traditions provide detailed accounts of religious coping (Lincoln & Mamiya, 1990), these topics have received little systematic empirical attention. For example, there is surprisingly little research in psychiatric epidemiology and the general mental health literature on religious coping, perhaps due to longstanding skepticism that these concerns are relevant for mental health practice (Chatters, 2000). Several ongoing programs of research (Ellison & Taylor, 1996; Koenig, Smiley, & Gonzales, 1988; Pargament, 1997) however, have directly examined these topic areas and found that they are significant for understanding how individuals, particularly older African Americans, cope with life adversities, including mental and physical health difficulties.

Several research studies indicate that prayer is an important form of coping among African Americans, particularly for women and persons who were coping with a health problem (Ellison & Taylor, 1996). In a comparative analysis, Levin and Taylor (1997) found that African Americans, older persons, and women pray on a more frequent basis than do their counterparts. Reasons for prayer were diverse and included endorsement of worldview/beliefs that favor frequent prayer, relevant prior experiences emphasizing prayer as a means to make connections to God or the spiritual world, and current social group memberships in which frequent prayer is normative. This work suggests that in addition to asking respondents about frequency of prayer, it is important to inquire about their beliefs concerning the importance of religious coping, under what circumstances they have used religious coping, whether religious coping is used in conjunction with other forms of coping, and if other types of religious coping are employed, in addition to prayer (Chatters, 2000).

Church-Based Informal Support

Programmatic research on the informal support networks of African Americans has investigated the use of church members as sources of assistance and issues such as size of the church member network, frequency of interaction with church members, type of support that church members provide to each other (both emotional and tangible), and support reciprocity (Ellison & George, 1994; Taylor & Chatters, 1986a, 1986b, 1988). As noted previously, distinctive norms and functions of religious groups and participant similarity on relevant social, belief and attitudinal factors may facilitate the provision of support and enhance perceptions of assistance in ways that contribute to positive perceptions of support (e.g., support satisfaction and anticipated assistance).

These initial background findings are suggestive of a number of important measurement concerns in relation to church support. First, research and measurement strategies for church support have typically focused on providing a general profile of the social determinants, types, and overall patterns of supportive exchanges, while relatively less attention was paid to the consequences of supportive relationships. Church support relationships might be profitably examined in relation to issues of support mobilization in response to emergent life problems or as a form of religious coping. In this way, more direct attention can be paid to issues of the specific conditions under which support is offered (e.g., reciprocity, helper orientations) and their potential associations with the efficacy of these exchanges and recipient satisfaction.

Second, with few exceptions, research in this area has focused on the presumed positive aspects of church support (Ellison & Levin, 1998). Recent research in both the general social support (Ingersoll-Dayton, Morgan & Antonucci, 1997; Krause, 1995; Rook, 1984) and the congregation-based support literatures (Krause, Chatters, Meltzer, & Morgan, 2000; Krause, Ellison, & Wulff, 1998) have explored the negative aspects of social relationships. Research in this area generally focuses on problematic social relationships and negative interactions with members of an individual's social network. With regards to congregational settings, feelings of being unwelcome, embarrassment, invasions of privacy, and criticism and gossip are the types of negative interactions that can undermine psychological well-being. Other aspects of problematic social relationships include the sense of burden (both time and money) that individuals may have when they feel overcommitted to interpersonal activities. Krause and colleagues (Krause, Ellison, & Wulff, 1998) found that among a sample of Presbyterians, negative interaction among church members significantly reduced psychological well-being. In another recent article Krause and colleagues (Krause, Chatters, Meltzer, & Morgan, 2000) provide a focus group analysis of negative interaction among church members. This article, one of the most extensive investigations in this area to date, suggests that interpersonal problems with fellow church members, conflict between church members and their pastors and conflict over church doctrine are some of the problematic personal interactions that arise in religious settings.

Assistance From Ministers

Finally, as part of a general strategy to assess church-based assistance, it is important to determine when and how individuals seek assistance from the clergy (e.g., ministers, pastors) and for what types of problems (Neighbors, Musick, & Williams, 1998). For example, individuals may seek out clergy for assistance with basic problems of daily life (e.g., family relations, acute illness), but may be more reluctant to approach clergy for more serious problems that involve some degree of stigma (e.g., mental illness, domestic violence). There are undoubtedly individual differences in the willingness to seek aid from the clergy that may be associated with basic social categories (e.g., age and gender status) and/or with differences in relation to religious orientation and commitments. It is also important to assess the specific types of assistance that clergy provide, whether assistance from other sources (i.e., health and mental health professionals) is also solicited, and whether assistance from ministers is viewed as useful in addressing the problem.

IMPLICATIONS FOR HEALTH AND MENTAL HEALTH RESEARCHERS

One of the limitations of many large-scale surveys of health and mental health is the lack of sufficient measures of religiosity. Most large-scale national surveys include only two or three items tapping religious involvement. For instance, the major aging (Health and Retirement—AHEAD) and mental health (National Survey of Health and Stress) surveys each only have one or two religious items (i.e., denomination, attendance). Obviously, this is insufficient to measure the construct of religiosity and has lead to many of the measurement difficulties (i.e., overreliance upon church attendance) discussed here.

The challenge for health and mental health researchers is to decide how many items within identified domains are necessary to adequately measure religiosity. These measurement considerations must be balanced against the various time and budgetary constraints of adding items to a major survey. We recommend, at a minimum, the inclusion of measures of denomination, organizational, nonorganizational and subjective religiosity in any set of items measuring religiosity. Measures of religious coping should also be included with any coping checklist. We also recommend use of the Brief Multidimensional Measure of Religiousness/Spirituality: 1999 (BMMRS) as a starting point for items on religiosity (Fetzer Institute/NIA Report, 1999). This measure was created by some of the leading experts in the field of religion, health and aging and is already being widely used by a variety of health and mental health researchers.

Presently, it is difficult to determine the degree to which established measures of religiosity are equally valid for older Blacks and Whites. There are simply too few investigations of the psychometric properties of these measures within samples that provide adequate representation of older Blacks and Whites. Research indicates that Blacks report higher levels of religious participation than do Whites (Taylor et al., 1996). Overall, though, the patterns of findings with respect to antecedent factors (e.g., age, gender, SES) are similar across racial groups. For these reasons, we speculate that the basic measures of religious participation are valid for both Blacks and Whites. Religiosity is intertwined with factors such as culture, race, ethnicity, denomination and social class. Consequently, without adequate and representative samples of both Blacks and Whites, it is difficult to determine valid race effects for religious participation.

On a substantive level, there are reasons to suspect that the nature and functions of religious involvement for Blacks and Whites may differ qualitatively. Both historical and ethnographic investigations of religious involvement within African American communities point to the distinctive roles of Black religion and religious institutions for improving the social, emotional, psychological and spiritual well-being of Black Americans (Frazier, 1974; Lincoln & Mamiya, 1990; Taylor, Thornton, & Chatters, 1987). This includes the operation of social networks and supportive exchanges within churches, the beneficial aspects of individual and group religious worship, and the use of religious coping strategies and resources (Chatters, 2000).

Clearly, these features of religious involvement and participation characterize White religious expression as well. However, African Americans historically have encountered significant racial and economic discrimination and had limited access to institutions and resources (e.g., medical, educational) within secular realms. As a consequence, the Black church has been pivotal in addressing pressing economic, political, and social welfare needs of Black individuals, families, and communities. Similarly, Black religious institutions have framed distinctive theologies and religious discourses that address the ongoing problems of alienation and marginalization, racial discrimination, and the pursuit of social and economic justice. Black churches and religious thought uniquely address the emotional, psychological and spiritual needs of individuals suffering from varying levels of disenfranchisement.

Finally, it is important to acknowledge that under particular circumstances, there may be points of convergence with respect to Black and White religious involvement and commitment. In particular, social class, denominational affiliations (e.g., Baptists, Conservative Protestants) and regional distinctions (i.e., the South) may function in such a manner that Blacks and Whites within these categories are more similar than they are different in terms of their religious orientations. Information on religious commitment from large, representative samples of Black Americans will help us understand the antecedents and consequences of religious involvement (independent of the effects of other social status characteristics), as well as the extent to which Black religious expression embodies a distinctive viewpoint.

A number of current research efforts are attempting to understand the nature and consequences of religious involvement for African Americans. The authors of this article are actively engaged in two investigations that attempt to gain a better understanding of the effectiveness of measures of religiosity in accurately representing the religious experiences of Black Americans. One study uses a focus group methodology to explore the nature and functions of religious participation among Black Americans, with a specific emphasis on religious coping efforts (Taylor, Neighbors, & Chatters, 1998). Respondents were assigned to focus groups that were stratified by age (18-54 years vs. 55 years and older) and gender (i.e., older women, older men, younger women, younger men) to investigate the potential influence these factors may have on the nature and functions of religious involvement. The second study investigates the religious experiences of elderly Whites and Blacks (Krause, Chatters, Meltzer, & Morgan, 2000). Again, focus groups were stratified, this time by race (i.e., White versus Black), in order to investigate the potentially different ways that respondents of different groups describe their religious experiences. Ongoing work using the initial data from the focus groups is currently focused on developing religious involvement items for use in community surveys of Black and White elderly.

SUMMARY AND CONCLUSIONS

Research on religion and health has benefited from a long tradition of research and writing on African American religious traditions and experiences, as well as early interest in these topics within the field of social gerontology. The combined influences of these research traditions has shaped not only a basic appreciation of the diverse nature of religious phenomena, but also an understanding of the importance of social factors (e.g., race/culture, age status) for the meaning and patterns of religious involvement. Over the past several years there have been significant advances in the measurement of religious involvement. These improvements have directly informed and furthered efforts to investigate religion-health relationships within diverse groups of the population, including older African Americans. Recent programmatic efforts reflect greater clarity in defining religious involvement (e.g., conceptual definitions, multidimensionality) and the research methodologies and procedures (e.g., measurement, sampling, study design) used to investigate these questions. In addition, current research efforts are focused on developing conceptually based and empirically validated measures of religious involvement and testing explicit theoretical models that link religious involvement and mental and physical health outcomes.

These ongoing efforts will significantly advance knowledge concerning the measurement and meanings of religious involvement within diverse populations. However, consideration of several methodological issues and concerns will further capitalize on these measurement developments. First, it is important to recognize that the types of relationships between religion and health that are of interest to researchers are best examined using longitudinal analyses. At present, the field is dominated by studies that are based on cross-sectional data. Longitudinal analyses will address issues of change in mental and physical health outcomes that occur as a consequence of religious involvement and help to resolve a number of seeming paradoxes in these associations (Levin & Taylor, 1998). Second, the interpretation of religion and health relationships should give careful consideration to the possible impact of social and demographic factors that are known to be associated with both religious factors and mental health and which may be differentially distributed within diverse populations. For example, differences in the age or gender compositions of study samples may have an impact on levels of overall religious involvement, as well as the presence and strength of observed associations between religion and health measures.

Overall, the current state of the art in the measurement of religious involvement points to the emergence of more rigorous and systematic programs of research that will enhance our understanding of the meaning of religion across diverse population groups. Owing to the important contributions of research and writings on older and minority populations in the development of this work, this research promises to extend our understanding of the measurement of religion and the nature of religion-health relationships among older African Americans. A continued focus on issues of multiple dimensions of religious involvement, subgroup variations, research methodologies and procedures, and the development and testing of explicit theoretical linkages between religion and mental and physical health outcomes will assure the development of valid, reliable and conceptually relevant measures of religious involvement.

REFERENCES

Ainlay, S. C., & Smith, D. R. (1984). Aging and religious participation. *Journal of Gerontology, 39*, 357-363.

Ahmed, F., Brown, D. R., Gary, L. E., & Saadatmand, F. (1994). Religious predictors of cigarette smoking: Findings from African American women of childbearing age. *Behavioral Medicine, 20,* 34-43.

Bearon, L. B., & Koenig, H. G. (1990). Religion cognitions and use of prayer in health and illness. *The Gerontologist, 30,* 249-53.

Bensley, R. J. (1991). Defining spiritual health: A review of the literature. *Journal of Health Education, 22,* 287-90.

Brown, D. R., & Gary, L. E. (1994). Religious involvement and health status among African-American males. *Journal of the National Medical Association, 86,* 825-831.

Brown, D. R., Gary, L. E., Greene, A. D., & Milburn, N. G. (1992). Patterns of social affiliation as predictors of depressive symptoms among urban Blacks. *Journal of Health & Social Behavior, 33,* 242-253.

Brown, D. R., Ndubuisi, S. C., & Gary, L. E. (1990). Religiosity and psychological distress among Blacks. *Journal of Religion and Health, 29,* 55-68.

Bryant, S., & Rakowski, W. (1992). Predictors of mortality among elderly African Americans. *Research on Aging, 14,* 50-67.

Chatters, L. M. (2000). Religion and health: Public health research and practice. *Annual Review of Public Health, 21,* 335-367.

Chatters, L. M., Levin, J. S., & Taylor, R. J. (1992). Antecedents and dimensions of religious involvement among older Black adults. *Journals of Gerontology: Social Sciences, 47,* S269-S278.

Chatters, L. M., & Taylor, R. J. (1989). Age differences in religious participation among Black adults. *Journals of Gerontology: Social Sciences, 44,* S183-S189.

Chatters, L. M., Taylor, R. J., & Lincoln, K. D. (1999). African American religious participation: A multi-sample comparison. *Journal for the Scientific Study of Religion, 38,* 132-145.

Colantonio, A., Kasl, S. V., & Ostfeld, A. M. (1992). Depression symptoms and other psychosocial factors as predictors of stroke in the elderly. *American Journal of Epidemiology, 136,* 884-94.

Cornwall, M. (1989). The determinants of religious behavior: A theoretical model and empirical test. *Social Forces, 68,* 572-592.

Craigie, F. C., Larson, D. B., & Lieu, I. Y. (1990). References to religion in the journal family practice: Dimensions and valence of spirituality. *Journal of Family Practice, 30,* 477-80.

Diaz, D. P. (1993). Foundations for spirituality: Establishing the viability of spirituality within the health disciplines. *Journal of Health Education, 24,* 324-26.

Dwyer, J. W., Clarke, L. L., & Miller, M. K. (1990). The effect of religious concentration and affiliation on county cancer mortality rates. *Journal of Health and Social Behavior, 31,* 185-202.

Ellison, C. G. (1994). Religion, the life-stress paradigm, and the study of depression. In J. S. Levin (Ed.), *Religion and aging and health: Theoretical foundations and methodological frontiers* (pp. 78-121). Thousand Oaks, CA: Sage.

Ellison, C. G. (1995). Race, religious involvement and depressive symptomatology in a southeastern U. S. community. *Social Science & Medicine, 40*, 1561-1572.

Ellison, C. G. (1999). Religious preference. In *Multidimensional measurement of religiousness/spirituality for use in health research* (pp. 81-84). Kalamazoo, MI: Fetzer Institute.

Ellison, C. G., & Gay, D. A. (1990). Region, religious commitment, and life satisfaction among Black Americans. *Sociological Quarterly, 31,* 123-147.

Ellison, C. G., Gay, D. A., & Glass, T. A. (1989). Does religious commitment contribute to individual life satisfaction? *Social Forces, 68,* 100-123.

Ellison, C. G., & George, L. K. (1994). Religious involvement, social ties, and social support in a southeastern community. *Journal for the Scientific Study of Religion, 33,* 46-61.

Ellison, C. G., & Levin, J. S. (1998). The religion-health connection: Evidence, theory and future directions. *Health, Education & Behavior, 25,* 700-720.

Ellison, C. G., Levin, J. S., & Taylor, R. J. (1997). *Religious involvement and psychological distress in a national panel study of African Americans.* Paper presented at the joint meetings of the Society for the Scientific Study of Religion and the Religious Research Association, San Diego, CA.

Ellison, C. G., & Sherkat, D. E. (1995). The "semi-involuntary institution" revisited: Regional variations in church participation among Black Americans. *Social Forces, 73,* 1415-1437.

Ellison, C. G., & Sherkat, D. E. (1993). Conservative protestantism and support for corporal punishment. *American Sociological Review, 58,* 131-144.

Ellison, C. G., & Taylor, R. J. (1996). Turning to prayer: Social and situational antecedents of religious coping among African Americans. *Review of Religious Research, 38,* 111-131.

Ferraro, K. F., & Albrecht-Jensen, C. M. (1991). Does religion influence adult health? *Journal for the Scientific Study of Religion, 30,* 193-202.

Fetzer Institute/NIA Report. (1999). *Multidimensional measurement of religiousness/spirituality for use in health research.* Kalamazoo, MI: John E. Fetzer Publication.

Frazier, E. F. (1974). *The Negro church in America.* New York: Schocken Books.

Gartner, J. D., Larson, D. B., & Allen, G. D. (1991). Religious commitment and mental health: A review of the empirical literature. *Journal of Psychology and Theology, 19,* 6-25.

Greeley, A. M. (1989). *Religious change in America.* Cambridge, MA: Harvard University Press.

Hadaway, K., Marler, P., & Chaves, M. (1993). What the polls don't show: A closer look at U. S. church attendance. *American Sociological Review, 58,* 741-752.

Hill, P. C., & Hood, R. W., Jr. (1999). *Measures of religiosity*. Birmingham, AL: Religious Education Press.

Hummer, R. A., Rogers, R. G., Nam, C. B., & Ellison. C. G. (1999). Religious involvement and U. S. adult mortality. *Demography, 36,* 273-85.

Idler, E. L., & George, L. K. (1998). What sociology can help us understand about religion and mental health. In H. G. Koenig (Ed.), *Handbook of religion and mental health* (pp. 22-29). San Diego, CA: Academic Press.

Idler, E. L., & Kasl, S. V. (1997). Religion among disabled and nondisabled persons II: Attendance at religious services as predictors of the course of disability. *Journals of Gerontology: Social Sciences, 52B,* S306-S316.

Ingersoll-Dayton, B., Morgan, D., & Antonucci, T. C. (1997). The effects of positive and negative social exchanges on aging adults. *Journals of Gerontology: Social Sciences, 52B(4),* S190-S199.

Kark, J. D., Shemi, G., Friendlander, Y., Martin, O., & Blondheim, S. H. (1996). Does religious observance promote health? Mortality in secular and religious kibbutzim in Israel. *American Journal of Public Health, 86,* 3431-3446.

Kennedy, G. J., Kelman, H. R., Thomas, C., & Chen, J. (1996). The relation of religious preference and practice to depressive symptoms among 1,855 older adults. *Journals of Gerontology B: Psychological Sciences, 51,* P301-P308.

King, M. B., & Hunt, R. A. (1969). Measuring the religious variable: Amended findings. *Journal for the Scientific Study of Religion, 8,* 321-323.

King, M. B., & Hunt, R. A. (1972). Measuring the religious variable: Replication. *Journal for the Scientific Study of Religion, 11,* 240-251.

Koenig, H. G., Smiley, M., & Ganza, J. (1988). Religion, Health, and Aging. Westport, CT. Greenwood Press.

Koenig, H. G. (1998). Religious attitudes and practices of hospitalized medically ill older adults. *International Journal of Geriatric Psychiatry, 13,* 213-224.

Koenig, H. G., George, L. K., & Peterson, B. L. (1998). Religiosity and remission of depression in medically ill older patients. *American Journal of Psychiatry, 155,* 536-542.

Koenig, H. G., Hays, J. C., George, L. K., Blazer, D. G., Larson, D. B., & Landerman, L. R. (1997). Modeling the cross-sectional relationships between religion, physical health, social support, and depressive symptoms. *American Journal of Geriatric Psychology, 5,* 131-145.

Krause, N. (1991). Stress, religiosity, and abstinence from alcohol. *Psychology and Aging, 6,* 134-144.

Krause, N. (1993). Measuring religiosity in later life. *Research on Aging, 15,* 170-197.

Krause, N. (1995). Negative interaction and satisfaction with social support among older adults. *Journals of Gerontology: Psychological Sciences, 50B,* P59-P73.

Krause, N. (1998a). Neighborhood deterioration, religious coping, and changes in health during later life. *Gerontology, 38,* 653-664.

Krause, N. (1998b). Stressors in highly valued roles, religious coping, and mortality. *Psychology of Aging, 13,* 242-255.

Krause, N., Chatters, L. M., Meltzer, T., & Morgan, D. L. (2000). Negative interaction in the church: Insights from focus groups with older adults. *Review of Religious Research, 41*(4), 510-533.

Krause, N., Ellison, C. G., & Wulff, K. M. (1998). Church-based emotional support, negative interaction, and psychological well-being: Findings from a national sample of Presbyterians. *Journal for the Scientific Study of Religion, 37*(4), 725-741.

Larson, D. B., Koenig, H. G., Kaplan, B. H., Greenberg, R. F., Logue, E., & Tyroler, H. A. (1989). The impact of religion on blood pressure status in men. *Journal of Religion & Health, 28*, 265-278.

Larson, D. B., Sherrill, K. A., Lyons, J. S., Craigie, F. C. Jr., & Theilman, S. B. (1992). Associations between dimensions of religious commitment and mental health reported in the American Journal of Psychiatry and Archives of General Psychiatry: 1978-1989. *American Journal of Psychiatry, 149*, 557-559.

Levin, J. S. (1994). *Religion in aging and health: Theoretical foundations and methodological frontiers.* Thousand Oaks, CA: Sage Publications.

Levin, J. S. (1999). Private religious practices. In *Multidimensional measurement of religiousness/spirituality for use in health research* (pp. 39-42). Kalamazoo, MI: John E. Fetzer Publications.

Levin, J. S., & Chatters, L. M. (1998a). Research on religion and mental health: An overview of empirical findings and theoretical issues. In H. G. Koenig (Ed.), *Handbook of religion and mental health* (pp. 34-50). San Diego, CA: Academic Press.

Levin, J. S., & Chatters, L. M. (1998b). Religion, health, and psychological well-being in older adults: Findings from three national surveys. *Journal of Aging & Health, 10*, 504-31.

Levin, J. S., Chatters, L. M., & Taylor, R. J. (1995). Religious effects on health status and life satisfaction among Black Americans. *Journals of Gerontology: Social Sciences, 50B*, S154-S163.

Levin, J. S., Chatters, L. M., Ellison, C. G., & Taylor, R. J. (1996). Religious involvement, health outcomes, and public health practice. *Current Issues in Public Health, 2*, 220-225.

Levin, J. S., & Markides, K. S. (1985). Religion and health in Mexican Americans. *Journal of Religion & Health, 24*, 60-69.

Levin, J. S., & Markides, K, S. (1986). Religious attendance and subjective health. *Journal for the Scientific Study of Religion, 25*, 31-40.

Levin, J. S., & Markides, K. S. (1988). Religious attendance and psychological well-being in middle-aged and older Mexican Americans. *Sociological Analysis, 49*, 66-72.

Levin, J. S., Markides, K. S., & Ray, L. A. (1996). Religious attendance and psychological well-being in Mexican Americans: A panel analysis of three-generations data. *The Gerontologist, 36*, 454-463.

Levin, J. S., & Schiller, P. L. (1987). Is there a religious factor in health? *Journal of Religion & Health, 26,* 9-36.

Levin, J. S., & Taylor, R. J. (1997). Age differences in the patterns and correlates of the frequency of prayer. *The Gerontologist, 37,* 75-88.

Levin, J. S., & Taylor, R. J. (1993). Age and gender differences in religiosity over the life cycle among Black Americans. *The Gerontologist, 33,* 16-23.

Levin, J. S., & Taylor, R. J. (1998). Panel analysis of religious involvement and well-being in African-Americans: Contemporaneous vs. longitudinal effects. *Journal for the Scientific Study of Religion, 37,* 695-709.

Levin, J. S., Taylor, R. J., & Chatters, L. M. (1994). Race and gender differences in religiosity among older adults: Findings from four national surveys. *Journals of Gerontology: Social Sciences, 49,* S137-S145.

Levin, J. S., Taylor, R. J., & Chatters, L. M. (1995). A multidimensional measure of religious involvement for African Americans. *Sociological Quarterly, 36,* 901-919.

Levin, J. S., & Tobin, S. H. (1996). Religion and psychological well-being. In M. A. Kimble, S. H. McFadden, J. W. Ellor, & J. J. Seeber (Eds.), *Aging, spirituality, and religion: A handbook* (pp. 30-46). Minneapolis, MN: Fortress Press.

Levin, J. S., & Vanderpool, H. Y. (1987). Is frequent religious attendance really conducive to better health?: Toward an epidemiology of religion. *Social Science & Medicine, 24,* 589-600.

Levin, J. S., & Vanderpool, H. Y. (1992). Religious factors in physical health and the prevention of illness. In K. I. Pargament, K. I. Maton, & R. E. Hess (Eds.), *Religion and prevention in mental health: Research, vision, and action* (pp. 83-103). New York: Haworth.

Lincoln, C. E., & Mamiya, L. (1990). *The Black Church in the African American Experience.* Durham, NC: Duke.

Matthews, D. A., McCullough, M. E., Larson, D. B., Koenig, H. G., Swyers, J. P., & Milano, M. G. (1998). Religious commitment and health status. *Archives of Family Medicine, 7,* 118-24.

Meador, K. G., Koenig, H. G., Turnbull, J., Blazer, D. G., George, L. K., & Hughes, D. C. (1992). Religious affiliation and major depression. *Hospital & Community Psychiatry, 43,* 1204-1208.

Mindel, C. H., & Vaughan, C. E. (1978). A multidimensional approach to religiosity and disengagement. *Journals of Gerontology, 33,* 103-108.

Musick, M. A. (1996). Religion and subjective health among Black and White elders. *Journal of Health & Social Behavior, 37,* 221-37.

Musick, M. A., Koenig, H. G., Hays, J. C., & Cohen, H. J. (1998). Religious activity and depression among community-dwelling elderly persons with cancer: The moderating effect of race. *Journals of Gerontology: Social Sciences, 53B,* S218-S227.

Neighbors, H. W., Musick, M. A., & Williams, D. R. (1998). The African American minister as a source of help for serious personal crises: Bridge or barrier to mental health care? *Health, Education & Behavior, 25*(6), 759-777.

Ortega, S. T., Crutchfield, R. D., & Rushing, W. A. (1983). Race differences in elderly personal well-being. *Research on Aging, 4,* 101-117.

Oxman, T. E., Freedman, D. H., & Manheimer, E. D. (1995). Lack of social participation or religious strength and comfort as risk factors after cardiac surgery in the elderly. *Psychosomatic Medicine, 57,* 5-15.

Packer, S. (1997). Letter to the editor. *Journals of Gerontology: Psychological Sciences, 52B,* P156.

Pargament, K. I. (1997). *The psychology of religion and coping: Theory, research, practice.* New York: Guilford.

Poloma, M. M., & Gallup, G. H. (1991). *Varieties of prayer: A survey report.* Philadelphia, PA: Trinity Press International.

Presser, S., & Stinson, L. (1998). Data collectiion mode and social desirability in self-reported religiious attendance. *American Sociologist Review, 63*(1), 137-145.

Pressman, P., Lyons, J. S., Larson, D. B., & Strain, J. S. (1990). Religious beliefs, depression, and amputation status in elderly women with broken hips. *American Journal of Psychiatry, 147,* 758-60.

Propst, L. R., Ostrom, R., Watkins, P., Dean, T., & Mashburn, D. (1992). Comparative efficacy of religious and nonreligious cognitive-behavioral therapy for the treatment of clinical depression in religious individuals. *Journal of Consulting & Clinical Psychology, 60,* 94-103.

Rook, K. S. (1984). The negative side of social interaction: Impact on psychological well-being. *Journal of Personality and Social Psychology, 46*(5), 1097-1108.

Schiller, P. L., & Levin, J. S. (1988). Is there a religious factor in health care utilization: A review. *Social Science & Medicine, 27,* 1369-1379.

St. George, A., & McNamara, P. H. (1984). Religion, race, and psychological well-being. *Journal for the Scientific Study of Religion, 23,* 351-363.

Strawbridge, W. J., Cohen, R. D., Shema, S. J., & Kaplan, G. A. (1997). Frequent attendance at religious services and mortality over 28 years. *American Journal of Public Health, 87,* 957-961.

Taylor, R. J. (1988a). Correlates of religious noninvolvement among Black Americans. *Review of Religious Research, 30,* 126-139.

Taylor, R. J. (1988b). Structural determinants of religious participation among Black Americans. *Review of Religious Research, 30,* 114-125.

Taylor, R. J., & Chatters, L. M. (1986a). Church-based informal support among elderly Blacks. *The Gerontologist, 26,* 637-642.

Taylor, R. J., & Chatters, L. M. (1986b). Patterns of informal social support to elderly Black adults: Family, friends and church members. *Social Work, 31,* 432-438.

Taylor, R. J., & Chatters, L. M. (1988). Church members as a source of informal social support. *Review of Religious Research, 30,* 193-203.

Taylor, R. J., & Chatters, L. M. (1991a). Religious life of Black Americans. In J. S. Jackson (Ed.), *Life in Black America* (pp. 105-230). Newbury Park, CA: Sage.

Taylor, R. J., & Chatters, L. M. (1991b). Non-organizational religious participation among elderly Black adults. *Journals of Gerontology: Social Sciences, 46,* S103-S111.

Taylor, R. J., Chatters, L. M., Jayakody, R., & Levin, J. S. (1996). Black and White differences in religious participation: A multi-sample comparison. *Journal for the Scientific Study of Religion, 35,* 403-410.

Taylor, R. J., Thornton, M. C., & Chatters, L. M. (1987). Black Americans' perceptions of the socio-historical role of the church. *Journal of Black Studies, 18,* 123-38.

Taylor, R. J., Neighbors, H. W., & Chatters, L. M. (1998). Appraisals of religiosity, coping and church support. Research proposal submitted to the National Institute of Mental Health.

Thomas, M. E., & Holmes, B. J. (1992). Determinants of satisfaction for Blacks and Whites. *Sociological Quarterly, 33,* 459-472.

Waite, P. J., Hawks, S. R., & Gast, J. A. (1999). The correlation between spiritual well-being and health behaviors. *American Journal of Health Promotion, 13,* 159-62.

Wallace, J. M., Jr., & Forman, T. A. (1998). Religion's role in promoting health and reducing risk among American youth. *Health Education and Behavior, 25,* 721-741.

Williams, D. R. (1994). The measurement of religion in epidemiologic studies. In J. S. Levin (Ed.), *Religion in aging and health: Theoretical foundations and methodological frontiers* (pp. 125-48). Thousand Oaks, CA: Sage Publications.

Woodberry, R. D., & Smith, C. S. (1998). Fundamentalism et al.: Conservative protestants in America. *Annual Review of Sociology, 24,* 25-56.

Wright, L. S., Frost, C. J., & Wisecarver, S. J. (1993). Church attendance, meaningfulness of religion, and depressive symptomatology among adolescents. *Journal of Youth & Adolescence, 22,* 559-568.

Afterword

A Long-Range Innovative Approach to Reducing Health Disparities: The National Institute on Aging's Resource Centers for Minority Aging Research

Sidney M. Stahl

The health status of racial and ethnic groups in the U.S. has improved steadily over the last several decades. At the same time, however, health disparities between minority and non-minority groups have increased. As part of its mission to improve the health of older Americans, the National Institute on Aging (NIA) is committed to reducing this minority/non-minority differential and its social sequelae. Both the NIA Strategic Plan and the NIA Health Disparities Strategic Plan commit the Institute to reducing health disparities among older persons and to enhancing resources to support high-quality research by training and attracting a diverse work force. To these ends, NIA focuses research and training directly on identifying the determinants of health disparities and designing interventions to minimize these disparities. Disparity reduction is a long-term and multidisciplinary activity. Therefore, NIA initiated a program to reinforce the scientific infrastructure addressing health promotion, disease and disability prevention, the management of disease, and access to services for minority aging populations. NIA, with participation from the National Institute of Health's Office of Research on Minority Health and the National Institute of Nursing Research, funds six Resource Centers for Minority Aging Research (RCMAR). The Appendix lists RCMAR locations and investigators. These Centers address social science, clinical, methodological, and health services research issues among the largest minority groups throughout the U.S.

OBJECTIVES AND ORGANIZATION

RCMAR objectives addressing infrastructure creation are to:

1. establish mechanisms for mentoring researchers for careers in research relevant to the health of minority elders;
2. enhance the diversity of the professional research workforce conducting research on the health of minority elders;
3. develop and deploy strategies for recruiting and retaining older minority group members for epidemiological, psychosocial, and/or biomedical research; and
4. develop and deploy racially/ethnically sensitive and standardized measures for use in diverse populations.

The impressive accomplishments of the RCMARs in addressing this last objective during the first three years of program experience led, in part, to the publication of this book. The volume on measurement is consistent with the scientific goals of the RCMAR program. Valid measurement is a prerequisite to accurate assessment of medical needs and outcomes. Several of the contributors and associate editors of this book are RCMAR investigators linked to the various RCMAR Cores.

Each RCMAR is organized around integrated Cores, each with their own objectives. The mentoring objectives (numbers 1 and 2, above) are accomplished through Center-controlled funding processes: each RCMAR solicits, mentors and evaluates three to six new pilot investigators per year. An Investigator Development Core at each Center is responsible for this function. Mentored research projects generally involve the recruitment of minority subjects (Objective 3, above). Responsibility for this function belongs to the Community Liaison Core. This Core is also responsible for the collaborative functions between communities hosting research and RCMAR researchers. NIA is committed to the goal that its funded RCMARs maintain strong and positive relationships with research-targeted communities. The creation and maintenance of trust is further facilitated by "translating" research findings into practice to serve groups providing members as research participants. To these ends, each RCMAR participates in community education, community service (e.g., screening programs), or other "translation" activities appropriate to the ethnic/racial group(s) served by the RCMAR. Additionally, the Community Liaison Core is responsible for research on strategies for recruitment and retention of minority subjects.

The Measurement Core further facilitates mentoring. This Core has responsibility for developing and disseminating racially/ethnically sensitive measurement related research tools (Objective 4, above). There is a need to understand both within- and between-group variability in health and health-related behaviors. Therefore, NIA has charged the RCMAR Measurement Cores with the task of developing and evaluating appropriate measurement tools that can be standardized across groups. Until this is accomplished, it is impossible to guarantee the accurate measurement of health disparities. The measurement of health outcomes and their determinants is a central task for the RCMARs in their attempt to reduce minority/ non-minority health disparities. The Measurement Core also serves as a resource of methodological and statistical expertise for pilot investigators and other RCMAR-affiliated researchers. An Administrative Core completes the required intraorganizational RCMAR structure while a Coordinating Center is responsible for interCenter liaison.

ACCOMPLISHMENTS AND FUTURE DEVELOPMENT

During their brief history, the RCMARs have exceeded NIA's expectations in meeting program objectives. RCMAR investigators collaboratively authored a "Program Emphases and Outcomes" document (available on the RCMAR website: http://rcmar.musc.edu) serving to highlight accomplishments. Detailed program accomplishments can be viewed at the website. A few notable achievements in the program's first two-and-one-half years include: over 200 professional and innumerable community publications; over 50 additional research projects funded; measurement development (16 new measures) and evaluation (14 existing measures) using a trans-RCMAR template to assure racially/ethnically sensitive assessment (all found on the website under the Measurement Core); mentoring of over 70 new investigators; and extensive community outreach activities. Additionally, the RCMARs have begun to serve as resources for other NIA-supported research activities. Notable is the development of the recruitment and retention strategies of minority subjects in some of the NIA Alzheimer's Disease Centers.

The primary objective of building and strengthening an infrastructure for minority aging research is, of course, a long-term and evolving process. The achievements to date are strong evidence of the viability of this activity. NIA remains committed to reducing health disparities for older persons. The RCMARs represent one avenue for meeting this goal. Health disparity reduction is not subject to rapid resolution nor can a single program be expected to accomplish this goal. The RCMAR program is a viable, and potentially highly productive, long-range strategy for addressing the social problem of minority/nonminority health disparities.

APPENDIX

The location and Principal Investigators of the six RCMARs follow: Columbia University (Rafael Lantigua); Henry Ford Health System (Glenn Davis); University of Michigan/Wayne State University (James Jackson); University of Colorado (Spero Manson); University of California San Francisco (Eliseo Pérez-Stable); University of North Carolina (Elizabeth Mutran). A Coordinating Center is funded at the Medical University of South Carolina (Barbara Tilley) under a subcontract from Henry Ford.

Index

Aging in Good Health
Multidisciplinary Perspectives
Sue E. Levkoff, ScD, Yeon Kyung Chee, PhD, and Shohei Noguchi, BA, Editors

"...provides a comprehensive look at how psychological, social, and physical factors influence the aging process. ...much useful information on how to better understand and improve the quality of life of a rapidly increasing older population."

—**Kyriakos S. Markides,** Director
Division of Sociomedical Sciences
University of Texas

Most older adults lead productive, happy lives, without significant levels of disability or illness. In this well-written text, the editors integrate concepts of healthy aging with larger salient issues of aging from the psychological, social and biomedical fields. Topics include: stressful life events and late life adaptation, family dynamics and caregiving, retirement, medication use, geriatric rehabilitation, patient-provider communication and much more.

Partial Contents:
- Stressful Life Events and Late Adulthood Adaptation, *X. Cui and G.E. Vaillant*
- Spirituality in Later Life, *M.N. Sheehan*
- Emotional Health and Socioeconomic Stress, *L.E. Storck*
- The Role of Music Therapy in Successful Aging, *S.B. Hanser*
- Family Dynamics and the Flow of Caregiving, *A.J. Lieberman*
- Understanding and Planning for Retirement, *R. Bosse*
- Issues in Rural Aging, *P.F. Weitzman, K.Y. Chee,* and *S.E. Levkoff*
- Elder Abuse, *R.S. Wolf*
- Medication Use in Older Individuals, *J.H. Gurwitz* and *P.A. Rochan*
- The Integration of Exercise and Nutrition in Geriatric Medicine, *M.A.F. Singh*
- Falls Among the Elderly, *J. Howland, E.W. Peterson,* and *M.E. Lachman*
- Geriatric Rehabilitation, *L. Thalheimer*

Nurse's Book Society Selection
2000   392pp   0-8261-1366-4   hard $48.95 (outside US $53.80)

536 Broadway, New York, NY 10012 • Telephone: 212-431-4370
Fax: 212-941-7842 • Order Toll-Free: 877-687-7476 • Order On-line: www.springerpub.com